An Introduction to Anglo-Saxon Church Architecture
Anglo-Saxon & Anglo Scandinavian Stone Sculpture

AN INTRODUCTION TO ANGLO-SAXON CHURCH ARCHITECTURE
&
ANGLO-SAXON & ANGLO-SCANDINAVIAN STONE SCULPTURE

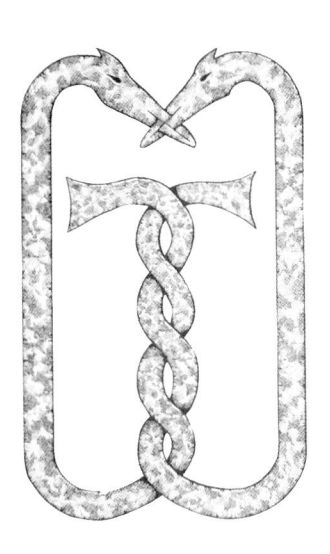

GUY POINTS

AN INTRODUCTION TO ANGLO-SAXON CHURCH ARCHITECTURE & ANGLO-SAXON & ANGLO-SCANDINAVIAN STONE SCULPTURE

First Published in Great Britain in 2015 by the author as
RIHTSPELL PUBLISHING

ISBN 978-0-9930339-0-2

© Guy Points 2015

All rights reserved. No part of this publication may be reproduced, stored in a retrievable system, or transmitted, in any form or by any means, electronic, mechanical, photocopying, recording or otherwise, without the prior written permission of the author and copyright owner.

The right of Guy Points to be identified as the author of this work has been asserted in accordance with the Copyright, Designs and Patents Act 1988.

By the same Author:
The Combined Anglo-Saxon Chronicles: A Ready-Reference Abridged Chronology (2013)
A Gazetteer of Anglo-Saxon & Viking Sites: County Durham & Northumberland (2012)
Yorkshire: A Gazetteer of Anglo-Saxon & Viking Sites (2007)
A Concise Guide to Historic Northumberland and Tyne & Wear (1987)
A Concise Guide to Historic Shetland (1984)
A Concise Guide to Historic Orkney (1981)

Marketed and Distributed in the UK and Rest of the World by:
Oxbow Books Limited
10 Hythe Bridge Street
Oxford
OX1 2EW
www.oxbowbooks.com

Marketed and Distributed in North America by:
The David Brown Book Company
PO Box 511 (Main Street)
Oakville CT 06779
USA
queries@dbbconline.com

Printed by Binfield Print & Design Ltd
www.binfield.com

PREFACE

This book is for the reader who wishes to learn more about Anglo-Saxon church architecture and Anglo-Saxon and Anglo-Scandinavian stone sculpture. Intended for the student and non-specialist alike, as well as those who already have some knowledge of the subjects covered, it bridges the divide between an academic approach and that of the interested general public.

The content has three objectives.

First, to provide an introduction to Anglo-Saxon church architectural features and Anglo-Saxon stone sculpture.

Second, to provide illustrative and photographic examples so that the reader will be more readily able to recognise church architectural features and stone sculptural artefacts identified.

Third, to provide a gazetteer of places which are excellent examples of the church architectural features and stone sculptural artefacts identified.

An Introduction to Anglo-Saxon Church Architecture &
Anglo-Saxon & Anglo Scandinavian Stone Sculpture

CONTENTS

Part 1 – BACKGROUND INFORMATION

Glossary of Terms	11
Who were the Anglo-Saxons?	27
Who were the Vikings?	28
The Hiberno-Norse	29
The Celtic and Roman Church Practices, and the Synod of Whitby	30
Church Building Styles and Architecture	31
Suggested Reading	32

Part 2 - ANGLO-SAXON CHURCHES

Anglo-Saxon churches	37
Plans of Anglo-Saxon Churches	38
1. Simple Church Plan	38
2. Church Plan with Variations and Additions	39
3. Cruciform Church Plan	40
Construction of Anglo-Saxon Churches	41
1. Walling	41
2. Quoining	43
A. Side Alternate Quoining	44
B. Face Alternate Quoining	45
C. Long and Short Quoining	45
D. Escomb Quoining	46
E. Long and Short Quoining – "Sussex" variation	47
3. Archways, Doorways, Windows and Belfry Openings	48
A. Commonalities	48
(i) Openings with Lintel Heads	48
(ii) Openings with Semi-Circular Heads	48
(iii) Openings with Flat-Heads	50
(iv) Openings with Triangular-Heads	50
B. Additional characteristics of Windows	50
C. Additional characteristics of Belfry Openings	53
4. Hood Moulding and Strip-Work	54
5. Pilaster Strips, including "Pilaster-Buttresses"	56
6. String Courses	57
7. Plinths	57
8. Stairways	57
9. Upper Doorways	58
10. Porticos	58
11. Crypts	59
12. Roofs	59

CONTENTS

Excellent Examples of Anglo-Saxon Construction Features	61
Identifying Anglo-Saxon Fabric and Features Among Later Buildings	67
Anglo-Saxon Fonts	68
Anglo-Saxon Sundials	69
Anglo-Saxon Stone Furniture	71
Other Anglo-Saxon Stone Features, including decorative altar panels, architectural decorative friezes, wall panels, shrine covers, roods.	71

Part 3 – ANGLO-SAXON & ANGLO-SCANDINAVIAN STONE SCULPTURE

Anglo-Saxon/Anglo-Scandinavian Crosses	77
Crossheads including Finials	79
Free-Arm Crossheads	79
Ring or Wheel-Head Crossheads	80
Plate or Plate-Ring Crossheads	81
Disc-Head Crossheads	82
Cross-Shafts	82
Cross-Bases	83
Anglo-Saxon/Anglo-Scandinavian Grave Markers – "Grave Slabs"	84
Grave Markers	84
Pillow Stones and Name Stones	86
Grave Covers and Grave Slabs	86
Hogback Grave Covers or Hogback Tombstones	87
Sarcophagus	88
Anglo-Saxon/Anglo-Scandinavian Decoration	88
Moulding – Flat, Grooved, Roll, Cable-Pattern (Rope-Work), Key-Pattern, Stepped-Pattern, Pellet.	90
Interlace Design – Basket-Plait Design or Basket-Ware Design, Cats-Cradle Design, Gridiron Design, Knot-Work Design, Plait-Work Design, Ring-Chain Design or Ring-Twist Design, Ring-Knot Design, Scroll-Design, Spiral-Scroll Design, "Stopped" Plait-Work Design, Strap-Work Design, Zigzag Design.	91
Plant Design. Plant-Scroll Design - Bush-Scroll, or Vine-Scroll, or Tree-Scroll. Inhabited Plant-Scroll Design. Palmette Design.	95
Other Designs: Balusters. Chequer-Board Designs. Chevron-Pattern Design. Pellet Design	96
Anglo-Scandinavian Decoration	96
Borre Design	96
Jellinge Design	97
Ringerike Design	97
Ryedale Design	97
Urnes Design	97
Excellent Examples of Anglo-Saxon and Anglo-Scandinavian Stone Sculpture	98

An Introduction to Anglo-Saxon Church Architecture &
Anglo-Saxon & Anglo Scandinavian Stone Sculpture

Part 4 – RECOMMENDED EXEMPLAR CHURCHES AND MUSEUMS

Access to Churches   107

Alphabetically listed and numbered recommended exemplar churches and museums with summarised information on Anglo-Saxon church architectural features to be seen, and/or Anglo-Saxon or Anglo-Scandinavian sculpture and their decoration.   108

PHOTOGRAPHIC ACKNOWLEDGEMENTS
(Note: all photographs are taken by the author and remain the copyright of Guy Points.)

With thanks to the Clergy, Churchwardens and Parochial Church Councils for their agreement to reproduce photographs taken at the following churches:

St Bartholomew's Church, Aldbrough, East Yorkshire.
St Andrew's Church, Bishop Auckland, County Durham.
St Mary's Church, Breamore, Hampshire.
St Mary and St Hardulph Church, Breedon-on-the-Hill, Leicestershire.
St Bridget's Church, Brigham, Cumbria.
Bristol Cathedral, Gloucestershire.
St Thomas's Church, Brompton-in-Allertonshire, North Yorkshire.
St Andrew's Church, Burton Pedwardine, Lincolnshire.
St Peter's Church, Codford St Peter, Wiltshire.
St Andrew's Church, Colyton, Devon.
Church of the Holy Rood, Daglingworth, Gloucestershire.
St Mungo's Church, Dearham, Cumbria.
Church of St Edmund King and Martyr, Dolton, Devon.
St Lawrence's Church, Eyam, Derbyshire.
St Margaret's Church, Fletton, Cambridgeshire.
St Mary's Church, Gosforth, Cumbria.
St Michael's Church, Great Urswick, Cumbria.
St Hilda's Church, Hartlepool, County Durham.
Hexham Abbey, Northumberland. All photographs reproduced by kind permission of the Rector and Churchwardens of Hexham Abbey, Northumberland.
St Peter's Church, Heysham, Lancashire.
All Saints Church, Hough-on-the-Hill, Lincolnshire.
All Saints Church, Ilkley, West Yorkshire.
Lichfield Cathedral, Staffordshire.
St Oswald's Church, Lythe, North Yorkshire. With permission of the Rector & PCC of St Oswald's, Lythe, North Yorkshire.
St Mary's Church, Melbury Bubb, Dorset.
St Chad's Church, Middlesmoor, North Yorkshire.
St Andrew's Church, Middleton, North Yorkshire.
St Mary & All Saints Church, Nassington, Northamptonshire.
St Mary and St Helen's Church, Neston, Cheshire.
St Mary's Church, Newent, Gloucestershire.
Peterborough Cathedral, Cambridgeshire.

Holy Cross Church, Ramsbury, Wiltshire.
St Wystan's Church, Repton, Derbyshire.
Romsey Abbey, Hampshire.
St Mary's Church, Stow-in-Lindsey, Lincolnshire.
St Peter's Church, Monkwearmouth, Sunderland, County Durham.
St Michael & All Angels Church, Thornhill, West Yorkshire.
St Oswald's Church, Thornton Steward, North Yorkshire.
St Michael's Church, Thursley, Surrey.
All Hallows Church, Whitchurch, Hampshire.
St Michael's Church, Winterbourne Steepleton, Dorset.
St Peter's Church, Wootton Wawen, Warkwickshire.
St Nicholas Church, Worth, Sussex.

ALSO with thanks to the Authorities:
Derby Museum & Art Gallery, Derby.
English Heritage: St Peter's Church, Barton-on-Humber, Lincolnshire
Historic Scotland: Whithorn Priory Museum, Wigtownshire.

PART I

BACKGROUND INFORMATION

GLOSSARY OF TERMS

ABACUS – A flat slab forming the top of a capital.

ADDORSED - Two figures or features placed symmetrically back-to-back.

ADZE – A tool used in woodworking for chipping or slicing away the surface of the wood – a variation of an axe. The blade attached to the end is at right-angles and curves inwards towards the handle.

AFFRONTED – Two figures or features placed symmetrically with their bodies facing and their heads turned back away from each other.

AISLE – Part of the church running alongside the nave, choir or transepts. It is separated from the nave, choir or transepts by columns or piers. It can also be a central passageway in the nave, choir or transepts.

ALCOVE – A vaulted recess.

ALTAR – A table made of wood or stone usually situated at the eastern end of the chancel, or the nave; also at the eastern end of side chapels. The altars are consecrated for the purpose of the celebration of the Eucharist (the sacrament of the Lord's Supper, the Communion).

AMBULATORY – An open or enclosed walkway - mostly at the east end of the chancel surrounding an apse.

ANIMALS OR BEASTS – The two terms animals or beasts are often used to describe the same thing. Where animals or beasts were depicted on metalwork, woodwork and stonework they were rarely exact representations; often with stylised curving and/or with entwined bodies, necks and legs.

ANNULAR – A description for a complete ring; often used when describing a brooch or a representation forming part of a decorative design. See **PENANNULAR**.

APSE - A vaulted semi-circular, sometimes polygonal, eastern end of the nave or chancel.

ARCADE – A series of freestanding arches supported by columns or piers between a nave and an aisle. When not freestanding and incorporated into walling they are described as blind arcades.

ARCH - Stonework over a void intended to support other arches and the weight of the wall above.

ARCHITRAVE – A collective name for the features of stonework – lintel, jambs, mouldings – which surround an opening, doorway or window.

ARTEFACT (Artifact) – A useful or decorative man-made object.

ASHLAR – Stonework prepared and trimmed with a finished surface, "dressed", comprising smooth-faced square or rectangular blocks laid with fine joints in regular courses.

AUMBRY – A recess or cupboard within a wall specifically to hold sacred vessels.

BALUSTER – A turned, usually short vertical pillar, sometimes with a bulbous centre and at other times with a plain cylindrical shape. Often with spaced raised bands and spaced grooves. Some examples may also have distinct capitals and bases. They were used to support imposts of doors and windows, often as the central support in a double window or belfry opening. They were also used as decorative supporting features in coping and balustrades. Often referred to as "baluster shafts".

BALUSTRADE – A series of balusters supporting a handrail.

BAND – A strip of either flat or thin material used to hold things together or bind around an object. Also commonly used for a strip of stonework providing a vertical and horizontal border to enclose decoration within a panel, or to separate one decorative panel from another, or to separate decoration within an individual panel. Moulding is often described as a "band(s) of moulding".

BAPTISTRY – An area for baptism designed to include the font. It is usually near the entrance to the church, at the west end of the south aisle or nave, or on the ground floor of the tower. It can also be located at the east end of the south aisle or in the south transept.

BARREL VAULTED – A descriptive term for a building or room with a semi-cylindrical roof.

BAS RELIEF – Shallow moulding or sculpture in wood or stone where a figure, less than half its true proportion, protrudes from the background.

BASE – The bottom or foot of a column or pilaster-strip or strip-work. The base may be chamfered, stepped, moulded or sculptured.

BASILICA – A rectangular building with aisles separated by colonnades or arcades from a nave.

BASKET-PLAIT DESIGN OR BASKET-WARE DESIGN – A variation of Interlace Design. A design representing the appearance of plaited wickerwork. See **INTERLACE DESIGN**.

BATTLEMENT – An indented parapet at the top of a wall often used as a decorative feature. The original purpose was as a fortified feature so that archers could shoot through the indentations between the projecting solid sections of masonry.

BAY – A section of an interior space divided by vertical columns or arches or windows or walling.

BELFRY – The stage of the tower where the bells are hung, usually the highest stage of the tower.

BELL-COTE – An ornamental structure designed to house one or two church bells usually on the roof of a church.

BEVELLED – A sloping edge or surface greater than a right angle.

BILLET – A term used to describe the additional small circular plate or roll of metalwork, woodwork or stonework identifiable at the junctures of the arms of some free-arm crosses.

BLOCKED - The description attached to a doorway, arch or window, where it is no longer open and used for its original purpose and where stonework of some description has been inserted to fill in the former void.

BORRE DESIGN - A design distinguished by a symmetrical pattern with concentric circles held together by bands. Animal heads, gripping paws, knot-work and chain work motifs are typical. The design was in use from the mid ninth century to the late tenth century. It was named after the designs on artefacts found in a rich ship burial in Borre, Norway.

BOSS – A square or round projecting area of stonework often found in the centre of crossheads which can vary in height considerably. It is also more commonly used to cover the intersections of the ribs in a vaulted ceiling. It may also be a feature of a shield, brooch or other artefact.

BRACKET – A small projecting block of stonework or woodwork used as a support e.g. the beam of a roof or an arch.

BRICK – A block of clay that has been kneaded, moulded and hardened to form a definite size and shape (usually rectangular).

BRICKWORK – A structure formed by using bricks.

BUSH-SCROLL DESIGN – See **PLANT-SCROLL DESIGN**.

BUTTRESS – A section of masonry or brickwork supporting or projecting from a wall. Its purpose is to provide extra strength.

CABLE-PATTERN DESIGN/CABLE-PATTERN MOULDING OR ROPE-WORK DESIGN - A design consisting of a series of distinctive thick diagonal lines in relief which take on a distended curved shape.

CAME(S)/CALMES - A strip of lead with a groove on each side which holds window glass in place to facilitate a design.

CANOPY - A projection, a hood, over a doorway, niche, statue, altar or pulpit.

CAPITAL - The head or the top part of a column. Capitals may be decorated and/or chamfered, stepped, moulded or sculptured.

CASTELLATED - A feature decorated with battlements.

CATHEDRAL - The principal church of a diocese, containing the "cathedra" or throne of a bishop - the chair of office.

CATS-CRADLE DESIGN - A variation of Interlace Design. A design consisting of a series of ribbon-like strands intricately entwined, producing an elaborate symmetrical pattern. See **INTERLACE DESIGN**.

CEILING - An under covering or lining of a roof or of one of the floors of a room or building which conceals timbers, plaster, etc.

CELL - A small chamber or room. It can also refer to a dependent subsidiary of (usually) a monastery.

CELTIC DESIGN - Like Anglo-Saxon design, this may be summarised as including interlace, knot-work, scrolls, spirals, key patterns, lettering, zoomorphic, plant forms, animals and human figures. There is great difficulty in distinguishing Celtic design from Anglo-Saxon since there was considerable cross-fertilisation of ideas.

CELTS - The Celts were the indigenous peoples who retained or acquired land in the western and highland areas of present day Scotland, Cumbria, the Isle of Man, Wales, Cornwall, Ireland and Brittany and other regions of Europe. Many spoke what might be described as an early form of Welsh. Many accepted Christianity during the fourth and fifth centuries.

CHAMFER - A design feature where a square edge or corner has been cut off to provide a surface with a sloping, angled edge.

CHANCEL - The east end of the church beyond the nave where usually the altar is located. The part of the church intended for use by the clergy and the choir.

CHANCEL ARCH - A large arch over a void forming the division between the eastern end of the nave and the western end of the chancel. The supporting pillars or columns or jambs and the surrounding stonework and the decoration where this occurs often provide dating evidence.

CHANTRY CHAPEL - A separate chapel within or attached to a church specifically for saying Mass for the soul(s) of the dead.

CHAPEL - A place of worship usually dependent on, or subordinate to, a church: a subdivision of a larger church containing its own altar.

CHEVRON-PATTERN DESIGN - A distinctive pattern comprising a series of "V" shapes, one under another, in an upright, curving, or inverted sequence.

CHI-RHO - A descriptive term applied to the representation of the first two letters (XP) of the word in Greek for Christ, ΧΡΙΣ(C)ΤΟΣ(C). The "X" and the "P" are depicted in different combinations.

CHOIR - The part of the church, cathedral, or monastery, where services are sung by an organised body of singers ("the choir").

CLERESTORY - The upper (top) storey of the nave or chancel walls pierced by windows.

CLERGY - Persons who have been ordained to conduct religious services in a Christian church: a collective term for such people.

CLOISONNÉ - A geometric or schematic design whereby silver or gold wire is soldered or glued and set on edge onto a metal object dividing its surface into a number of compartments; these are then filled with cut gemstones or glass, paste or enamel, or any mixture of these. The compartments edged with silver or gold wire thus remain distinctive when the object is complete. Cloisonné design is found on jewellery, fittings for clothing, weaponry and on other high status items.

COLONNADES – A series of columns.

COLUMN – A vertical structure, either round, angled or polygonal in shape. It usually has an added capital and base.

CONFRONTING – A description used to indicate that the decoration on stonework or woodwork includes at least two (the usual number) figures of saints, humans or animals, standing or meeting face to face with both heads and bodies facing each other.

CONGREGATION – A gathering of usually lay people into a single body or assembly. Sometimes members of the clergy may be in the congregation and sometimes the congregation may exclusively consist of the clergy.

CONSECRATION - The act of making a solemn dedication for a sacred or religious purpose.

CONSECRATION CROSS – Painted or carved crosses on the fabric of the church indicating the place(s) where the walls were touched with holy oil during the consecration of the church.

COPING – The course of masonry or brickwork covering the top of a wall which slopes in a downward direction to throw off rain. It is also used as an adjective (coped) to describe the shape of an artefact such as a shrine or grave cover.

CORBEL – A block of stone or wood projecting from a wall to provide support to a beam.

CORNICE – A projected horizontal moulded feature at the very top of a building or immediately below the ceiling in a room.

COURSE – A continuous row or layer of stones, brick or timber at a similar height in a wall or face of a building.

CROSS – The standard Latin cross comprises a horizontal line placed across a vertical line. The representation of a cross signifies a sacred mark or symbol. A generic term used to describe a crosshead with its attached cross-shaft; sometimes with its cross-base.

CROSS-BASE – A section of ground or floor-standing stonework specifically designed to support a cross-shaft in a vertical position. Examples can vary in height, width, depth, shape and decoration.

CROSS DESIGN – A design depicting the shape of a cross.

CROSSHEAD – A section of stonework or a design with four arms connected to a common centre. Examples can vary in height, width, depth, shape and decoration.

CROSS-SHAFT – A four-sided angular vertical section of stonework, comprising two wider faces and two narrower sides usually for supporting a crosshead. They vary in height, width and depth and usually taper from the ground upwards. They can also be circular in shape or have a circular lower half and an angular upper half with the join between the two shapes separated by distinctive pendulous swag(s), and/or, by distinctive collar(s).

CROSSING – The central area in a cruciform church forming the junction of the nave, chancel and transepts.

CRUCIFIX – An image depicting Christ on the Cross.

CRUCIFORM – The ground plan of a church shaped in the form of a cross.

CRYPT – An underground vaulted chamber usually provided to house shrines or relics.

CUSHION-CAPITAL – A capital formed by a cube whose lower horizontal edges have been shaped as semi-circles.

DAMAGED – Some part of the artefact, section of stonework, survives and it can be identified despite the obvious damage.

DECORATED – Where it is possible to identify an artefact or section of stonework that has been decorated with some design.

DESIGN – A combination of details that together go to make up a decorative form of art.

DIOCESE – The district under the pastoral care of a bishop.

DISC-HEAD CROSSHEAD – Disc-Head Crossheads are usually identified by their large circumference and lack of depth. The band of moulding around the edges continues around the "eyelets" between the junctions of the arms, often highlighting the eyelets. The eyelets can surround voids, a sunken section of stonework, or a very large round pellet-like feature. They have similarities in design with Plate or Plate-Ring Crossheads. See **PLATE** OR **PLATE-RING CROSSHEADS**.

DOORFRAME – A structure providing the skeleton for hanging a door.

DOUBLE WINDOWS/DOUBLE OPENINGS – Often used to describe two windows or openings which share the same interior (central) column or other stonework.

DRESSED – Stonework whose surface(s) have been prepared or worked on with an implement by craftsmen. Such a description can be applied to individual stones, to sections of walling, and to entire walls. It can also apply to stonework which has been specifically incorporated or added for decorative purposes.

DROP-SPINDLE – A short, slender and rounded piece of wood (usually) – "rod-like" - that tapers at both ends with its greatest diameter towards one end. A spindle-whorl was placed around it. (See **SPINDLE-WHORL**.) The end of a thread formed by taking a few fibres out from the wool or flax and twisting them together was attached to a notch at the top of the drop-spindle. With the wool or flax in one hand and the spindle in the other, the spindle was twisted, and as the spindle-whorl dropped – hence "drop-spindle" - towards the ground, the "yarn" (the spun fibre, threads individually or collectively) was drawn out and additional fibres of wool or flax added. When the spindle reached the ground yarn was wound round its base allowing enough to make another thread at the top notch of the spindle. The process was then repeated. Note: All spinning during the Anglo-Saxon period used drop-spindles; spinning wheels were not known in England until later.

EAVES – The projecting edge of a roof that overhangs the sidewalls of a structure.

ESCOMB QUOINING/ESCOMB JAMBS – A description applied to quoining where the construction technique is similar to that employed in the jambs supporting the chancel arch in the Anglo-Saxon church at Escomb, County Durham. Ostensibly similar to "Long" and "Short" Quoining, the critical difference is that the "Longs" comprise demonstrably large vertically placed quoins displaying a long face: they are not narrow, column or pillar-like "Longs" encountered with typical "Long" and "Short" quoining. See **LONG AND SHORT QUOINING**.

FACE(S) – The two widest and opposite sides of an individual piece or section of stonework, including crossheads and cross-shafts. It can also be used to describe the wider side of a building, often the front.

FACE ALTERNATE QUOINING – This is where quoins are laid alternately so that on one wall one quoin displays horizontally one long side above another quoin displaying one short side horizontally, whilst on the adjoining walling the same quoins display a horizontal short side above a horizontal long side. The quoins are laid horizontally lying flat on their faces - hence the name "Face Alternate".

FETTERED – A description applied to where the main object – usually an animal – is ensnared by ribbon-like strands which are not part of its body.

FINIAL – An architectural decoration on a church, often in the shape of a cross, placed on the apex of a roof or gable, or on each corner of a tower. It is also used to describe decorative features at the apex of woodwork or stonework e.g. pew ends.

FLAG – A flat slab of any fine grained rock which can be split into flagstones.

FOLIATE – Decoration which represents a leaf.

FONT – A bowl for holding the consecrated water used for baptisms.

FREE-ARM CROSS – The stonework comprises a representation of a standard Latin cross. The horizontal arms are supported by centrally-placed vertical arms.

FRIEZE – A band of painted or sculptured decoration set into or protruding from an architectural feature, stone furnishing, or the surface of a wall.

GABLE – The vertical end of the wall at the end of a ridged roof, from the level of the eaves to the summit, often triangular in shape.

GALLERY – An additional storey usually at first floor level.

GESSO – A preparation of finely-ground chalk base made up into a paste-like plaster of Paris used for certain types of painting.

GNOMON – An axial pillar, rod, or pin, in the centre of sundials which by its shadow indicates the time of day. When missing, the central hole into which it was inserted remains.

GRAVE MARKERS - A generic definition including Pillow Stones, Name Stones, Grave Covers and Grave Slabs for marking the site of a grave or commemorating an individual. They vary in size, shape and decoration; some stood upright, others were laid flat.

GRIDIRON DESIGN – A variation of Interlace Design. A design consisting of parallel ribbon-like strands running in squared-off horizontal and vertical directions to pass over and under each other. See **INTERLACE DESIGN**.

GROOVE – A design made by a channel cut into (usually) stone, wood or metal.

GROZE/GROZING – The process of trimming the edge of glass with a pair of pincers called grozing irons.

GRUBENHAUS – A building constructed above a pit in the ground which was probably used as a grain store or workshop rather than a dwelling. There is some debate as to whether these buildings had floor planks at or above ground level.

HAMMER-HEAD – Hammer-shaped item with an unusually expanded head. Crossheads with hammer-heads have two additional horizontal arms integrated into and extending from each side of the top of the vertical arm.

HERRINGBONE – Where the building material, stone, flints, tiles, bricks, are laid diagonally in rows of parallel lines in opposite directions to provide a pattern in the shape of the letter V or an inverted letter V. On occasions only one – or an incomplete – row of diagonals survive.

HOGBACK GRAVE COVER OR HOGBACK TOMBSTONE – A recumbent grave cover in the shape of an elongated house with a convex profile comprising a pitched roof above long side walls; often the roof has a curved top ridge. The overall effect is reminiscent in shape to a hog's back. Many have inward-facing bear-like animals at each "gable" end gnawing at the roof and holding the long side walls and roof of the house with their paws.

HOOD MOULDING – A section of moulded stonework integral to, or protruding from, the face of the stonework over, or parallel to, the head of an archway, doorway, window or belfry opening; it can also be described as "strip-work". See **STRIP-WORK** and **PILASTER-STRIPS**.

An Introduction to Anglo-Saxon Church Architecture &
Anglo-Saxon & Anglo Scandinavian Stone Sculpture

IMPOST - A horizontal section of stonework which supports the bottom of an arch (one each side) spanning an archway, doorway, window or belfry opening. Imposts often project from the underside of the arch and overhang the jambs. Imposts may be decorated and/or chamfered, stepped, moulded or sculptured.

INCISED - Lines or a design cut into, or engraved in, an object.

INTERLACE DESIGN - A generic term for a design which consists of a pattern of ribbon-like strands intricately entwined and woven together constantly passing over and under each other. It may include strands which change direction and turn back on themselves to avoid crossing the strands below and above. Some designs may also include strands with an incised groove running in the centre running parallel to its long borders.

IRREGULAR ANGLO-SAXON WALLING - This is where the walling comprises irregularly-shaped roughly-faced rubble which is randomly sized and placed and not in recognisable courses.

JAMB(S) - The straight vertical side of an archway, doorway, window or belfry opening. Jambs can comprise rubble or roughly-dressed stones; some, where particularly large stones are used are referred to as "megalithic".

JELLINGE DESIGN - A design distinguished by ribbon-like reptilian S-shaped creatures who are fettered. The design was in use in the tenth century. It is named after the animal which decorates a small silver cup found at the royal burial ground in Jellinge in Jutland in Denmark.

JOISTS - Horizontal timbers carrying a floor or ceiling.

KEY-HOLE WINDOW - Mostly found in Lincolnshire. A window whose head is shaped into more than half a circle resulting in the overall shape resembling a key-hole.

KEY-PATTERN DESIGN - A design depicting a row of distinctive alternating key-shapes placed together in a regular pattern.

KEYSTONE - The central stone in an arch.

KNOT-WORK DESIGN - A variant of Interlace Design. It entwines a pattern of ribbon-like strands, usually wider and more angular than those found in common Interlace Design. See **INTERLACE DESIGN.**

LABEL-STOPS - A protruding three-dimensional (usually) stonework often in the shape of an animal or human head used to decorate both terminals of hood moulding. Occasionally found, but St Mary's Church, Deerhurst, Gloucestershire provides the "classic" Anglo-Saxon examples.

LANCET - Pointed arches known as lancet enable arches to be high and windows large. Characteristic of the Early English Gothic period circa 1180 to 1275.

LIGHT - A window opening.

LINEAR DESIGN - A design involving the use of a line or series of lines.

LINTEL - A horizontal beam bridging an archway, doorway, window or opening.

LITURGY - The service of the Holy Eucharist; a form of public worship.

LONG AND SHORT QUOINING - This is where quoins are laid alternately so that on one wall one quoin displays horizontally one long or short side above another quoin displaying one long face or side vertically, whilst on the adjoining walling the same quoins display a horizontal long or short side above a vertical long face or side.

LONG AND SHORT QUOINING - "SUSSEX" VARIATION - A variation found in some churches, predominantly in Sussex but also in other counties - its use is not uniform. It is where more than one flat quoin forms the "short" between the "long" narrow-sided quoins standing upright in long and short quoining. The short quoins are laid so that on each wall a long horizontal side alternates with a short horizontal side. The number of flat "short" quoins between the upright "long" quoins can vary within the same angle of walling.

LONGHOUSE – A house long in overall physical appearance and often of low height in comparison to its length. Originally, on one side of the entrance there was a living room – sometimes subdivided – and on the other side a byre (a house for cattle).

LOOM – A wooden-framed mechanism enabling yarn or thread to be woven into fabric by interweaving the "warp" (threads extended lengthwise) and "weft" (threads which cross from side to side – at right angles to the warp). The warp threads are held in parallel under tension by tying them into small bunches to "loom weights". See **LOOM WEIGHTS**.

LOOM WEIGHTS – Weights made from a spool-like piece of stonework with a hole through the centre; they can be made of baked clay/pottery. They were used to provide the tension to the warp threads when weaving. See **LOOM**.

MASS – A service to celebrate the Lord's Supper or Sacrament of the Body and Blood of Christ, the Eucharist – Holy Communion. See **CHANTRY CHAPEL**.

MASS DIAL OR SCRATCH DIAL – A device for measuring the passing of the time to indicate the time for the liturgy (service or mass) of the Eucharist (The Sacrament of the Lord's Supper, the Communion). It usually consists of a stone slab incorporated into the fabric of the church, on whose vertical face there is an incised semi-circle with its horizontal line having lines radiating often below but sometimes above. At the central intersection of these lines dividing the day into segments there would be a wooden or metal peg or stele – the "gnomon". The gnomon would cast a shadow and thus denote the time for the service or mass, usually 9 am, noon and Vespers (Evensong). The gnomon is now usually missing but the hole in which it was housed is still identifiable. Often the hole for the missing gnomon assists in identifying the weathered scratches on a vertical slab of stonework as being those from a mass or scratch dial. Mass Dials or Scratch Dials are usually located on the south side of the church often on stonework in the walling near, or to the east of, the south side entrance.

MEGALITHIC – A description used to identify distinctive larger than average sized stones which are not uniform in size or shape used in the construction of quoining, and the jambs of archways, doorways and windows. Sometimes they are used individually on the corners of a building where the quoining above is formed of smaller more manageable stones. The lower courses of walling may include the occasional random megalithic stone, or comprise mostly of megalithic stonework.

MILLEFIORI (Glass) – A process involving fusion of fine strands of coloured glass which are then cut across to provide the required detail for decorative purposes. Millefiori glass inserted into metalwork was used to decorate the covers of illuminated manuscripts and books.

MISERICORD – A bracket placed under a hinged seat to provide support to the occupant when standing. Under this hinge there can be elaborate carvings.

MINSTER – The church of a monastery. (See **MONASTERY**.)

MONASTERY – A place of residence and prayer for a community of monks and secular clergy.

MONOLITH – A single large block of stonework.

MORTAR – A mixture of cement or lime, sand and water used to make the joints between stones and bricks and seal them together.

MOULDING (MOULDED) – A continuous section of metalwork, woodwork or stonework with defined parallel borders. Moulding is often used as decoration on artefacts and architectural features; it can be in a single band, a pair of adjacent bands, or two bands separated by a groove, or a series of alternating grooves and bands. (See **BAND**.) The edges of the moulding may be flat, rounded, chamfered or bevelled. Also refers to the shaping of the surface of a piece of metalwork, woodwork or stonework by the use of an implement.

NAME STONES - A small stone denoting a grave usually with a cross and inscribed with the name of the individual in letters, sometimes in runes. Similar but larger than Pillow Stones.

NARTHEX - A covered porch or portico spanning the whole width of the west end of a church separated from the nave by a wall.

NAVE - The main body of the church from west to east intended for the congregation.

NEWEL - The central pillar from which the steps of a winding stairway radiate. Also the post at the head or foot of a stairway supporting a hand-rail.

NICHE - A vertical arched recess usually intended to house a statue.

OGEE - An S-shaped moulding consisting of a continuous double curve, convex above and concave below.

OPUS SIGNINUM - A red flooring material made by mixing very hard waterproof cement with crushed brick and tile. In Britain this type of flooring was first used by the Romans.

ORATORY - A small room or chapel intended for private prayer.

ORDER - An architectural term used when classifying stonework leading up to and surrounding an opening, doorway or window in terms of classical architecture. Classical architecture evolved in terms of differences in height, lightness and decoration from Tuscan, Doric, Ionic, Corinthian through to Composite.

ORNAMENTED - Something embellished with decoration.

PALMETTE DESIGN - A design consisting of a series of adjacent, narrow-stemmed leaf shapes.

PANEL - A self-contained area having a defined border or frame within a larger construct or design. It can be in relief or recessed within the overall design and may encompass a wide range of decoration, sometimes including an inscription.

PARAPET - A low wall to provide protection where there is an abrupt drop.

PARCLOSE SCREEN - A screen which separates a chapel from the rest of the church.

PARVISE CHAMBER - A room over the porch.

PATTERN-WELDED SWORDS - These are swords where the blade comprises a centre core of iron rods twisted together and forge-welded, with additional strips of iron welded on to form the cutting edges. This process differentiated pattern-welded blades from those more widely and simply produced which were liable to break easily. The composite blade was then tempered and re-heated until the desired level of hardness and flexibility was achieved. The blade was then ground into shape and polished; acid was used to etch wording or runes. The extended hilt of the blade was provided with fittings made of wood or bone, metal or leather, gold or silver, often highly decorated and ornamented including garnets and other gems.

PELLET(S) - A moulding or design on which there is a single or a row of small rounded sometimes elongated shapes in relief.

PENANNULAR - A description for an incomplete ring; often used when describing a brooch or a representation forming part of a decorative design. See **ANNULAR**.

PEW - A seat for worshippers, usually a wooden or stone bench with a long back and square-ends.

PIER - A large section of stonework which supports an arch.

PILASTER-STRIP - A vertical strip of stonework protruding from a wall intended to assist in the bonding of the stonework, the application of plaster and for decorative purposes. See **STRIP-WORK**.

PILLAR - A vertical section of usually circular, angular or polygonal stonework whose height is much greater than its diameter.

PILLAR-STONE – A stand alone, irregularly-shaped, section of stonework whose only consistent characteristics are that it is slender in proportion to its height, and that it is incised with lettering on one face only. Additionally, some examples may have a Chi-Rho (see **CHI-RHO**) monogram depicted in different combinations. Pillar-Stones usually date from the fifth to the eighth centuries. Note: from the eleventh century "Stone Pillars" appear similar in physical characteristics, and with abstract and figurative designs poorly depicted, sometimes on more than one side.

PILLOW STONE – A small stone denoting a grave incised with a cross and inscribed with the name of the individual concerned in letters, sometimes in runes. Similar but smaller than Name Stones.

PISCINA – A basin, with a drainage hole, incorporated into the fabric of a wall, used for washing Communion vessels.

PITCH – The shape or angle of a roof.

PLAIT-WORK DESIGN – A variation of Interlace Design where a pattern of ribbon-like strands all advance towards the base of the design without diverging. Like Interlace Designs the strands are woven together regularly passing over and under each other. Unlike some Interlace Designs the strands do not change direction and turn back on themselves. In addition, often each strand has an incised groove in the centre running parallel to its long borders. See **INTERLACE DESIGN**.

PLANT-SCROLL DESIGN – A variation of Scroll Design. Plant-Scroll Designs resemble a circuitous design representing the branches or trunks of a plant or bush, vine or tree. Plant-Scroll design can be sub-divided into "Bush-Scroll", "Tree-Scroll" or "Vine-Scroll". See **SCROLL DESIGN**.

PLASTER – A composition of lime, sand and other material, used for covering walls and ceilings.

PLATE OR PLATE-RING CROSSHEADS – This is where the ring of a Ring-Head Crosshead comprise solid stonework from the spaces between the junctures of the arms to near or at the top of the ring. See **RING-HEAD CROSSHEAD**.

PLINTH – The projecting part of a wall immediately above the ground. Also, stonework or any other material at ground level whose specific purpose is to support or display artefacts, for example, a cross-shaft or font.

POINTING – The mortar jointing between blocks of stonework or bricks.

PORCH – The structure surrounding and enclosing an entrance. Used for both secular and religious purposes; sometimes there is an upper chamber.

PORTICO/PORTICOS – A structure up to two storeys high adjacent and attached to the north and south walls of the main body of a church, including the porch and tower; sometimes overlapping both nave and chancel. A portico can be a single structure or a series of attached structures similar in effect to an aisle.

PORTRAIT – A representation of a figure, including Christ, angels, saints, humans and gods, animals or some hybrid, as seen from the front in full face.

PRIEST – A minister of religious worship.

PRIESTS – When priests or monks were depicted on stonework they are shown with either a Celtic or Roman tonsure (see **TONSURE**) and usually hold a book, often The Bible, or sometimes a cross. Additionally those following the Celtic form of Christianity were often carved with a reliquary or book satchel hanging from their neck and with both feet pointing the same way sideways.

PROFILE – A representation of a face or figure, including Christ, angels, saints, humans and gods, animals or some hybrid, as seen from the side.

PROKROSSOS – A corbel-like feature projecting from a wall decorated with the head, and usually the neck, of an enigmatic beast.

PULPIT – A raised and sometimes enclosed structure used for the preaching of sermons.

QUARRY WINDOWS/QUARRIES – Pieces of window glass trimmed to a shape so that they could be placed in a design for a window.

QUERNSTONE(S) – Two circular-shaped stones used in the hand-grinding of corn. The upper stone is turned to crush the corn poured between it and the lower stone.

QUILL(S) – A hollow stem or stalk usually cut from the wing feather of a duck or goose used as a writing implement to apply ink to the pages of a manuscript or book. Ink was mixed from both carbon (charcoal or soot) and gum, or from oak galls (a fluid caused by the activities of insects on oak) mixed with sulphates of copper, zinc and iron.

QUOIN(S) – Collectively "quoining" are sections of stonework which supports the corners of a church or building. Individually, one side of a quoin forms the last stone in one wall and another side of the same quoin forms the last stone in the wall adjoining. Usually quoins are distinctly larger than other individual stones in the rest of the walling and are not always uniform in shape and size. Quoins are also used in the stonework forming the jambs to archways, doorways, windows and belfry openings. Quoins are usually "dressed". See **DRESSED**.

REBATE – A small section of stonework cut out of a jamb of an archway, doorway, window or opening to enable the insertion and retention of a door, shutter or window.

RECESS – A niche or alcove.

REGULAR ANGLO-SAXON WALLING – This is where the walling comprises shaped, unevenly-faced and differently-sized stonework or rubble placed in discernible regular courses.

RELIEF – A design protruding from the surface of the main material being used.

RENDERED – A process resulting in the shape of a section of stonework being altered and smoothed to fit in a particular place, for example, the side of a cross-shaft being rendered so that it can fit into a particular section of walling, or to provide a lintel or sill for an archway, doorway, window or belfry opening. This often results in any decoration being damaged or completely removed.

RENDERING – Where a coat of plasterwork or whitewash has been applied to stone surfaces, usually for protective purposes. Often covering a wall to provide a uniform surface.

REREDOS – Usually a painted or carved screen or wall behind and above an altar.

RESPOND – A half-column supporting a single arch or pier at the end of an arcade.

RHENISH HELM – A square stone tower having four triangular gables on to which a pyramidal roof is affixed, thus giving the impression of a hood or helm. This is achieved by constructing the roof of four diamond shapes conjoined to form a pyramid-shaped steeple, while the open triangles at the base are built directly on to the four matching gables of the tower walls.

RIBBON-SHAPED ANIMAL – An animal whose body and features are long and narrow; usually depicted in profile.

RING-CHAIN DESIGN OR RING-TWIST DESIGN – A variant of interlace design. It consists of ribbon-like strands forming a pattern containing an outer and inner pair of concentric circles. These circles are entwined with single or pairs of distinctly longer, curving or angular and diagonally placed, ribbon-like strands connecting them to similar pairs of concentric circles. Some examples may have more angular or squared-off components rather than circles. See **INTERLACE DESIGN**.

RING-HEAD CROSSHEAD – A crosshead where the four arms of a free-arm crosshead are linked to each other by curved sections of metalwork, woodwork or stonework – known as quadrants – to give the overall appearance of a ring; they are often also referred to as "wheel-head" crossheads. There are voids between the junctures of the arms of the crosshead and the underside of the quadrants forming the ring.

RING-KNOT DESIGN – A variant of Interlace Design. It consists of a curving pattern of ribbon-like strands forming a series of connected circular or angular patterns. Often the circular varieties form a "figure of eight" pattern. Such patterns are entwined with distinctly longer, curving or angular and diagonally placed, ribbon-like strands connecting them to similar figure of eight or other patterns. See **INTERLACE DESIGN**.

RINGERIKE DESIGN – A design distinguished by a large quadruped or bird with extensions from its body erupting in fans and taking on a foliate appearance. The design was in use in the late tenth and eleventh centuries. It is named after a group of animal and plant motifs on ornamental slabs in the Ringerike district in Norway.

ROLL MOULDING – A band (length) of moulding comprising a three-quarter circle in its cross section.

ROMAN TOOLING – Found on re-used Roman stonework and referred to as such in information leaflets, booklets and guidebooks. Such a description usually refers to the actions of craftsmen who have applied their skills to produce incised, angled or feathered striations on the surface(s) of the stonework.

ROOD OR HOLY ROOD – Usually a sculptural representation of Christ on the Cross, sometimes including other figures such as The Virgin Mary, St John the Evangelist, the spear-bearer Longinus and the sponge-bearer Stephaton. It can be in wood, in stonework, or painted onto walling. Such a representation may sometimes be used to decorate crossheads or cross-shafts.

ROOD LOFT – A gallery built above the rood screen (See **ROOD SCREEN**). Sometimes used by singers during a service, also used to maintain the Rood Screen.

ROOD SCREEN – A wooden, stone, or wrought iron screen separating the nave from the chancel supporting a sculptural representation of Christ on the Cross, sometimes with other figures such as The Virgin Mary and St John the Evangelist. Many would have elaborate carved or applied designs.

ROPE-WORK DESIGN – See **CABLE-PATTERN DESIGN**.

ROSETTE – A decorative ornamental design resembling a rose with a distinctive centre with flower-like petals radiating from it.

RUBBLE – Rough and ready building material comprising irregularly-shaped, roughly-faced, and randomly-sized stone or flint, or reused broken or unbroken Roman bricks and tiles – on occasions some or all of these components may be mixed together.

RUDE – A description used when the stonework or design is simple, or where poor quality workmanship is exhibited.

An Introduction to Anglo-Saxon Church Architecture & Anglo-Saxon & Anglo Scandinavian Stone Sculpture

RUNES OR RUNIC OR FUTHORC ALPHABET – A form of early writing incised on wood or stone. Futhorc denotes the first six letters of the alphabet f, u, "th" being a thorn, i.e. "þ" or "ð" (hence one letter), and o, r, and c. The Anglo-Saxon runic alphabet contained thirty-one characters. These are:

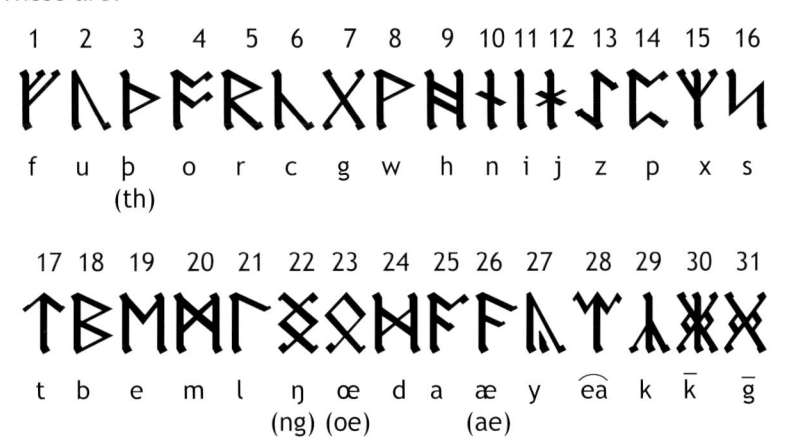

1	2	3	4	5	6	7	8	9	10	11	12	13	14	15	16
f	u	þ (th)	o	r	c	g	w	h	n	i	j	z	p	x	s

17	18	19	20	21	22	23	24	25	26	27	28	29	30	31
t	b	e	m	l	ŋ (ng)	œ (oe)	d	a	æ (ae)	y	ea	k	k̄	ḡ

RYEDALE DRAGON DESIGN - A design usually comprising a single, bound beast or dragon shown in S-shape with its jaws open. Similar to the Jellinge Design (see **JELLINGE DESIGN**). The design features on a number of examples of cross-shafts and grave covers in the Ryedale area in North Yorkshire – hence the name.

SACRISTY - Now more commonly known as the vestry. Used for storing sacred vessels and vestments.

SANCTUARY – The area immediately around the main altar of a church.

SCEAT (singular) and **SCEATTAS** (plural) – These were small, thick silver pennies similar in size, weight and appearance to Thrymsas (see below). They were in general circulation between 680 and 760. Wider silver pennies first introduced during the reign of King Offa of Mercia (757-796) gradually replaced them. The silver content of later sceattas was often debased.

SCRAMASAX - A term sometimes used to describe a single-edged knife, a "seax" (see **SEAX**), used as a weapon rather than for hunting or domestic use. No Old English source material uses this term; it probably comes from a single description in the "History of the Franks" by Geoffrey, Bishop of Tours, AD 539-594.

SCROLL DESIGN – A variation of Interlace Design. A design where a pattern of ribbon-like strands resembles a circuitous design. (See **INTERLACE DESIGN**.) A variant of this design is "Plant-Scroll Design" (see **PLANT-SCROLL DESIGN**).

SEAX (SÆX/SAEX) – A single-edged knife, large dagger or short sword used for hunting or domestic purposes. This weapon gave its name to the people known as the "Sæx" – the Saxons. See **SCRAMASAX**.

SEDILIA – A seat for officiating priests usually on the south side of the chancel.

SHAFT - A vertical round, angled or polygonal section of stonework forming a column or pillar between the base and capital.

SIDE ALTERNATE QUOINING – This is where the quoins are laid alternately so that on one wall one quoin displays horizontally one long face or side above another quoin displaying one short side vertically, whilst on the adjoining walling the same quoins display a vertical short side above a horizontal long face or side. The quoins stand on their sides hence the name "Side Alternate".

SILL - The horizontal section of stonework or woodwork at the bottom of a window or doorframe.

SLAB - A flat and broad section of stonework.

SOFFIT - The underside of a lintel, vault or arch.

SOUND-HOLE - A recognisable "hole" in the stonework in the belfry stage of a tower intended to assist in the amplification of the sound of the bells.

SPANDREL - The triangular space between adjacent arches in a wall or the arms of a cross.

SPINDLE-WHORL - The whorl is a small wheel-shaped piece of stonework with a hole through its centre used as a weight in hand spinning and placed on one end of a wooden spike - a "spindle". It was used to maintain or regulate speed when spinning raw flax and wool into thread for the production of woven material. Once the flax or wool had been spun into a yarn, it was then dyed or bleached, woven into cloth, cut and sewn into clothing. See **DROP SPINDLE**.

SPIRAL-SCROLL DESIGN - A variation of Interlace Design. A design where a pattern of ribbon-like strands coil in a cylindrical, conical or helical way. The designs includes strands which may or may not be connected, may form "bands", or may form an idiosyncratic design within a panel containing other designs. See **INTERLACE DESIGN**.

SPLAY(ED) - An angled jamb of a window or doorway used to increase the amount of light coming into a building. Usually found on the internal face of a single-splayed window or doorway but also found on the external face of a double-splayed window.

SPRING(ING) - The point where an arch rises from its supports.

SQUINT (HAGIOSCOPE) - A hole in a wall to allow sight of an altar from a position in the church otherwise blocked by stonework.

STAGE - A storey or floor of a building.

STELE - An upright, often cylindrical, section of stonework sometimes decorated with sculptured designs or inscriptions.

STEPPED-PATTERN OR STEPPED-WORK DESIGN - A design depicting a row of distinctive steps placed together in a regular pattern whose central feature is noticeably thicker than the attached extensions.

STONEWORK - Masonry comprising stones sometimes without mortar.

"STOPPED" PLAIT-WORK DESIGN - A variation of Interlace Design and more specifically of Plait-Work design. This is where the individual ribbon-like strands within the design usually have rounded ends and "stop" just before the point where they meet other strands; they do not give the appearance of passing over and under each other. In addition, often each strand has an incised groove in the centre running parallel to its long borders. See **INTERLACE DESIGN**.

STOREY - A stage of a building at one level.

STOUP - A recess or niche to hold holy water.

STRANDS/STRANDED - The ribbon-like threads in an Interlace Design. See **INTERLACE DESIGN**.

STRAP-WORK DESIGN - A variation of Interlace Design. A plain design resembling a flat band or strap. See **INTERLACE DESIGN**.

STRING COURSE - A distinctive line of horizontal stonework which protrudes around the external fabric of a wall intended to assist in the bonding of stonework, to divert rainwater from running down the face of a wall, or for decorative purposes. It often separates the various stages of a tower.

STRIP-WORK - A long narrow section of moulded stonework which may arch over, or be parallel to, the top of an archway, doorway, window or belfry opening, and continue vertically parallel to both jambs towards the base, floor or ground level. It may be integral or protrude from the wall. It is often used as a generic term including Hood Moulding and Pilaster-Strips as well. See **HOOD MOULDING** and **PILASTER-STRIPS**.

STYCAS – A copper coin or debased sceat that contained no silver, issued in Northumbria. It was in circulation towards the end of the eighth century up until the mid ninth century.

STYLUS (STILUS) – An implement made from bronze, iron or bone, used to write on wax tablets. It had one pointed end, for writing, and one flat end, for smoothing out mistakes. Writing on wax tablets was used for practice purposes, preparing drafts, and for making notes.

SUNDIAL – A device for measuring the passing of the time of the day scratched on metalwork, woodwork or stonework.

SWAGS – A distinctive pendulous decorative feature with a lower semi-circular centre linked to two higher "ends". These are found on some cross-shafts, particularly near the juncture of those with a circular lower half and an angular upper half.

SYNOD – An assembly of the clergy, sometimes including representatives of the laity, held for the purposes of discussing and deciding ecclesiastical affairs.

TEGULATED – A design comprising, or arranged like, a series of overlapping tiles similar in effect to roofing tiles and plate-armour.

TERRACOTTA – Moulded and fired unglazed clay.

"THE FOUR EVANGELISTS" DESIGN – A decorative design depicting the Four Evangelists: Matthew represented by a winged man or angel symbolising the Incarnate Christ; Mark represented by a winged lion symbolising the triumphant resurrected Christ; Luke represented by a winged ox or bull or calf symbolising the atonement made by Christ's sacrifice on the Cross; and John represented by an eagle symbolising the ascended Christ of the Second Coming.

THROUGH-STONE – A stone which may extend right through the depth of a wall, extend halfway through the wall - "half-through-stones" or three-quarters of the way through the wall - "three-quarter-through-stones". Half or three-quarter through-stones require additional stonework to form the remaining depth of the wall.

THRYMSAS – A small, thick gold coin minted from around the 630s; also known as gold shillings. They were superseded by thin silver pennies known as sceattas which were made from pure silver and were the same size and weight and general appearance as thrymsas.

TILES – Thin flat slabs of burnt clay (unglazed) or stone or slate covering the roof or floor of a building.

TOMB-CHEST – A large stone coffin (like the size of a chest piece of furniture) often decorated.

TONSURE – For ecclesiastical figures two types of tonsure are likely to be encountered, Celtic and Roman. The Celtic Tonsure is where the head is shaved at the front, across the forehead, from ear to ear – the hair covers the rest of the top and the back and sides. The Roman Tonsure is where the head is shaved on the crown in a circular fashion so that the surrounding hair might symbolise the Crown of Thorns.

TOOLED – Where the surface and/or shape of a piece of stonework, woodwork, leatherwork or metalwork, have been worked with an implement.

TORUS – A roll moulding design used on a column base.

TOWER – A structure taller in height than its width, mostly square in plan but also circular. It may be built on top of and incorporate in its lower stages (see **STAGE**) an earlier porch (see **PORCH**). A tower is usually attached to the west end of the church, occasionally detached. In a cruciform church the tower is more centrally placed, between the east end of the nave and the west end of the chancel. The tower usually houses the church bells. Towers sometimes provided accommodation for a priest, acted as a schoolroom, and provided a secure refuge in times of danger.

TRACERY - Intricate ornamental stonework separating the lights (encased windows) in the upper part of Gothic (circa 1180 to 1520) windows. The stonework to support glass within a large window aperture.

TRANSEPT - The transverse sections (arms) of a cruciform church.

TRANSOM - The horizontal bar across the openings of a window.

TREE-SCROLL DESIGN - See **PLANT-SCROLL DESIGN**.

TRIFORIUM - An arcaded wall passage below the clerestory.

TYMPANUM - A solid semi-circle of stone directly above the lintel which may not always be capped by voussoirs. They are most often found above doorways but also above double belfry openings. The tympanum may be decorated.

URNES DESIGN - A design that is distinguished by elongated stylised animals entwined with spiral and scroll strands. The design was in use during the second half of the eleventh century and the first half of the twelfth century. It is named after the wood carvings on Urnes Church in Norway.

VAULT - An arched stone ceiling.

VELLUM - A prepared skin from a calf, lamb or kid (goat) which was stretched and scraped with a stone (a "smoother"). It was then folded into quires - a set of four sheets that are doubled over to form eight leaves, one within another. It was then cut and stitched into a book. Vellum was marked with a stylus, pricker (sharp-pointed instrument or tool) or compass to assist the writing or design. Ink was then applied with a quill. Vellum was used as pages for an illuminated manuscript or book.

VESTRY - A room primarily now used as a robing room by the clergy and choir. Formerly, it also stored the church plate and church records.

VINE-SCROLL DESIGN - see **PLANT-SCROLL DESIGN**.

VOLUTE - A scroll-like curve used to decorate a capital.

VOUSSOIR - Each of the wedge-shaped, tapered, stones forming an arch. Some voussoirs may comprise stones (rubble), flints and tiles which are laid radially round an arch though not wedge-shaped.

WEATHERED OR WEATHERING - An artefact, or section of stonework, seasoned by the weather rather than deliberately damaged.

WHEEL-HEAD CROSSHEAD - See **RING-HEAD CROSSHEAD**.

WHETSTONE - A hard fine-grained shaped stone used to sharpen cutting tools or weapons. Also called a "Hone".

WHITEWASH - A liquid composition of lime and water to provide a lighter colouration to built surfaces.

ZOOMORPHIC DESIGN - A design representing or imitating animals.

WHO WERE THE ANGLO-SAXONS

The Anglo-Saxon period is defined as the years from 400 up to 1100 AD.

The predecessors to the Anglo-Saxons in Britain were the Romans with the native British; how much these peoples could be accurately described as "Romano-Britons" and how much the native British retained their separate identity is a matter of conjecture.

Around 428 AD Vortigern, a British ruler, invited the Angles and Saxons in to the country to help fight the Picts who at that time dominated modern day Scotland. Traditionally these Angles and Saxons were led by Hengist and Horsa. In return for their services Vortigern offered them land. On seeing how rich and sparsely populated the country was, the Angles and the Saxons rebelled around 441 AD and took land on their own behalf. Growing populations in the Anglo-Saxon homelands, the need for farmers to seek better land for their crops, and for some, the fear of their land being flooded by the rising North Sea, prompted migration of the Anglo-Saxons to Britain.

Initially the Anglo-Saxons crossed the North Sea in relatively small groups in the late fourth and early fifth centuries, but subsequently their numbers increased so that during the later fifth and sixth centuries they began to dominate the population. As well as warriors the settlers were predominantly arable farmers wanting better and more land for their crops and families. As the number of Anglo-Saxon settlers increased, the language of the native Romano-Britons/British population was replaced by English, reflecting the domination of the newcomers. In lowland Britain this was exemplified by the use of English to describe names for topographical features, settlements and groups of settlers. In response, some Romano-Britons/British intermingled with the newcomers whilst others moved westwards into Cornwall, Wales and Brittany either as a result of warfare or their own volition.

THE ANGLES came from the Danish peninsula, some of the islands in the Danish archipelago and southern Norway. They settled north of the River Thames and established the kingdoms of Bernicia (roughly modern day Northumberland, Durham, parts of Cumbria and parts of southern Scotland), and Deira (roughly modern day Yorkshire). After 600 AD Bernicia and Deira were united to become the kingdom of the "people north of the River Humber", "Northanhymbre" -Northumbria. The kingdom of Northumbria extended from the Rivers Humber and Mersey in the south up through all the land south of the Firth of Forth in modern day Scotland, including Edinburgh. ("Edwin's burgh", named after King Edwin of Northumbria who reigned 616-633. He was baptised in 637 at York.)

The Angles also established the kingdoms of Lindsey (roughly modern day Lincolnshire), Mercia (roughly modern day Cheshire, Derbyshire, Nottinghamshire, Leicestershire, Staffordshire, Shropshire, Herefordshire, Worcestershire, Warwickshire, Northamptonshire, Bedfordshire, Hertfordshire, Greater London, Middlesex, Buckinghamshire, Oxfordshire and Gloucestershire), and East Anglia (roughly modern day Norfolk, Suffolk and Cambridgeshire).

THE SAXONS came from North Germany; they lived to the southwest of the Angles on the North Sea coastal plain around and up to the River Weser. They settled south of the River Thames and established the kingdoms of Wessex (roughly modern day Devonshire, Somersetshire, Dorsetshire, Wiltshire, Berkshire and Hampshire), Essex (roughly modern day Essex but with parts of Greater London, Hertfordshire and possibly parts of Surrey), and Sussex (roughly modern day Sussex but extending into parts of Hampshire and Surrey).

THE JUTES came from Jutland in Denmark. The Jutes settled in Kent, the Isle of Wight and the coastal lands in Hampshire opposite the Isle of Wight.

THE FRISIANS were from the north of Holland; their numbers were increased by Angles and Saxons who used Frisia as a staging point in their migration. The Frisians settled mostly in Kent. Franks from the German Rhineland also settled in Kent.

WHO WERE THE VIKINGS

The Viking period is defined as the years from 793 to 1100 AD.

The Vikings were people from modern day Denmark, Norway and Sweden. The "Age of the Vikings" was prompted by:

1. Economic factors. The populations were expanding; there was not enough land and wealth for everyone in the homelands.

2. The climate. The northern hemisphere was experiencing a periodic improvement in climate, making formerly inhospitable land desirable. In contrast, some areas experienced a rise in water levels making the land less hospitable.

3. Political factors. Warfare, consolidation and enlargement of kingdoms resulted in numbers of people becoming displaced.

4. Technological factors. The improvement of their ships in terms of construction, speed and manoeuvrability, and their ability to navigate.

Among the first recorded attack of the Vikings on England is the one on Lindisfarne off the Northumberland coast in 793. Initially, these raids by both Danish and Norwegian Vikings comprised a series of small-scale raids on undefended coastal sites by a few ships intent on acquiring portable wealth for either trade or use at home. As the success of these early raids became known, larger groups of between thirty and forty ships became involved. These targeted rich trading centres and developed a systematic pattern of raiding. These larger groups had the advantage over any who opposed them in that they could land and attack wherever they chose; unlike their opponents they did not have to stretch their resources to defend everywhere from surprise attack. Raids by these larger groups developed into attempts at conquest of the country by armies involving hundreds of ships.

Viking conquest of England began in 865 with "The Great Army" led by two sons of Ragnar Lothbrok, Ivar "the Boneless" and Halfdan. They landed in East Anglia and in the succeeding years the army moved back and forth between York, Mercia, East Anglia (where they killed King (Saint) Edmund the Martyr of East Anglia in 869), Wessex, London and Northumbria. In 874 the Great Army divided into two. One part, under the leadership of Halfdan went to the area around the mouth of the River Tyne in Northumbria. This resulted in 876 with the settlement of many of his soldiers in lands in modern day Yorkshire. The second part of the Great Army under the leadership of Guthrum, Oscytel and Anund moved to the Cambridge area. In 876, this part of the army attacked Wessex, moving between Wessex and Mercia in succeeding years. King Alfred's Treaty of Wedmore with Guthrum in 886 divided much of England between Saxon Wessex and Anglian south and west Mercia, with Viking "Danelaw" covering much of England north and east of a line from London to the Mersey. Part of northern Northumbria, with its capital at Bamburgh, Northumberland, remained English (Anglian) rather than Viking. Over the next eighty years the English gradually re-imposed their authority over the areas settled by the Great Army and their descendants.

During 900-925 Norwegian settlements extending from west of the Pennines to York were augmented by displaced Vikings from Ireland.

In 1014 the Vikings conquered all of England under Sweyn Forkbeard, King of Denmark and Norway. Shortly after his success Sweyn died and was succeeded by Canute who initially battled with King Edmund II "Ironside" for control of the country. With Edmund's death in 1016, Canute reigned as the unopposed King of England until 1035. He was succeeded as King of England by Harold I (1035-1040). Harold I was in turn succeeded by Hardecanute (1040-1042). On Hardecanute's death in 1042 Viking rule of England ceased. Hardecanute was succeeded by Edward the Confessor (1042-1066) who was one of the sons of King Æthelred II (the Unræd – The Unready) of England and Emma of Normandy.

The next Viking attempt at conquering England occurred in 1066. A Norwegian led army under Harald III "Hardrada" of Norway landed in Yorkshire. After initial success at the battle of Fulford Harald Hardrada and his army were comprehensively defeated by King Harold II of England at the battle of Stamford Bridge.

In 1069 King Sweyn Estrithson of Denmark sent a composite fleet of Danes and Norwegians to join the English in their attempts to overthrow William I. After testing defences in Dover, Sandwich, Ipswich and Norwich the fleet went to safe anchorages in the River Humber. In 1070 King Sweyn himself led another Viking fleet to join the fleet he had sent in 1069. These Vikings were involved in the events orchestrated by Hereward leader of the English in the Isle of Ely. In the summer of 1070 Sweyn and William made a peace treaty involving William paying money to Sweyn to leave the country. There were no further attempts by the Vikings to effect a conquest of England.

Those Vikings who settled in England, whilst retaining their language, laws and customs, gradually adopted Christianity and adapted their life-style and culture to those they found prevailing in Anglo-Saxon England. This resulted in their becoming "Anglo-Scandinavian" similar, but not the same, as their relations in the Scandinavian homelands. Thus in this book the term "Anglo-Scandinavian" is used rather than "Viking". This signifies, for example, that a section of stonework has been commissioned by, or shows subject or stylistic influences of, Scandinavians who have settled in England.

THE HIBERNO-NORSE

This is a term often used to describe the similarities and influences between the culture of the Norse and other Scandinavian settlers living in Ireland with the Isle of Man, the Western Isles (Hebrides), Western and South-Western Scotland, Cumbria and parts of Lancashire and Cheshire, with each other and with the indigenous Celts, Irish, British, and Anglo-Saxon peoples. The amalgam of these cultures began in the mid tenth century and continued into the twelfth century.

THE CELTIC AND ROMAN CHURCH PRACTICES, AND THE SYNOD OF WHITBY

In 664 King Oswy of Northumbria called a Synod at Whitby to resolve differences creating tension between the followers of the Celtic or Irish and the Roman practices of Christianity. Both were derived from the same Latinised Western European conversion sponsored by the Popes in Rome. But the very different circumstances of land-holding and political power in Ireland had given rise to different practices and patterns of development.

Celtic or Irish Christian communities were locally sponsored by highly segmented political dynasties. As there was no single regional or national central authority these communities were indifferent to conformity and did not adhere to a particular "Rule". Local variations of liturgy and ritual and a system of penitential discipline developed.

In contrast, Roman Christianity was propagated by missions from Rome whose members were trained in the traditions of the Benedictine Rule (written advice by Saint Benedict of Nursia in Italy, 480-547, on the precepts for monks living in a community headed by an abbot). Roman Christianity was organised on a centralised, hierarchical structure, aiming at universality rather than insularity and parochialism. It was imposed on a "top-down" basis stemming from the conversion of regional kings. Its promotion was dependent on the activity of bishops who were responsible for the "state" religion within their diocese. Bishops undertook both an evangelical and administrative role. They were head of a retinue which confirmed and maintained his importance. An abbot of a monastery answered to their bishop for their actions. This markedly contrasted with bishops from the Celtic or Irish communities who avoided special treatment and lived simply like the rest of their community. They undertook a ministerial role in their diocese whilst administrative authority within a monastery remained with the abbot who answered only to their patron, not to a bishop.

Irish missionaries had contributed to the process of conversion to Christianity of the Anglo-Saxons especially in the north of England. When Colman (of the Celtic or Irish tradition) was appointed Bishop of Northumbria in 660, disputes came to a head. The principal arguments related to the calculation of the date of Easter; details of church liturgy and canon law; the style of the monastic tonsure; the Celtic or Irish practice of following the example of the "Desert Fathers" who lived as hermits, ascetics and monks in the Egyptian desert (Saint Anthony the Great who died in 356 became known as the father and founder of desert monasticism); and also baptismal and fasting practices.

King Oswy's synod took place at Whitby (Streanaeshalch) where the monastery was ruled by Abbess Hild (later Saint Hilda). The principal advocate of the "Roman" party was Wilfrid (later bishop and Saint) and the principal advocate of the "Irish" party was Colman. Regarding the method of calculating the timing of Easter, Colman based his arguments on the authority of Saint John the Apostle, the teachings of the church in Iona and the tradition of Saint Columba. Wilfrid based his arguments on the authority of Saint Peter the keeper of the "Keys of Heaven" whose authority had been inherited by his church in Rome; the folly of only the two "outer" islands of Christianity each using a different method of calculating Easter; and the advantages of conformity across the Christian world. The Synod determined that the "Roman" rather than the "Celtic or Irish" form of Christianity would be adhered to in England. Most accepted the decision but Colman, many of his Irish clergy, and some English monks, left for Iona.

CHURCH BUILDING STYLES AND ARCHITECTURE

Churches are the main providers of extant fabric of Anglo-Saxon or Anglo-Scandinavian origin. However, much of what survives is incorporated into later work when substantial additions, rebuilding and restorations took place. As a general guide, characteristics of church building styles and architecture can be described as:

1. **"Celtic or Irish" Christian settlements from the third to the seventh century.** Although in England structural evidence of these settlements is lacking, later, church-centred oval churchyards reflect the Celtic or Irish tradition of Christian community layout. These could comprise a church within an oval enclosure in which there were groups of circular huts for monks who lived in hermit-like cells with an outer enclosing earth bank and ditch. The church was the only substantial structure. Sometimes wooden preaching crosses were erected instead of churches. All the buildings were made of wood, wattle and daub and thatch.

2. **The Anglo-Saxon period 410-1066.** Church building began in the seventh century and continued until the 1060s. Whilst some churches were built in stone from their seventh century origin the majority were built in wood. An extensive building and rebuilding of churches in stone took place in the late tenth and early eleventh centuries. However, throughout the Anglo-Saxon period many more churches were built in wood.

    Typical Anglo-Saxon churches were rectangular in plan with thin and tall walls with the nave in particular being high in relation to its length and width. Doorways, arches and windows were generally narrow in comparison with their height. Some churches had a western porch or a square or round tower and some an eastern apse or chancel. Other churches were cruciform in shape with a tower rising above the central crossing. Anglo-Saxon churches often have distinctive features such as large or megalithic quoining, walling with irregular stonework, splayed windows, hood-moulding and strip-work (see Part 2, Anglo-Saxon Churches, Pages 41 to 60).

    The Anglo-Saxons also raised crosses to denote preaching places, places of prayer and contemplation within a monastic community, and memorials to the dead sometimes accompanied by a surrounding graveyard including both vertical crosses and recumbent grave covers. They were also used to commemorate places in the life of a saint or their funeral route, and as markers for boundaries and wells.

3. **The combined Anglo-Saxon/Anglo-Scandinavian (including Danish/Norse) period 793-1100.** With the coming of the Danes in the ninth century and the Norse in the tenth century many churches were abandoned or destroyed in whole or in part. When the Danes and Norse were converted to Christianity, churches were rebuilt in the Anglo-Saxon architectural style and crosses raised for similar reasons as in "2" above.

4. **Saxo-Norman 1066-1100.** During this period characteristic Anglo-Saxon building features can sometimes be identified in new works built under the direction of the Normans.

5. **Norman or Romanesque 1066-1170.** The use of ashlar became widespread and the tops of the arches and windows were semi-circular in shape. Typically, the building style emulated the Roman style; known as "Romanesque" in mainland Europe.

6. **Transitional 1170-1200**. The period when the style of architecture changed from Norman/Romanesque to Early English Gothic displaying characteristics of both building styles.

7. **Gothic period**. Typified by tall, narrow pointed arches, vaulted roofs, buttresses, large windows and spires. It is divided into three often overlapping phases:

    (i) **Early English Gothic circa 1180 to 1275**. Typified by tall and narrow "lancet" windows terminating in a pointed head. This enabled arches to be higher than before and windows larger.

    (ii) **Decorated Gothic circa 1275 to 1380**. Typified by tracery (ornamental stonework separating the glass) in the upper part of the window. Latterly, window heads became more curving but still terminated in a point although less pronounced than before. Columns became taller and vaulting became more intricate.

    (iii) **Perpendicular Gothic circa 1380 to 1520**. Typified by even taller arches and larger windows with more complex tracery and stained glass.

8. **Tudor, Elizabethan, Stuart, Jacobean 1520 to 1714**. Few churches were built during this period. However, many monuments and brasses do survive. Elizabeth 1, who reigned 1558-1603, decreed that the congregation should no longer have to stand in church but be provided with seating.

9. **Georgian 1715 to 1837**. Churches were built in the "classical" style based on Ancient Greek and Roman styles of architecture.

10. **Victorian 1837 to 1901**. Many churches were restored or rebuilt during this period, often in a style imitating work of an earlier period particularly medieval Gothic.

SUGGESTED READING

Anglo-Saxon England: Sir Frank Stenton. Oxford University Press. First Published 1943.

The Anglo-Saxons: James Campbell. Phaidon Press Limited. First Published 1982.

Anglo-Saxon Architecture: H M Taylor and Joan Taylor. (Three Volumes.) Cambridge University Press. First Published 1965.

Anglo-Saxon Architecture: Mary and Nigel Kerr. Shire Publications Ltd. First Published 1983.

Church Archaeology: Warwick Rodwell. B T Batsford/English Heritage. First Published 1981.

The Corpus of Anglo-Saxon Stone Sculpture Series published by Oxford University Press:
Grammar of Anglo-Saxon Ornament: A General Introduction to the Corpus of Anglo-Saxon Stone Sculpture: Rosemary Cramp. 1991.
Volume I: County Durham and Northumberland: Rosemary Cramp. 1984.
Volume II: Cumberland, Westmorland and Lancashire North-of-the-Sands: Richard N. Bailey & Rosemary Cramp. 1988.
Volume III: York and Eastern Yorkshire: James Lang. 1991.

Volume IV: South-East England: Dominic Tweedle, Martin Biddle & Birthe Kjølbye-Biddle. 1995.
Volume V: Lincolnshire: Paul Everson & David Stocker. 1999.
Volume VI: Northern Yorkshire: James Lang. 2001.
Volume VII: South-West England: Rosemary Cramp. 2006.
Volume VIII: Western Yorkshire: Elizabeth Coatsworth. 2008.
Volume IX: Cheshire and Lancashire: Richard N. Bailey. 2010.
Volume X: *The Western Midlands*: Richard Bryant. 2012.

Northumbrian Crosses of the Pre-Norman Age: by W G Collingwood. First Published 1927, Reprinted by Llanerch Enterprises. 1989.

Anglo-Saxon Sculpture: James Lang. Shire Publications Ltd. First Published 1988.

The Arts in Early England: G Baldwin Brown. John Murray Ltd. First Published 1903, 1915 and 1921.

PART 2

ANGLO-SAXON CHURCHES

ANGLO-SAXON CHURCHES

Minster or Mother Churches were built as part of an organised clerical settlement whose members may or may not have followed a disciplined "Rule" of the Church. Founded by kings and landowners the head of such an establishment was often related to the founder's family, with the hereditary principal continuing thereafter. These settlements were endowed with grants of land with rights and entitlements in a defined territory, exempt from certain obligations – primarily military. The settlements varied in nature, some containing a community of monks whose primary purpose was contemplative study, the production of books and manuscripts, and the maintenance of the "Daily Offices of Prayer". Others contained mainly secular clergy who undertook pastoral or missionary work. Monks were not necessarily ordained as priests, secular clergy were. Some of the monastic Minster or Mother Churches became economic and strategic centres taking on the attributes of a town, others were occupied as royal residences or administrative centres where the literate monks provided the proto-civil service.

The network of local churches was expanded in a number of different ways. One of the duties of a bishop was considered to be the foundation of churches within his diocese to bring teaching and baptism to the inhabitants of the surrounding countryside; it was their responsibility to provide the priest(s) and ensure funding. In addition, local landowners' established churches (usually with graveyards) or oratories (usually without an altar and graveyard), endowing them with land and income, and appointing one priest to service them. Such churches were often regarded as the hereditary property of the landowner who determined the disposal of church income and the appointment of the priest. Instead of a church some local landowners built crosses on their lands served by a single priest to act as a focal point for worship; churches were also built at these sites when it was justified. These smaller churches and crosses were primarily for the benefit of the families of the local landowner.

Note: Crosses were also raised as places of prayer and contemplation within a monastic community, and memorials to the dead sometimes accompanied by a surrounding graveyard including both vertical crosses and recumbent grave covers. They were also used to commemorate places in the life of a saint or their funeral route, and as markers for boundaries and wells.

PLANS OF ANGLO-SAXON CHURCHES

The three numbered church plans following (key below) illustrate common variations in plan in Anglo-Saxon churches or churches retaining Anglo-Saxon features and fabric despite later alterations, additions, rebuilding and restorations.

KEY TO CHURCH PLANS

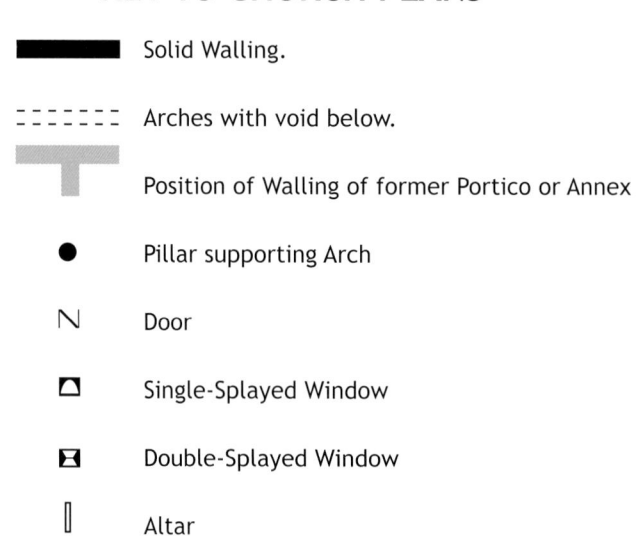

■■■■ Solid Walling.

------- Arches with void below.

┳ Position of Walling of former Portico or Annex

● Pillar supporting Arch

И Door

◨ Single-Splayed Window

⊟ Double-Splayed Window

▯ Altar

1. SIMPLE CHURCH PLAN

A single storey building comprising a rectangular nave with a smaller rectangular chancel attached – often termed "two-cell". At the east end of the nave, a void with the "chancel arch" above gives entry to the chancel area. Single-splayed windows (see Pages 51 to 52) provide light throughout the church. The only door is in the south wall of the nave; the only altar is at the east end of the chancel. A font is close to the centre of the west wall of the nave. See below, PHOTO 1, Escomb Church, County Durham.

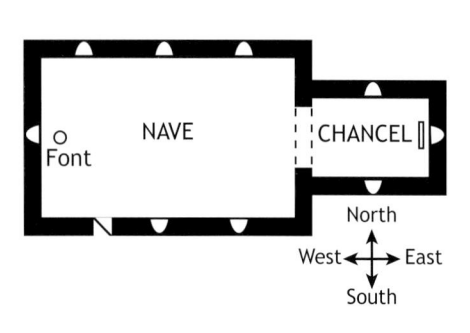

PHOTO 1 – *Example of Simple Church Plan: Nave and Chancel. Escomb Church, County Durham. See: Page 124, Site 47.*

An Introduction to Anglo-Saxon Church Architecture &   **39**
Anglo-Saxon & Anglo Scandinavian Stone Sculpture

2. CHURCH PLAN WITH VARIATIONS AND ADDITIONS

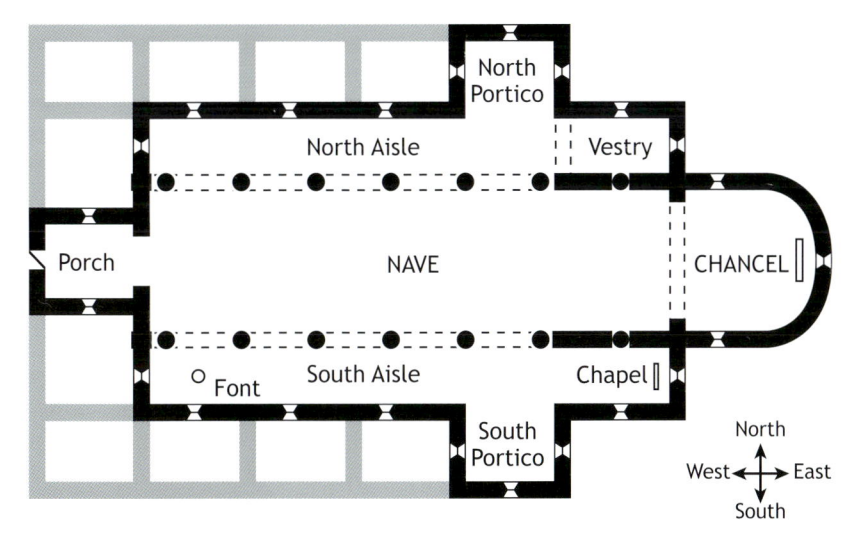

A single or two-or-more storied building comprising a rectangular nave with a smaller semi-circular ended chancel attached to its eastern end – sometimes referred to as "apsidal". A void in the east wall has a "chancel arch" above giving access to the chancel itself. The west end of the nave has an attached porch with an entry door. Note: There are examples where former porches have been incorporated into the later towers built on top of them by the Anglo-Saxons. See adjacent, PHOTO 2, All Saints Church, Brixworth, Northamptonshire, and Page 66, PHOTO 47, St Peter's Church, Monkwearmouth, Sunderland County Durham.

Both the north and south walls of the nave have attached aisles with access provided from the nave by voids with arches above. Such aisles may occupy part or all of the positions of a number of former porticos or annexes (see Page 58, 10. Porticos). Plan 2 shows the aisles occupying only part of the area occupied by the former porticos and annexes with their remaining walling (now outside the church) indicated by grey lines – nothing may now be visible. In this example "North" and "South" porticos now equate to

PHOTO 2 - *Example of Church with Variations and Additions: Stair Turret, Square Tower incorporating earlier Porch, Nave. All Saints Church, Brixworth, Northamptonshire. See: Page 114, Site 23.*

transepts and mostly survive as integral to the current structure. Originally the porticos would have been entered through a narrow doorway in an inward-facing wall rather than an open arch as in a transept; this example shows doorway and walling removed.

This church is lit by double-splayed windows (see Pages 52 to 53). The only door into the church is in the porch at the west end of the nave. The main "High Altar" is at the east end of the chancel and there is another, smaller altar in the chapel at the east end of the south aisle. There is a vestry at the east end of the north aisle. A font is located towards the west end of the south aisle.

3. CRUCIFORM CHURCH PLAN

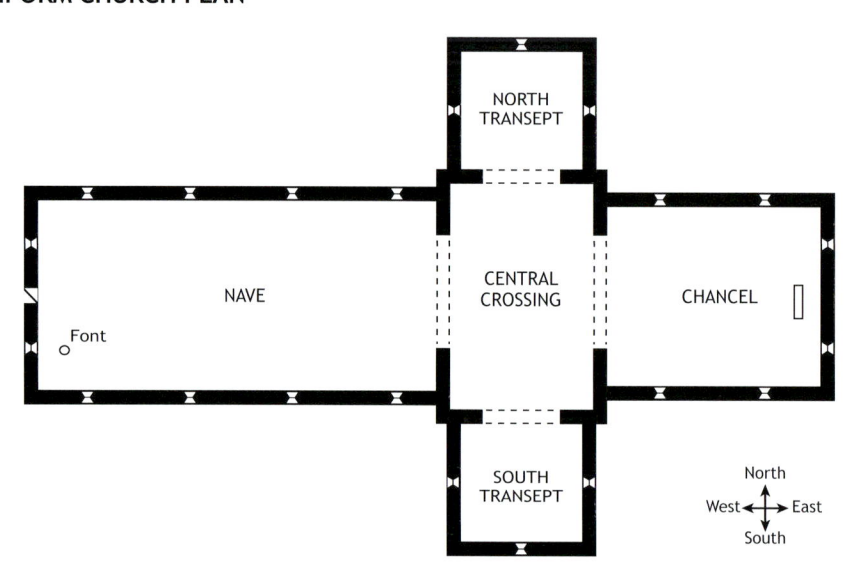

Churches which are cruciform in shape comprise a long rectangular nave, transepts extending at right angles, a sizeable chancel, and a central "crossing" whose pillars, arches and walling often support a tower. Access to and from the nave to the north and south transepts and the chancel is provided by a central crossing where there are voids with arches above.

A characteristic of Anglo-Saxon cruciform churches was that the rectangle formed by the central crossing was larger than the width of any of the four buildings joined onto it resulting externally in the quoining – see Pages 43 to 47 – jutting out from the lines of walling forming the nave, transepts and chancel.

In this example the church is lit by double-splayed windows (see Pages 52 to 53). The door providing entry is at the west end of the nave. A font is located towards the southwest corner of the nave.

See adjacent, PHOTO 3, St Mary's Church, Breamore, Hampshire.

PHOTO 3 - Example of Cruciform Church: Nave. Central Square Tower with two receding pyramidal roofs separated by vertical walling. South Portico. St Mary's Church, Breamore, Hampshire. See: Page 113, Site 17.

CONSTRUCTION OF ANGLO-SAXON CHURCHES

Typical Anglo-Saxon churches consisted of a larger western rectangle – the nave - with a smaller eastern rectangle – the chancel or apse – attached. (See Page 38, PHOTO 1, Escomb Church, County Durham.) The walls were thin and tall, the nave in particular was high in relation to its length and width. Doorways, arches and windows were generally narrow in comparison with their height. Some churches had a western porch or a square or round tower; additionally some had north and south annexes attached to the porch or tower. Other churches were cruciform in shape with a tower rising above the central crossing. (See Page 40, PHOTO 3, St Mary's Church, Breamore, Hampshire). In some cases a crypt (See Page 59, PHOTO 33, St Wystan's Church, Repton, Derbyshire, and Page 59, PHOTO 34, Hexham Abbey, Northumberland); or additional chapels or porticos, were built as a mausoleum, to house shrines (See Page 40, PHOTO 3, St Mary's Church, Breamore, Hampshire, and Page 39, PHOTO 2, All Saints Church, Brixworth, Northamptonshire), or display relics.

Whilst many Anglo-Saxon churches would originally have been constructed in wood some were constructed in stone from the outset, often utilising stonework from nearby Roman buildings. There are no known wooden Anglo-Saxon churches surviving apart from the one at Greensted in Essex. At Greensted, most of the nave walls are formed by vertically split trunks of oak trees which date from Anglo-Saxon times. These trunks rest on a Victorian wooden sill supported by Victorian bricks. Fortunately many Anglo-Saxon stone churches survive in whole or in part often incorporated into extensive later (non-Anglo-Saxon) rebuilding and restoration programmes.

Anglo-Saxon mortar was of good quality, similar in mixture and particle size to that used today and this is one of the reasons why some fabric survives. This quality has assisted Anglo-Saxon walling to carry weight for which it was not originally intended. This is exemplified by the retention of original Anglo-Saxon walling in the nave walls above "new" arches inserted in later centuries; also the lower stages of original Anglo-Saxon porches and towers can support "new" stages of towers built on top of them in later centuries. The quality of the mortar also enables identification of courses of Anglo-Saxon stonework among later medieval ones which have poorer quality mortar.

Often Anglo-Saxon churches were plastered and/or painted inside and/or out.

Roofs were supported by a wooden framework and covered with mainly thatch or turf although some might have stone tiles. Monastic buildings would more likely be tiled; some might have lead roofing, or stone tiles with lead flashing along the edges.

Windows in most churches would be open with wooden or fabric shutters, whilst some might have plain and/or coloured glass.

The floors would be the soil on which the church stood, possibly covered with straw, whilst some floors might be covered with opus signinum. (See Glossary.)

1. WALLING
The thickness of the walls of a church is a characteristic of Anglo-Saxon workmanship. Apart from walls in the towers, most Anglo-Saxon walls were less than 36 inches/91 centimetres thick, although there are occasional exceptions where they were wider.

PHOTO 4 - All Saints Church, Appleton-le-Street, North Yorkshire. Square Tower: Coursed Stone Walling. See: Page 108, Site 2.

PHOTO 5 - St Michael's Church, Oxford. Square Tower: Random Rubble Walling. See: Page 140, Site 94.

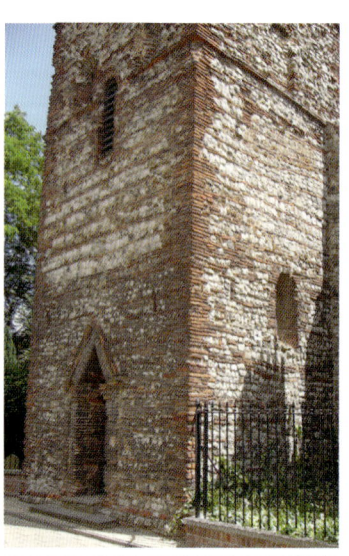

PHOTO 6 - Holy Trinity Church, Colchester, Essex. Square Tower: Random Rubble Walling including reused Roman Bricks and Tiles. See: Page 117, Site 31.

Anglo-Saxon walling may comprise shaped or irregularly-shaped, roughly-faced, and differently-sized stones, flints or rubble. Sometimes these are laid in discernible regular courses and termed "Coursed Stone" or "Coursed Rubble" - See above, top left, PHOTO 4, All Saints Church, Appleton-le-Street, North Yorkshire.

Alternatively, Anglo-Saxon walling may comprise irregularly-shaped, roughly-faced and randomly-sized rubble comprising any mixture of small pieces of stone, flint, brick or tile, not laid in discernible courses and termed "Random Rubble Walling" - See above, top centre, PHOTO 5, St Michael's Church, Oxford.

PHOTO 7 - St Andrew's Church, Wroxeter, Shropshire. North wall of nave: Coursed Stone Walling including Megalithic work from reused Roman Stonework. See: Page 150, Site 127.

Large "megalithic" stones may be randomly placed in both coursed and non-coursed stonework and rubble – their use is characteristic of Anglo-Saxon workmanship. On other occasions stonework may be laid in a herringbone pattern.

Where it was readily available tooled stonework or tiles and bricks from nearby Roman remains may be reused to form the walling itself or to decorate features such as archways, doorways and windows. See above, top right, PHOTO 6, Holy Trinity Church, Colchester, Essex, and, also see, above, middle right, PHOTO 7, St Andrew's Church, Wroxeter, Shropshire.

An Introduction to Anglo-Saxon Church Architecture & Anglo-Saxon & Anglo Scandinavian Stone Sculpture

Rarely did the Anglo-Saxons use uniform-shaped stones or use ashlar (see Glossary) stonework favoured in Norman and later periods. See adjacent, PHOTO 8, St Laurence Church, Bradford-on Avon, Wiltshire.

2. QUOINING

Quoins, collectively "quoining", are sections of stonework which support the corners of a building to assist and stabilise the construction; they also ameliorate the effects of damage, weathering and decay. Quoins are usually "dressed" - See Glossary. Individually, one side of a quoin forms the last stone in one wall and another side of the same quoin forms the last stone in the wall adjoining. Most sides of the quoins are hidden from view by the interior fabric of the walling.

PHOTO 8 – St Laurence Church, Bradford-on-Avon, Wiltshire. Nave and Chancel: Ashlar Walling. See: Page 112, Site 15.

Quoins are usually distinctly larger than other sections of stonework in the rest of the walling and may equate to two or three courses of the adjacent stonework. They are not usually uniform in shape and size and may include the use of distinctly large "megalithic" stones. The use of megalithic stones is characteristic of Anglo-Saxon workmanship.

Quoins may be made up of stone, flint, bricks, tiles or rubble, individually, or in combination; Roman material may be reused where available. Where quoining is made exclusively of small pieces of stone, flint, complete or broken brick or tile, this is described as "Rubble Quoining". See adjacent left, PHOTO 9, St Katherine's Church, Little Bardfield, Essex.

"Side Alternate Quoining", followed by "Long and Short Quoining", are the most frequently encountered and they, and the more common variations, are described in Pages 44 to 47. "Long" and "Short" quoins are characteristic of Anglo-Saxon workmanship – their use is not uniformly spread over the country.

Some churches may have two types of quoining reflecting a change of masons undertaking the work, or different periods of building work within the same structure – e.g. the tower and nave – see adjacent right, PHOTO 10, St Bartholomew's Church, Whittingham, Northumberland.

PHOTO 9 – St Katherine's Church, Little Bardfield, Essex. Rubble Quoining with Flints. See: Page 134, Site 77.

PHOTO 10 - St Bartholomew's Church, Whittingham, Northumberland. Square Tower and Nave: Coursed Rubble Walling. Side Alternate Quoining. Long and Short Quoining (some in "Sussex" fashion). See Pages 44 to 47. See: Page 148, Site 118.

An Introduction to Anglo-Saxon Church Architecture &
Anglo-Saxon & Anglo Scandinavian Stone Sculpture

Quoins are also used to define the construction of stonework forming the jambs to internal and external archways, doorways, windows and belfry openings – see Pages 48 to 54. When used to form through-stone jambs in archways, doorways, windows, or belfry openings each quoin displays three sides.

There are some examples of quoining which has been "cut-back". This is where on both sides of the corner of the angle formed by two joining walls, a (usually) narrow vertical band has been worked to remain standing in relief. Such examples may be described as "Cut-Back Side Alternate Quoining", (see below right, PHOTO 12, St Mary's Church, Stow-in-Lindsey, Lincolnshire), or "Cut-Back Long and Short Quoining" (see Page 46, top right, PHOTO 14, All Saints Church, Wittering, Cambridgeshire).

A. SIDE ALTERNATE QUOINING

Side Alternate Quoining is where the quoins are laid alternately so that on one wall one quoin displays horizontally one long face or side above another quoin displaying one short side vertically, whilst on the adjoining walling the same quoins display a vertical short side above a horizontal long face or side. The quoins stand on their sides, hence the name "Side Alternate". See the illustration in the centre below: black lines denote exposed stonework, grey lines denote hidden stonework. See below left, PHOTO 11, St Andrew's Church, Bywell, Northumberland. Side Alternate Quoining may include examples of "Megalithic Quoins" and "Cut-Back Side Alternate Quoining", see below right, PHOTO 12, St Mary's Church, Stow-in-Lindsey, Lincolnshire.

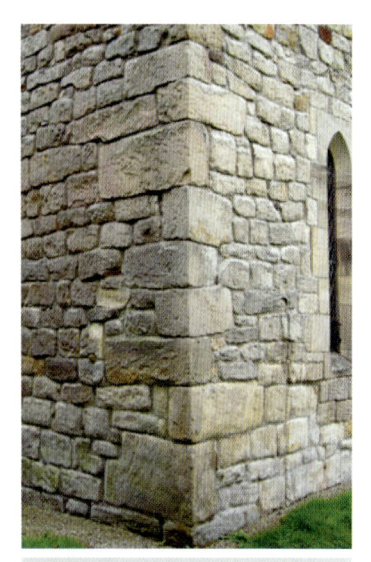

PHOTO 11 - St Andrew's Church, Bywell, Northumberland. Side Alternate Quoining. See: Page 116, Site 26.

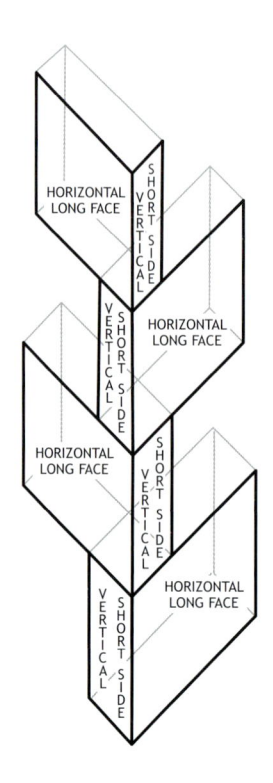

PHOTO 12 - St Mary's Church, Stow-in-Lindsey, Lincolnshire. Cut-Back Side Alternate Quoining. Central vertical grooves indicate "Cut Back". See: Page 144, Site 108.

An Introduction to Anglo-Saxon Church Architecture &   45
Anglo-Saxon & Anglo Scandinavian Stone Sculpture

B. FACE ALTERNATE QUOINING

Face Alternate Quoining is where the quoins are laid alternately so that on one wall one quoin displays horizontally one long side above another quoin displaying one short side horizontally, whilst on the adjoining walling the same quoins display a horizontal short side above a horizontal long side. The quoins are laid horizontally lying flat on their faces, hence the name "Face Alternate". See the adjacent illustration: black lines denote exposed stonework, grey lines denote hidden stonework.

Face Alternate Quoining may include "Megalithic Quoins" and "Cut-Back Face Alternate Quoining".

C. LONG AND SHORT QUOINING

Long and Short Quoining is where the quoins are laid alternately so that on one wall one quoin displays horizontally one long or short side above another quoin displaying one long face or side vertically, whilst on the adjoining walling the same quoins display a horizontal long or short side above a vertical long face or side. See illustration below left: black lines denote exposed stonework, grey lines denoting hidden stonework. See below right, PHOTO 13, St Mary's Church, Breamore, Hampshire.

The narrow vertical quoins are the "Long" and the wider horizontal quoins are the "Short". The "Longs" may sometimes be described as "column(s)" or "pillar(s)", particularly where the difference between the width of the long face and the long side is not easily apparent. There are also some examples of "Cut-Back Long and Short Quoining" – see Page 46 top right, PHOTO 14, All Saints Church, Wittering, Cambridgeshire.

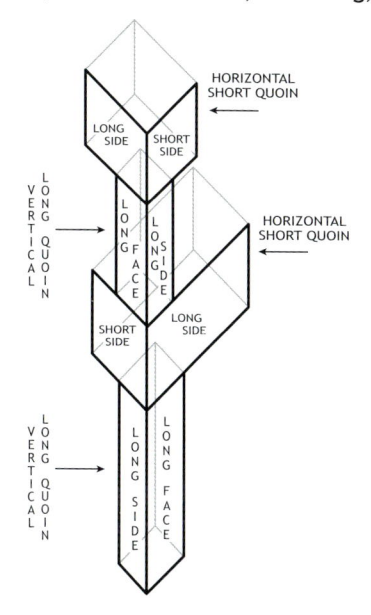

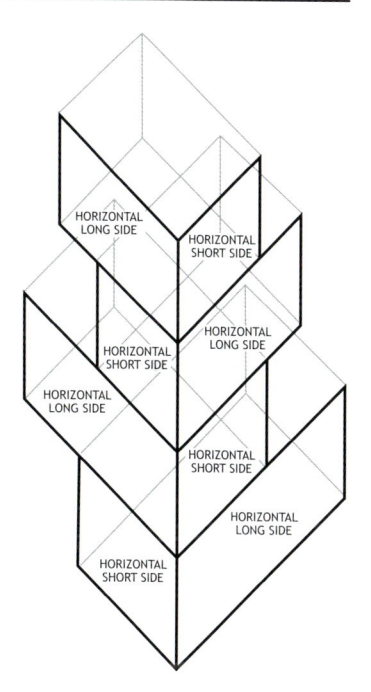

***PHOTO 13** – St Mary's Church, Breamore, Hampshire. Long and Short Quoining. See: Page 113, Site 17.*

D. ESCOMB QUOINING

Escomb quoining is a description applied to quoining where the construction technique is similar to that employed in the jambs supporting the chancel arch in the Anglo-Saxon church at Escomb, County Durham.

Ostensibly, similar to "long" and "short" quoining – see "C" above. The critical difference is that the "longs" comprise demonstrably large vertical quoins displaying a long face; they are not narrow, column or pillar-like "longs" encountered with typical long and short quoining.

The Illustration below shows quoins laid in "Escomb" fashion: black lines denote exposed stonework, grey lines denoting hidden stonework. See below PHOTO 15, St Mary's Church, Stow-in-Lindsey, Lincolnshire.

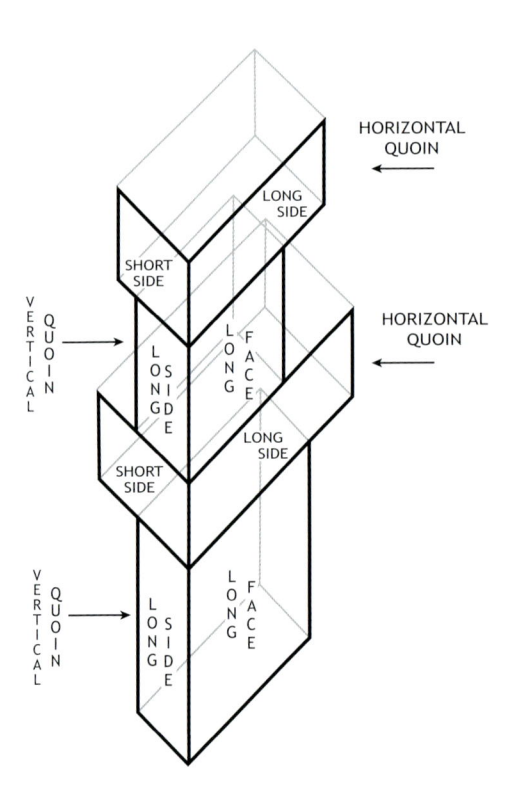

PHOTO 14 - All Saints Church, Wittering, Cambridgeshire. Cut-Back Long and Short Quoining – the distinctive grooves are near the right-hand sides of the "long" upright quoins. See: Page 149, Site 124.

PHOTO 15 - St Mary's Church, Stow-in-Lindsey, Lincolnshire. Doorway with "Escomb" Quoining forming the Jambs. See: Page 144, Site 108.

An Introduction to Anglo-Saxon Church Architecture &
Anglo-Saxon & Anglo Scandinavian Stone Sculpture

E. LONG AND SHORT QUOINING – SUSSEX VARIATION

The variation known as "Sussex" is where more than one flat quoin forms the "short" between the "long" narrow-sided quoins standing upright. Mostly found in Sussex – its use is not uniform; there are a few examples elsewhere.

Quoins are laid alternately so that on one wall two or more quoins display horizontally one long or short side above another quoin displaying one long face or side vertically, whilst on the adjoining walling the same quoins display a horizontal long or short side above a vertical long face or side.

The narrow vertical quoins are the "long", and collectively, the wider horizontal quoins are the "short". The number of flat "short" quoins between the upright "long" quoins can vary within the same angle of walling.

The illustration below shows three quoins in the lower "short" and two quoins in the upper "short". Black lines denote exposed stonework, grey lines denoting hidden stonework. See below, PHOTO 16, Holy Trinity Church, Bosham, Sussex.

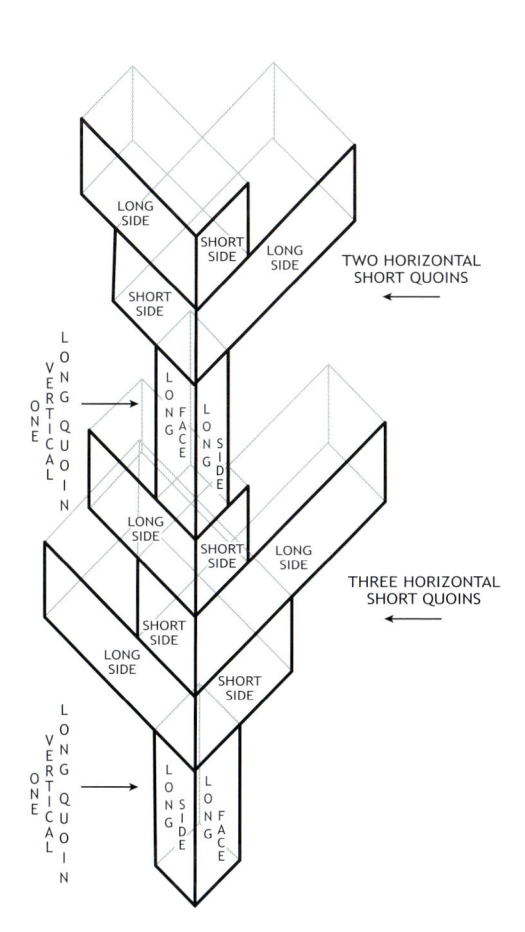

PHOTO 16 – Holy Trinity Church, Bosham, Sussex. Long and Short Quoining with "Sussex" variation. See: Page 112, Site 14.

3. ARCHWAYS, DOORWAYS, WINDOWS AND BELFRY OPENINGS

Archways, Doorways, Windows and Belfry Openings have many features in common as set out below in "A". Most will have some, but not all of the features identified. Characteristics additional to specific types of openings are then identified in "B" – Additional Characteristics of Windows, and in "C" – Additional Characteristics of Belfry Openings.

Archways, Doorways, Windows and Belfry Openings are narrow in proportion to their height and are usually faced with dressed stone (not to the uniformity of ashlar); some examples are entirely made up of rubble. They are mostly cut straight through the full thickness of the walls and constructed using "through-stones"; they are without recesses or rebates. (Through-stones may extend right through the depth of the wall, others extend halfway through the wall - "half-through-stones"- or three-quarters of the way through the wall - "three-quarter-through-stones". Both of these require additional stonework to form the remaining depth of the wall.) Tall and narrow Archways, Doorways and Belfry Openings, the use of through-stones, and the use of rubble rather than dressed stone to face some windows, are all characteristics of Anglo-Saxon workmanship.

Archways, Doorways, Windows and Belfry Openings may include particularly large "megalithic" stones which may be randomly placed. Often Round-Headed, they may also be Flat-Headed or Triangular (or Gable)-Headed. Both internally and externally, construction and design are similar.

A. COMMONALITIES

(i) OPENINGS WITH LINTEL HEADS

The heads are often formed by two large blocks of stone – sometimes "megalithic" in size - separated within the walling by rubble similar in nature to the fabric of the walling in which they are inserted. Only exceptionally are such heads through-stones, they are more likely half or three-quarter-through-stones. The heads often comprise a block of stone – the lintel - with a semi-circular head for the Archway, Doorway, Window or Belfry Opening, simply cut from the centre of the lower part of the horizontal side. With some examples, the heads may be "flat-headed" with no stonework cut away from the underside of the lintel.

The adjacent illustration identifies the main features likely to be found with a "megalithic" lintel head cut from a single block of stone. The jambs are made up of side alternate quoining (the number of quoins will often differ from one example to another).

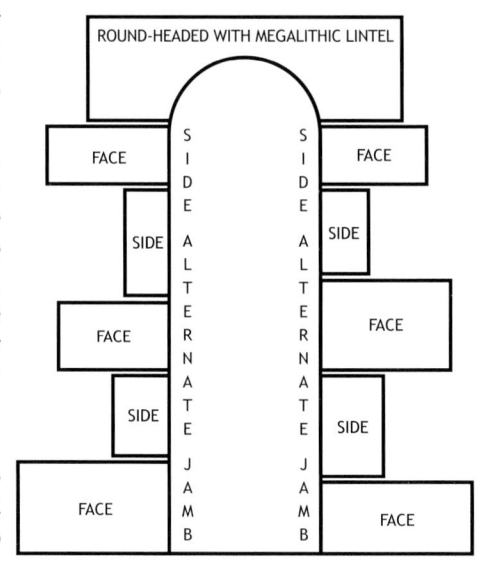

(ii) OPENINGS WITH SEMI-CIRCULAR HEADS
THE ARCH

Alternatively, the semi-circular head may be formed by "voussoirs" - generally wedge-shaped, tapered stones, flints or rubble but sometimes irregularly-shaped and sized. Roman tooled stonework or tiles and bricks were also used as voussoirs when they were available. The arch formed by the voussoirs is often not symmetrical with no obvious centrally-placed keystone; this, and the irregular shape and size of voussoirs are characteristics of Anglo-Saxon workmanship. See adjacent PHOTO 17, St Peter's Church, Wootton Wawen, Warwickshire. Arches can be quite broad and sometimes appear misshapen, at times distending to an almost horseshoe-like shape. The underside of the arch may also have an additional row(s) of smaller voussoirs forming a "soffit-roll".

Some openings with semi-circular heads may be formed of a mixture of stone, flint, brick and tile – "rubble" - with no indication of wedge-shaped voussoirs.

THE IMPOSTS
Most examples have imposts supporting each side of the arch spanning the opening; windows are usually the exception. Imposts often project from the underside of the arch and overhang the jambs; they may be through-stones. They are usually square in section and profile and sometimes may be chamfered and occasionally stepped, moulded or sculptured. They may also be decorated with a variety of designs: abstract, scroll, inhabited plant-scroll, and architectural designs, (for example, representations of balusters) etc.

PHOTO 17 - St Peter's Church, Wootton Wawen, Warwickshire. Voussoirs forming a Round-Headed Archway with Escomb Jambs. See: Page 149, Site 125.

THE JAMBS
The jambs may be made up of side alternate, or face alternate, or long and short, or "Escomb" quoins or rubble or roughly-dressed stones; they may be megalithic in size and be through-stones or half or three-quarter through-stones. Some examples may have columns or shafts with capitals (beneath the imposts) and bases all of which extend from and are integral to the walling forming the jambs. With such examples:

- The capitals take various forms and these may be square, rectangular, round, or trapezoid in shape, chamfered or moulded and sometimes may be described as a "cushion-capital" (See Glossary). Capitals may be decorated with designs similar to those used on imposts but with a more restricted choice.

- The columns or shafts themselves may be formed by one piece of stonework or a series of sections of stonework placed on top of one another. They may be circular, angled or polygonal in shape and sometimes decorated with designs similar to those used on imposts and capitals but with an even more restricted choice; some form of spiral decoration is quite common.

- The bases at the foot of the columns or shafts may be square, rectangular, round, or trapezoid in shape, chamfered or moulded.

- Sometimes, separating the base from the bottom of the column or shaft is an additional section of stonework which may be square, rectangular, round, or trapezoid in shape; it may also taper with concentric grooves indicating a reducing circumference.

(iii) OPENINGS WITH FLAT-HEADS

Whilst many examples are Round-Headed some are Flat-Headed with no cut out from the lintel. Flat-Headed examples are commonly formed by a single block of stone or, less frequently, by two or more stones in a row laid flat. Some may have round-heads externally and flat-heads internally and vice versa. See adjacent PHOTO 18, All Saints Church, Hough-on-the-Hill, Lincolnshire.

(iv) OPENINGS WITH TRIANGULAR-HEADS

Other examples have two stones placed to form a triangular-shaped (gable) head. Triangular-Headed archways, doorways, windows and belfry openings are indicative of Anglo-Saxon workmanship. See below right, PHOTO 19, St Peter's Church, Barton-Upon-Humber, Lincolnshire below with a Triangular-Headed Doorway with Hood Moulding and Strip-Work – See 4. Hood Moulding and Strip-Work, Pages 54 to 55.

B. ADDITIONAL CHARACTERISTICS OF WINDOWS

Many Anglo-Saxon windows were narrow, rectangular-shaped, with a Round-Head cut into the lower horizontal side of a lintel or with the Round-Head formed by voussoirs. Others were Flat-Headed, Triangular (Gable)-Headed, and some were Circular.

Most Anglo-Saxon windows were either "Single-Splayed" (see Pages 51 to 52) or "Double-Splayed" (see Pages 52 to 53). Double-Splayed windows are indicative of Anglo-Saxon workmanship and are rarely found in churches built in Norman and later periods.

Whilst the windows were often open to the elements some were shuttered with wood, animal horn, linen or glass (fragments of plain and coloured window glass survive). Wooden frames were made to insert into rebates constructed in both jambs "inside" (internally) the windows. With Single-Splayed Windows these rebates were close to the exterior face of the wall but with a sufficient gap between them to allow a shutter to be inserted; a gap resulted between the shutter and the exterior face of the wall. There are a few examples where the rebate is cut so close to the exterior face of the wall that the shutter is almost placed "outside". With Double-Splayed Windows the rebates were in the mid-wall and this has resulted in the wooden frames surviving in some cases – See Page 53, PHOTO 23 and PHOTO 24, both from St Michael's Church, Thursley, Surrey.

PHOTO 18 – All Saints Church, Hough-on-the-Hill, Lincolnshire. Flat-Headed Doorway. See: Page 130, Site 64.

PHOTO 19 – St Peter's Church, Barton-Upon-Humber, Lincolnshire. Triangular-Headed Doorway (blocked). See: Page 110, Site 6.

Some wooden frames appear to have "holes" in them to thread string to retain the animal horn, linen or netting (to keep birds out). Other wooden frames appear to have had iron nails to support the shutters.

Additionally, there are a few examples of where a stone slab has been pierced to form the exterior aperture of a window with the remaining stone of the slab providing the window

An Introduction to Anglo-Saxon Church Architecture &   51
Anglo-Saxon & Anglo Scandinavian Stone Sculpture

frame. See Page 58, PHOTO 32, All Saints Church, Hough-on-the-Hill, Lincolnshire.

SINGLE-SPLAYED WINDOWS
Single-Splayed Windows have their narrowest aperture at the outer (external) face of the wall of the church. The opening widens towards the interior of the church. The splay of the sill, jambs and window head continues through the full thickness of the wall; the angle of the splay is not very acute. (Single-Splayed Windows built in Norman and later periods have their splays recessed internally, behind the outer face of the wall; the sill, jambs and window head splay widely towards the interior of the church.) See adjacent PHOTO 20, Escomb Church, County Durham.

INTERIOR FACE
The illustration below left identifies the main features likely to be found in the interior of a Single-Splayed Window. This example shows a megalithic lintel with a semi-circular head cut into the centre of the lower horizontal side. The sill, jambs and window head are splayed outwards from the window towards the interior of the church. The jambs are made up of side alternate quoining; the number of quoins will often differ from one example to another.

PHOTO 20 – Escomb Church, County Durham. Interior of Round-Headed Single-Splayed Window with grooves for Shutter. See: Page 124, Site 47.

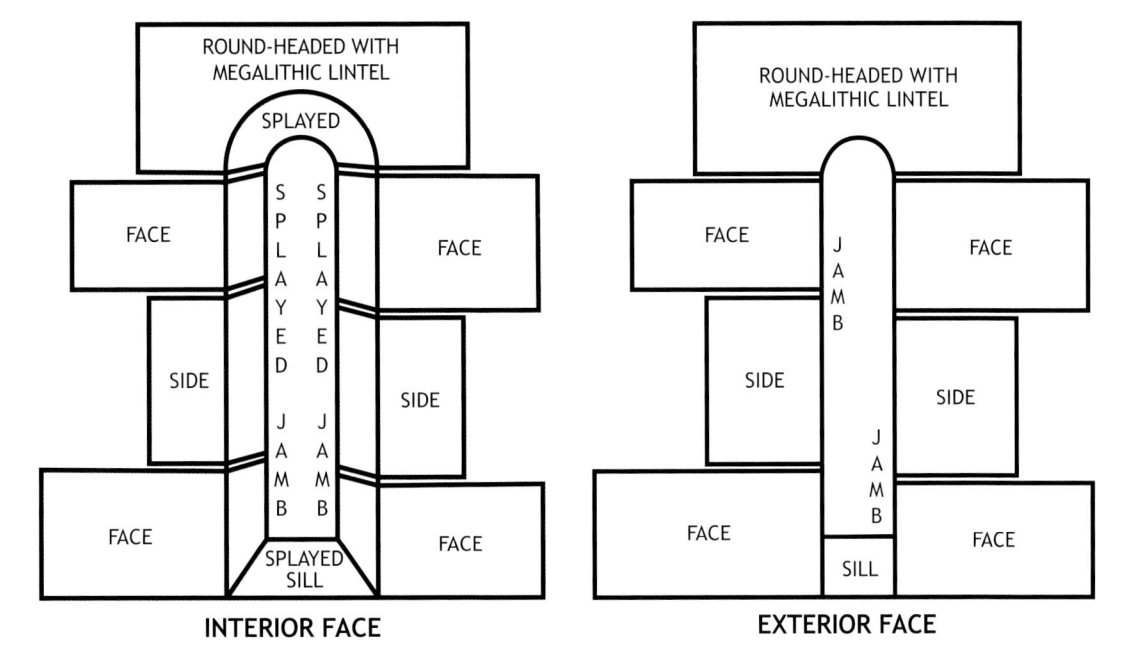

INTERIOR FACE

EXTERIOR FACE

EXTERIOR FACE
The illustration above right identifies the main features likely to be found in the exterior of a Single-Splayed Window. This example is round-headed with a megalithic lintel. The jambs are made up of side alternate quoining; the number of quoins will often differ from one example to another. The sill is identified. See Page 52 top left, PHOTO 21, St Paul's Church, Jarrow, County Durham.

PHOTO 21 - St Paul's Church, Jarrow, County Durham. Chancel: Round-Headed Single-Splayed Windows - exterior view. See: Page 132, Site 69.

PHOTO 22 - St Michael's Church, Glentworth, Lincolnshire. Exterior of Round-Headed "Key-Hole" Single-Splayed Window with Hood Moulding (See 4. Hood Moulding and Strip-Work, Pages 67 to 69), and decorated with "Palmette Design" (See Page 96.) See: Page 125, Site 51.

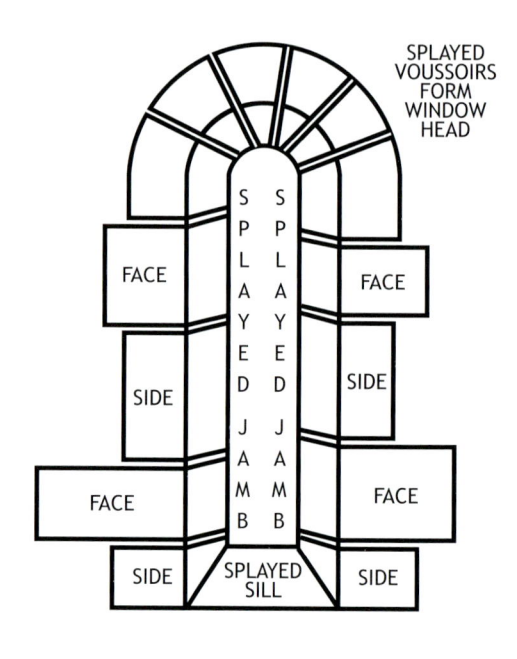

"KEY-HOLE" WINDOWS

In Lincolnshire in particular, the shape of the window head may be more than the usual half circle thus taking on the appearance of a key-hole; hence the description. Such windows are single-splayed. See above right, PHOTO 22, St Michael's Church, Glentworth, Lincolnshire.

DOUBLE-SPLAYED WINDOWS

Double-Splayed Windows have their narrowest aperture close to the centre of the wall of the church. The opening widens both outward towards the outer (external) face of the wall of the church and inward towards the inner (internal) face of the wall of the church. Double-Splayed Windows are mostly found in churches which have been built or rebuilt or altered from the ninth century onwards. (Double-Splayed Windows were rarely used in Norman and later periods.)

The adjacent illustration identifies the main features likely to be found in both the interior and exterior of a Double-Splayed Window. Both faces of this example have a round-head formed by voussoirs. The sill, jambs and voussoirs forming the window head are splayed outwards from the window towards the interior of the church. The jambs are made up of side alternate quoining; the number of quoins will often differ from one example to another. See Page 53, PHOTO 23 (interior) and PHOTO 24 (exterior) both from St Michael's Church Thursley, Surrey.

An Introduction to Anglo-Saxon Church Architecture &   53
Anglo-Saxon & Anglo Scandinavian Stone Sculpture

PHOTO 23 - St Michael's Church, Thursley, Surrey. Chancel. Round-Headed Double-Splayed Windows with Oak Mid-Wall Frames. Interior View. See Page 147, Site 114.

PHOTO 24 - St Michael's Church, Thursley, Surrey. Chancel. Round-Headed Double-Splayed Windows with Oak Mid-Wall Frames. Exterior View. See: Page 147, Site 114.

C. ADDITIONAL CHARACTERISTICS OF BELFRY OPENINGS

There are two basic types of Anglo-Saxon Belfry Openings - "Single" and "Double". Single-Belfry Openings are those where the two lights (openings) are separated by a central solid block of walling which runs through the entire thickness of the wall; this walling may comprise megalithic through-stones. Double-Belfry Openings are those where the two lights (openings) are separated from each other by a narrow "mid-wall" shaft (in the centre of the thickness of the wall) which may be formed by a baluster shaft, or by a section of stonework which is cylindrical, rectangular, or bulbous in shape. These mid-wall shafts support a large flat slab of stonework which runs through the entire thickness of the wall. These mid-wall shafts may have capitals and bases which take various forms and these may be square, rectangular, round, or trapezoid in shape, chamfered or moulded, and the capitals may be described as "cushion capitals" (see Glossary); capitals may be decorated.

Double-Belfry Openings cut straight through the wall, without being recessed from the face of the walling, and with a mid-wall shaft supporting a large flat slab running through the entire thickness of the wall, are characteristics of Anglo-Saxon workmanship.

The individual lights in a belfry opening may be:
- a semi-circular head cut from a lintel, occasionally the lintel may extend over both lights rather than individually over each light;
- a semi-circular headed arch formed by voussoirs;
- a semi-circular-headed arch formed by a mixture of stone, flint, brick and tile – "rubble" - with no indication of wedge-shaped voussoirs.
- a triangular-shaped (gable)-headed arch formed by two stones placed to form a triangle;
- flat-headed formed by a single horizontal stone.

Belfry Openings were not splayed like most Anglo-Saxon windows and they were left open, not glazed or shuttered.

Some Belfry Openings have circular-shaped Sound-Holes – sometimes described as "Circular Double-Splayed Windows". These may be placed singly, in pairs or evenly spaced, above, below or to the side of the lights; they may also be placed in the tympanum. In view of their small size their purpose was probably more ornamental than sound amplification.

The adjacent illustration identifies the main features likely to be found in a Double Belfry Opening. This example has two lights each with a round-head with a megalithic lintel head supported by imposts. The two lights are separated by a cylindrically-shaped column comprising a single shaft with an impost at its head and a base at the bottom. The jambs are formed of quoins laid in a random way. The opening sits on a distinctive sill and is framed by Strip-Work (See 4. Hood Moulding and Strip-Work, below) forming a curved arch above the heads of each of the two lights and continuing parallel to the jambs vertically to the base of the opening. There are three Sound-Holes, one in the centre of the tympanum and higher up one each side of the arch of the Strip-Work.

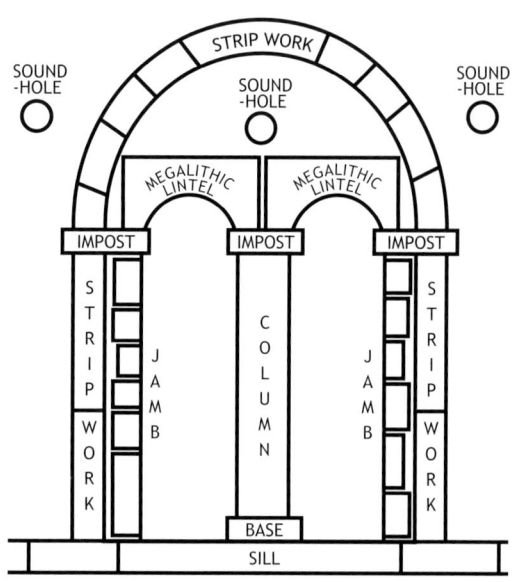

See Page 61, PHOTO 37, St Peter's Church, Barton-Upon-Humber, Lincolnshire, and Page 62, PHOTO 39, St Andrew's Church, Bywell, Northumberland.

4. HOOD MOULDING AND STRIP-WORK

The Arch, Imposts and Jambs of Openings with semi-circular or triangular heads may be accompanied by Hood Moulding and Strip-Work which usually comprise sections of moulded stonework integral to or protruding between 2 inches/5 centimetres and 3 inches/7 centimetres from the face of the stonework into which they are inserted.

Hood Moulding is above and concentric with the curved head or parallel to the triangular head of Archways, Doorways, Windows (rarely) and Belfry Openings. Strip-Work then extends from the bottom of both sides of the arch of the Hood Moulding vertically parallel to the jambs of the Archway, Doorway, Window or Belfry Opening down to the level of the sill, base, floor or ground.

Both Hood Moulding and Strip-Work usually decorate only one face of an Archway, Doorway, Window, or Belfry Opening, but there are exceptions where both faces are decorated. Where Hood Moulding is found externally it may act as a protective barrier to rain water.

Internally, the jambs of the arches of a crossing, or the jambs of a chancel arch, may be complemented by double rows of adjacent but separate Strip-Work (there may well have been similar double rows of Hood Moulding but no extant examples appear to have survived). There may be differences in construction between rows with one section of Strip-Work being "half-round", and the other being "half-square". The top of the Strip-Work may terminate in the imposts supporting the arches and the bases may terminate in bulbous corbels above a stepped plinth – see 7. Plinths, Page 57. See Page 56, PHOTO 29, St Mary's Church, Stow-in-Lindsey, Lincolnshire.

The illustration at the top of Page 55 identifies the main features likely to be found with a Round-Headed Archway, Doorway, Window or Belfry Opening, with a head formed by voussoirs supported by imposts, with capitals, and columns supported by stepped bases. Additionally, there is Hood Moulding and Strip-Work.

An Introduction to Anglo-Saxon Church Architecture & Anglo-Saxon & Anglo Scandinavian Stone Sculpture 55

In Norman and later periods Hood Moulding continued but Strip-Work parallel to the jambs and extending down to the sill, base, floor or ground was dispensed with.

Strip-Work is often used as a generic description for both Hood Moulding and Pilaster-Strips (see 5. Pilaster-Strips, Page 56.) Strip-Work on the surfaces of walls, whether described as "Strip-Work" or "Pilaster-Strips", are characteristics of Anglo-Saxon workmanship. See below left, PHOTO 25, All Saints Church, Wittering, Cambridgeshire; below centre, PHOTO 26, St John the Baptist Church, Barnack, Cambridgeshire; and below right, PHOTO 27, St Peter's Church, Barton-Upon-Humber, Lincolnshire.

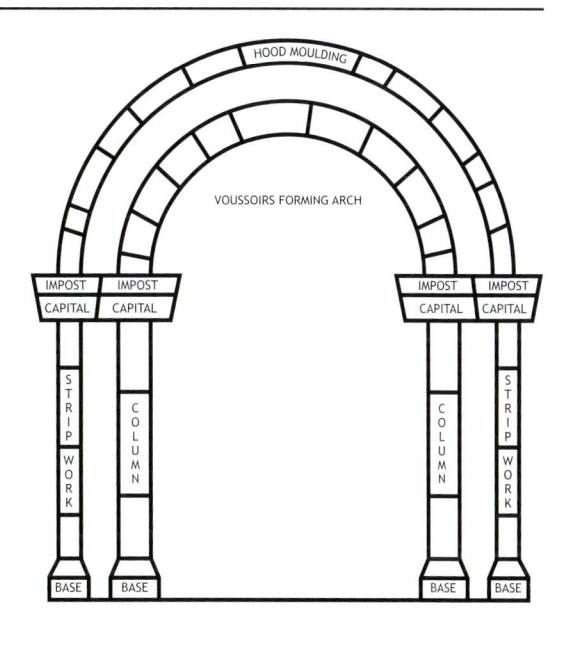

PHOTO 25 – All Saints Church, Wittering, Cambridgeshire. Chancel Arch with Hood Moulding and Strip-Work. See: Page 149, Site 124.

PHOTO 26 – St John The Baptist Church, Barnack, Cambridgeshire. Round-Headed Doorway with Hood Moulding and Strip-Work, and "Escomb" Jambs. Also Pilaster-Strips. See: Page 109, Site 5.

PHOTO 27 – St Peter's Church Barton-Upon-Humber, Lincolnshire. Round-Headed Tower Arches with semi-circular heads formed by wedge-shaped voussoirs with "Escomb" Jambs. The face of the Archway in the foreground is plain and the face of the Archway in the background additionally has, Hood Moulding and Strip-Work. See: Page 110, Site 6.

PHOTO 28 - St Andrew's Church, Great Dunham, Norfolk. Incomplete rows of Round-Headed Sunken Blind Arcading separated by Pilaster-Strips; some with decorated Imposts. See: Page 126, Site 53.

PHOTO 29 - St Mary's Church, Stow-in-Lindsey, Lincolnshire. Central Crossing: Round-Headed Arches with Hood Moulding. Jambs complemented by double rows of adjacent but separate Pilaster-Strips. Note: Ignore later fifteenth century "Perpendicular" arch. See: Page 144, Site 108.

5. PILASTER-STRIPS

Pilaster-Strips are usually plain, variable vertical lengths of dressed stone or rubble. They may be laid in simple lengths of upright material, or in similar fashion to the design of Long and Short Quoining, or laid in courses similar to the adjacent walling. They usually comprise sections of stonework integral to or protruding between 3 inches/7 centimetres from the face of the stonework into which they are inserted and measure between 6 inches/15 centimetres and 12 inches/30 centimetres wide.

Pilaster-Strips assist in the construction and preservation of the stonework, and in the application of plaster. They also ameliorate the effects of damaging, weathering and decay of the adjacent walling. They may be used to provide decoration – e.g. in Round-Headed or Triangular-Headed Arcading. Where the adjacent walling is formed by flints the Pilaster-Strips and the patterns associated with them are purely decorative in purpose.

Pilaster-Strips may also be referred to as Strip-Work which is often used as a generic description for both Hood Moulding and Pilaster-Strips (see 4. Hood Moulding and Strip-Work, Pages 54 to 55.) See above left, PHOTO 28, St Andrew's Church, Great Dunham, Norfolk, and see above right, PHOTO 29, St Mary's Church, Stow-in-Lindsey, Lincolnshire.

"PILASTER-BUTTRESSES"

Mostly in Kent, often where Roman bricks or tiles have been reused, some churches may have external small buttress-like pilaster-strips, particularly on or near the corners of walling; these are demonstrably wider than "standard" size Pilaster-Strips. See adjacent PHOTO 30, St Peter's-on-the-Wall, Bradwell-on-Sea in Essex has examples of these small buttresses.

PHOTO 30 - St Peter-On-The-Wall Church, Bradwell-on-Sea, Essex. Restored Nave. "Pilaster Buttresses". See: Page 112, Site 16.

An Introduction to Anglo-Saxon Church Architecture &   57
Anglo-Saxon & Anglo Scandinavian Stone Sculpture

6. STRING COURSES

String Courses are horizontal lengths of dressed stones or rubble which mostly protrude from the wall about 2 inches/5 centimetres to 4 inches/10 centimetres. They mostly measure between 6 inches/15 centimetres and 8 inches/20 centimetres in height. Their surviving length varies. String courses are mostly plain and square in section; these are characteristics of Anglo-Saxon workmanship. However, some are chamfered, others moulded, and a few may be decorated.

In addition to providing decoration String Courses assisted with the bonding of stonework and the application of plaster; they also diverted rainwater from running down the face of a wall.

String Courses were commonly used to help differentiate the stages of a tower. In some examples, the differences between the stages of a tower may also be emphasised by the face of the upper storey being "set-back" or "off-set" by around 6 inches/15 centimetres from the face of the stage below. See Page 64, PHOTO 43, St John the Baptist Church, Barnack, Cambridgeshire. Note: The walling of some towers may be uninterrupted by string courses or "set-backs/off-sets".

Sometimes String Courses formerly on the exterior face of (usually) nave walling may now be identified inside the church following the addition of aisles and towers in later centuries.

Internally, there are a few examples where the imposts of a tower arch or a chancel arch extend along the face of the walling in similar fashion to a String Course.

7. PLINTHS

Stone or Rubble Plinths at the bottom of walling may be Anglo-Saxon in origin where they accompany distinctive Anglo-Saxon features; large flat stones are particularly indicative. Whilst many comprise single, flat or square-shaped courses of stonework, some churches have stepped plinths comprising stonework several courses high – the lower course is usually flat or square with the upper courses often with chamfered tops. Whilst mostly surviving externally, there are examples internally. Note: Not all Anglo-Saxon walling has a plinth(s).

8. STAIRWAYS

Few examples of Anglo-Saxon spiral stairways survive but their construction distinctly differs from the methods used in Norman and later periods.

With Anglo-Saxon spiral stairways the central pillar - the newel - around which the steps radiate, consists of separate jointed sections of stonework rising above several steps. The treads of the individual steps are formed from separate sections of stonework which have been notched into the newel (on their inner side) and into the surrounding walling (on their outer side). At Hough-on-the-Hill in Lincolnshire (see PHOTO 31 adjacent), the treads have no separate support and simply rest on the step below; the underside of the treads provide the ceiling of the stairway. In contrast, at Brixworth in Northamptonshire (see Page 114, Site 23), the underside of the treads have vaulted supports.

PHOTO 31 – All Saints Church, Hough-On-The-Hill, Lincolnshire. Stair Turret. Underside of Spiral Stairway with Steps formed separately from the Newel. See: Page 130, Site 64.

In Norman and later periods stairways were usually constructed in jointed sections comprising both the central newel and steps all formed from the same individual section of stonework.

For the exterior views and placement of stair turrets see adjacent PHOTO 32, All Saints Church, Hough-on-the-Hill, Lincolnshire, and Page 39, PHOTO 2, All Saints Church, Brixworth, Northamptonshire.

9. UPPER DOORWAYS
Some churches have doorways above ground level - at first, second and third floor levels. They provided internal and sometimes external access to towers, naves and porticos.

Upper Doorways were reached by permanent wooden stairways or ladders, and sometimes by stone stairways. There are a few examples where a stair turret was built abutting the tower to provide access to the floor levels in the tower.

PHOTO 32 - All Saints Church, Hough-On-The-Hill, Lincolnshire. Turret for spiral stairway. See: Page 130, Site 64.

Through the use of stairways or ladders, upper doorways facilitated communication between rooms at various floor levels in the (usual) western tower. However, at first floor level, some provided the only external access to the tower, while others provided access to a western gallery in the nave.

The purpose of upper doorways at second and third floor levels in the tower is a matter of ongoing debate, some simply assisted communication within the tower, whilst others provided access to galleries or rooms above the nave, porticos and chancel. The purpose of a few at high level, particularly those which open externally, may have been for the display of relics to the congregation below.

In a cruciform church, and where the tower is centrally placed, the existing or former central crossing below may include doorways providing access to former upper galleries including those above the nave, transepts/porticos, and chancel.

Upper rooms or galleries would have been used in connection with the liturgy, as a library, scriptorium, treasury, chapel, the storage and display of relics, and for accommodation by the clergy.

10. PORTICOS
Porticos (see Page 40, PHOTO 3, St Mary's Church, Breamore, Hampshire) could be up to two storeys high adjacent and attached to the north and south walls of the main body of a church, and sometimes overlapping both nave and chancel and porch and tower. They could be a single structure or a series of attached structures similar in effect to an aisle. Porticos were usually entered through a narrow doorway. Originally used as side chapels, those near the east end of the nave were often used for important burials – on the north side for ecclesiastics, on the south side for royalty. They were also used for the preparation of the Communion and storage of sacred vessels, to house books, to act as a vestry, a baptistry, an additional space for lay members of the congregation at important festivals, as schoolrooms, courtrooms and for accommodation for priests (often the upper room(s)).

An Introduction to Anglo-Saxon Church Architecture &   **59**
Anglo-Saxon & Anglo Scandinavian Stone Sculpture

11. CRYPTS

There are a few examples of Anglo-Saxon crypts surviving which were built as a mausoleum, to house shrines or display relics of saints and kings.

The crypt at St Wystan's Church, Repton in Derbyshire has ashlar walling with megalithic square quoins and a square-stepped triple plinth and string courses, pilasters and vestiges of windows. However, the most impressive feature are the four centrally placed free-standing decorated columns with bases and decorated capitals assisting in the support of the vaulted roof. The recesses in the outer walls could be for shrines, bones, relics, or tombs. The crypt was used as a mausoleum by Mercian kings including King Ethelbald (reigned 716-757), King Wiglaf (reigned 827-840), and his grandson St Wystan (murdered in 740). See above PHOTO 33, St Wystan's Church, Repton, Derbyshire.

PHOTO 33 - St Wystan's Church, Repton, Derbyshire. Crypt: Decorated Columns with bases and decorated Capitals. Vaulted Roof. See: Page 141, Site 98.

The crypts at Hexham Abbey, Northumberland, (see adjacent, PHOTO 34, Hexham Abbey, Northumberland), and Ripon Cathedral, North Yorkshire, were built at the instigation of Bishop Wilfrid in the seventh century. The ashlar walling in these structures included the reuse of Roman stonework; some with decoration, some covered with vestiges of coloured plasterwork, and two examples (in Hexham) with Roman inscriptions. These underground structures comprise: a main central barrel-vaulted chamber with niches for lamps and relics, with an ante chamber containing a ventilation shaft; flat-headed access passages (at Hexham the two flanking passages have triangular-headed ante chambers at their western ends); round-headed archways (doorways); and stairs.

At All Saints Church, Wing, Buckinghamshire a seven sided apsidal chancel – see Page 66, PHOTO 48 - overlies an octagonal crypt with a central chamber surrounded by an ambulatory. The crypt walling is built of coursed rubble. Passages – the ambulatory – are pierced by round-headed openings which provide access to the central chamber which housed shrines, bones, relics, or tombs; both the central chamber and the ambulatory are barrel-vaulted.

PHOTO 34 - Hexham, Abbey, Northumberland. Crypt: Ashlar Walling including reused Roman Stonework. Round-Headed Archway. Barrel-Vaulted Chambers. See: Page 128, Site 60.

12. ROOFS

Whilst no Anglo-Saxon roofs now survive, evidence remains in the form of clearly identifiable triangular (gable)-shaped "rooflines" on existing structures, often indicating the height of a former Anglo-Saxon nave abutting the walling of a tower, the height of a former portico incorporated into a transept, and the height of a former porch incorporated into a tower. Sometimes the angle of an Anglo-Saxon roofline may survive in the current roofline, albeit reconstructed in later, non-Anglo-Saxon material, but perhaps with some vestiges of Anglo-Saxon stonework included.

The "Rhenish Helm" (See Glossary) roof on the Anglo-Saxon square tower of St Mary The Virgin Church at Sompting in Sussex is thought to replicate its Anglo-Saxon predecessor. See below left, PHOTO 35, St Mary the Virgin Church, Sompting, Sussex.

PHOTO 35 - St Mary The Virgin Church, Sompting, Sussex. Square Tower: Random Rubble Walling with Flints. "Cut-Back" Long and Short Quoining. Square String Course. Pilaster-Strips. Round-Headed Double-Splayed Windows. Triangular-Headed Windows. Round-Headed Double-Belfry Openings. Triangular-Headed Single Belfry Openings. "Rhenish Helm" Roof. See: Page 143, Site 106.

PHOTO 36 - St Bene't's Church, Cambridge, Cambridgeshire. Square Tower: Random Rubble Walling. Square String Courses. "Cut-Back" Long and Short Quoining. Round-Headed Double-Belfry Openings with mid-wall baluster shafts. Round Sound Holes. Above the Belfry Openings, a centrally placed Pilaster-Strip above the centre which possibly originally extended to a gable forming a "Rhenish-Helm" Roof. See: Page 116, Site 27.

The Anglo-Saxon square tower of St Bene't's Cambridge may have vestiges of support stonework for a "Rhenish-Helm" Roof comprising the remains of centrally placed Pilaster-Strips above the belfry openings. See above right, PHOTO 36, St Bene't's Church, Cambridge, Cambridgeshire.

St Mary's Church at Breamore in Hampshire - see Page 40, PHOTO 3 - with its central square tower with two receding pyramidal roofs separated by vertical walling is thought to represent a cut down version of the towers of major churches and cathedrals described in Anglo-Saxon literature and depicted in illustrations.

An Introduction to Anglo-Saxon Church Architecture &
Anglo-Saxon & Anglo Scandinavian Stone Sculpture

EXCELLENT EXAMPLES OF ANGLO-SAXON CONSTRUCTION FEATURES

PHOTO 37 – St Peter's Church, Barton-Upon-Humber, Lincolnshire.
Western Annexe: Random Rubble Walling (plastered externally). Vestiges of Square Plinth. "Cut-Back" Long and Short Quoining. Round-Headed Double-Splayed Windows. Circular Double-Splayed Windows.
Square Tower: Random Rubble Walling (plastered externally). Coursed Stone Walling. Square Plinth. "Cut-Back" Long and Short Quoining. Side Alternate Quoining. Round-Headed and Triangular-Headed Pilaster-Strips in Long and Short Fashion. Square String Courses. Round-Headed Doorway with "Escomb" Jambs, Hood Moulding and Strip-Work. Round-Headed Double Windows with "Escomb" jambs, decorated mid-wall baluster shafts and Hood Moulding. Triangular-Headed Double Openings with "Escomb" Jambs, decorated mid-wall baluster shafts, Hood Moulding and Strip-Work. Round-Headed Double Belfry Openings with cylindrical and square-shaped decorated mid-wall shafts. See: Page 110, Site 6.

PHOTO 38 – St John The Baptist Church, Kirk Hammerton, North Yorkshire. Square Tower, Nave and Chancel: Coursed Stone Walling. Square Double and Square Single Plinth. Side Alternate Quoining. Round-Headed Doorway. Flat-Headed Single-Splayed Windows. Square String Course. Round-Headed Double Belfry Openings with cylindrical mid-wall shafts. Restored Doorway with Hood Moulding and Strip-Work. Vestiges of Blocked Round-Headed Doorway with Hood Moulding and Strip-Work. Vestiges of Blocked Round-Headed Single-Splayed Window. See: Page 132, Site 71.

PHOTO 39 – St Andrew's Church, Bywell, Northumberland. Square Tower: Coursed Rubble Walling. Side Alternate Quoining. Square String Course. Round-Headed Doorway with Hood Moulding and Strip-Work at second floor level. Round-Headed Double-Belfry Openings with cylindrical mid-wall shafts: with Hood Moulding, Strip-Work and Circular Sound Holes. See: Page 116, Site 26.

An Introduction to Anglo-Saxon Church Architecture & Anglo-Saxon & Anglo Scandinavian Stone Sculpture

PHOTO 40 – St Mary's Church, Deerhurst, Gloucestershire. Interior West Wall of Nave: Parts of moulded Corbels at first floor level supporting former western gallery. At first floor level, Blocked Round-Headed (east face)/Flat-Headed (west face) Doorway. Triangular-Shaped Windows or Squints. Double Triangular-Headed Opening with Hood Moulding, Stepped Imposts, Jambs and Mid-Wall Square-Shaped Shaft decorated with fluted columns, Chamfered Bases (north opening has had the chamfering cut back when it was enlarged to become a doorway). Rectangular Panel prepared for possibly painted Inscription or Decoration. See: Page 119, Site 39.

PHOTO 41 – St Peter's Church, Monkwearmouth, Sunderland, County Durham. Interior West Wall of Nave: Coursed Rubble Walling. Restored Round-Headed Doorway. Round-Headed Window now converted into Doorway. Round-Headed Single-Splayed Windows now ornamented with Baluster Shafts. See: Page 144, Site 109.

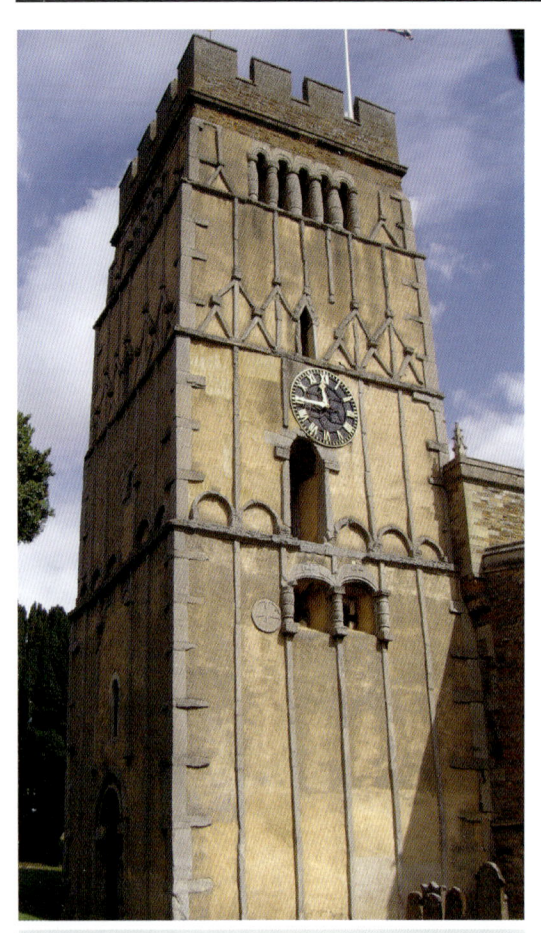

PHOTO 42 – All Saints Church, Earls Barton, Northamptonshire. Square Tower: Coursed Rubble Walling. Square Single Plinth. Long and Short Quoining. Pilaster-Strips. Chamfered and Square String Courses. Round-Headed Doorway with "Escomb" Jambs and Strip-Work. Restored Round-Headed Single-Splayed Window. Round-Headed (externally)/Flat-Headed (internally) Double-Splayed Double Windows with decorated heads and ornamented jambs and mid-wall shafts; vestiges of similar windows. Circular Stone Slab with Free-Arm Cross in relief. At Second Stage, Round-Headed Doorways with Strip-Work. Strip-Work providing interlinked semi-circular and diamond-shaped arcading. Triangular-Headed Windows. Round-Headed Quintuple Belfry Openings with mid-wall shafts externally ornamented with baluster shafts. See: Page 123, Site 45.

PHOTO 43 – St John the Baptist Church, Barnack, Cambridgeshire. Square Tower: Coursed Rubble Walling. Single Square Plinth. Square String Courses. "Set-Back"/"Off-Set" Upper Stage. Long and Short Quoining but some Face Alternate Quoins. Pilaster-Strips. Round-Headed Doorway with Hood Moulding and Strip-Work, and "Escomb" Jambs. Round and Triangular-Headed Single-Splayed Windows with "Escomb" Jambs. Triangular-Headed Doorway at second stage. Triangular-Headed Single Belfry Openings with decoration. Panels with decoration. Sundial. Prokrossos (see Glossary). See: Page 109, Site 5.

An Introduction to Anglo-Saxon Church Architecture & 65
Anglo-Saxon & Anglo Scandinavian Stone Sculpture

PHOTO 44 - St Peter's Church, Forncett St Peter, Norfolk. Round Tower: Coursed Rubble Walling with Flints. Circular Double-Splayed Windows. Triangular and Round-Headed (one restored) Double-Belfry Openings with cylindrical mid-wall shafts. Round-Headed Single-Splayed Windows - sometimes described as "Circular Sound Holes". Round-Headed Doorway (interior is original). See: Page 125, Site 50.

PHOTO 45 - St Mary's Church, Tasburgh, Norfolk. Round Tower: Coursed Rubble Walling with Flints. Round-Headed Single-Splayed Windows. One row of Round-Headed Sunken Blind Arcading separated by wide Pilaster-Strips, with above, another row of Headless (removed in building work above in 1385) Sunken Blind Arcading separated by wide Pilaster-Strips; the two rows provide an alternating pattern. See: Page 145, Site 110.

PHOTO 46 - St Katherine's Church, Little Bardfield, Essex. Square Tower: Coursed Rubble Walling with Flints. Part of Square Single Plinth. Rubble Quoining with Flints. Square String Courses. Indications of Blocked Doorway. Single Round-Headed Windows - some are blocked - including sets of two in pairs similar to double-belfry openings and separated by a thin mid-wall shaft. Nave: Coursed Rubble Walling with Flints. Part of Square Single Plinth. See: Page 134, Site 77.

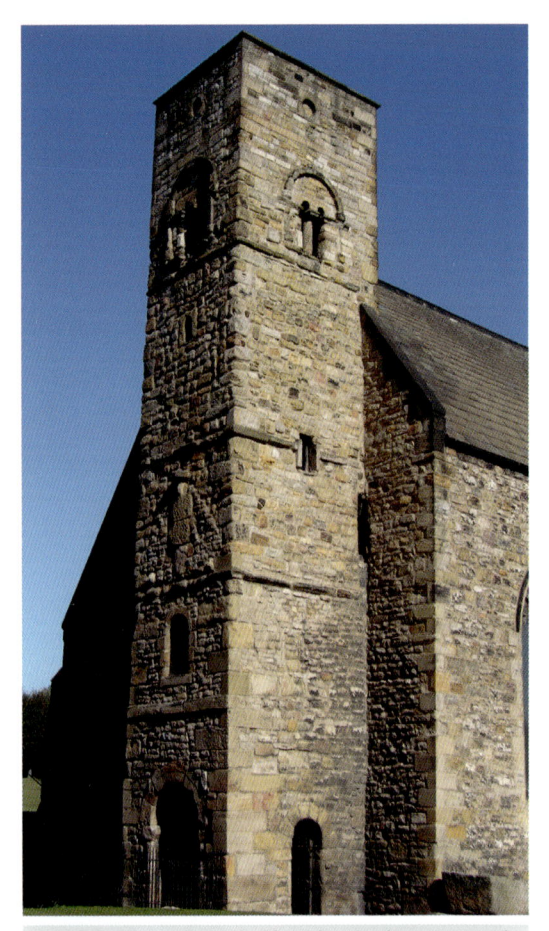

PHOTO 47 - St Peter's Church, Monkwearmouth, Sunderland, County Durham. Square Tower incorporating earlier Porch. Coursed Rubble Walling. Side Alternate including Megalithic Quoining. Round-Headed Archway with unique Decorated Jambs including Baluster Shafts. Round-Headed Doorways with "Escomb" Jambs. Square String Courses. Blocked Flat-Headed Window. Roofline of earlier Porch. Vestiges of a Statue. Flat and Round-Headed Single-Splayed Windows. Round-Headed Double-Belfry Openings with cylindrical mid-wall shafts, a single lintel covering both openings, Hood Moulding, Strip-Work. Round Sound Holes. Nave: Coursed Rubble Walling. Side Alternate including Megalithic Quoining. See: Page 144, Site 109.

PHOTO 48 - All Saints Church, Wing, Buckinghamshire. Seven Sided Apsidal Chancel: Coursed Rubble Walling. Pilaster-Strips and Strip-Work forming a Blind Arcade of tall Round-Headed Arches. Incomplete Blind Arcade of Triangular-Headed Openings. Blocked Round-Headed Single-Splayed Windows. Vestiges of Round-Headed Windows. Round-Headed Windows - one adapted to provide access to Crypt. See: Page 149, Site 121.

IDENTIFYING ANGLO-SAXON FABRIC AND FEATURES AMONG LATER BUILDING

Anglo-Saxon walling may survive both internally and externally in part rather than in whole. It is often found:

1. In the corners of the nave and the adjacent walling.
2. Above and between the arches later inserted into the nave walling to provide access to the north and south aisles.
3. On each side and above the chancel arch and below the current roof line.
4. Above the tower arch and below the current roof line.
5. As the lower courses of walling in the nave or chancel (less common) or in the lower stages of a tower.

Anglo-Saxon features such as Archways, Doorways and Windows may now be blocked by later (non-Anglo-Saxon) stonework, or cut into by later (non-Anglo-Saxon) archways, doorways and windows, and as a result Anglo-Saxon features survive only in part – for example, part of a window-head or part of one of the jambs. It may be possible to identify such features both internally and externally.

Some stonework from Anglo-Saxon features may be reused in a completely different context than their original intended use.

Megalithic archway, doorway or window heads may be used as infilling for walling or incorporated into the external face (more often) or internal face of walling in the tower, nave, porch, chancel, or vestry. They may be placed upside down, vertically or horizontally, at ground level, high up, or anywhere in between.

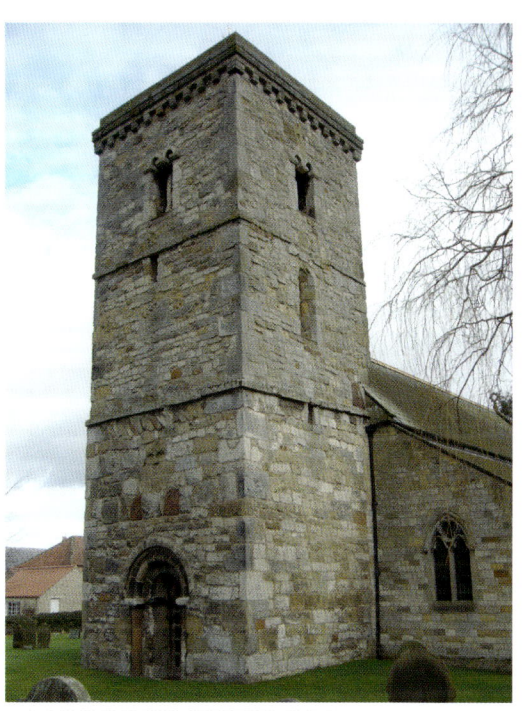

PHOTO 49 - All Saints Church, Hovingham, North Yorkshire. Square Tower: Coursed Stone Walling including Herringbone Masonry. Side Alternate Quoining (including window and door heads reused as quoins). Round-Headed Doorway. Flat-Headed Windows. Square String Courses. Round-Headed Double-Splayed Window. Round-Headed Double-Belfry Openings.
Externally, incorporated into the fabric of the tower: a Free-Arm Crosshead, and, a Plate-Ring Crosshead and part of its Angular Cross-Shaft both with abstract and figurative designs - see Pages 88 to 97. See: Page 130, Site 65.

See above, PHOTO 49, All Saints Church, Hovingham, North Yorkshire.

Occasionally, the outline plan of an Anglo-Saxon church is indicated in stone or brickwork where a church has been demolished, where the present church overlays, or is adjacent to, or near to the site, of an Anglo-Saxon Church. Where parts of the church have been demolished or where walling has been reduced in size or realigned, Anglo-Saxon material may survive in the foundations or in the lower courses of stonework in the present structure. During nineteenth century restorations, Anglo-Saxon and Anglo-Scandinavian material was often re-discovered and incorporated into new, or restored, fabric in the church; sometimes it was displayed.

ANGLO-SAXON FONTS

It is difficult to confidently state that a font is Anglo-Saxon unless it is decorated with an attributable design (occasionally) or a script (rarely). However, plain, circular or "tub" shaped, font bowls are sometimes identified as Anglo-Saxon and this may be the correct. Sometimes the "old", possibly Anglo-Saxon, font is retained somewhere inside the church – not necessarily near the font currently used or the baptistry. Others may be found outside the church abandoned in the churchyard often in the vicinity of the south porch.

PHOTO 50 – St Mary's Church, Potterne, Wiltshire. Font with incised lines bordering a Latin Inscription from Psalm 42.2. See: Page 140, Site 96.

See above, top right, PHOTO 50, St Mary's Church, Potterne, Wiltshire – font with an inscription. See below, bottom left, PHOTO 51, St Lawrence's Church, Eyam, Derbyshire – font decorated with architectural features. See below, centre, PHOTO 52, St Mary's Church, Deerhurst, Gloucestershire – font decorated with abstract designs. See below, bottom right, PHOTO 53, St Mary's Church, Melbury Bubb, Dorset – font decorated with abstract and figurative designs.

PHOTO 51 – St Lawrence's Church, Eyam, Derbyshire. Tub-Shaped Font decorated with Interlocking Arches with shared Columns, Imposts and Bases, similar to those of an Anglo-Saxon Chancel or Tower Arch. See: Page 124, Site 48.

PHOTO 52 – St Mary's Church, Deerhurst, Gloucestershire. Font and Stem with abstract and figurative designs including: Flat Moulding, Interlace Design, Plant-Scroll Design, Roll Moulding. Spiral-Scroll Design including Ribbon-Shaped Animals – see Pages 88 to 97. See: Page 119, Site 39.

PHOTO 53 – St Mary's Church, Melbury Bubb, Dorset. Part of a Round Cross-Shaft reused as a font with abstract and figurative designs, now upside down, including: Square-Shaped Pellets. Part of large Cat-Like Animal with open jaws, teeth and tongue, facing a Horse-Like Animal who holds the neck of a smaller Animal between them – see Pages 88 to 97. See: Page 135, Site 81.

ANGLO-SAXON SUNDIALS

Most Anglo-Saxon sundials were divided into four day segments sometimes subdivided. Some had four additional night segments – eight in total for day and night. Some sundials were divided into twelve day segments and twelve night segments – twenty-four in total for day and night. Dividing day and night into eight segments was a Germanic tradition rather than the Roman tradition of a twenty-four hour day and night.

Many consist of a stone slab incorporated into the fabric of the church, on whose vertical face there is an incised semicircle with its horizontal line having lines radiating below; in some examples these lines may be cut by another line to form a cross. Others with a more elaborate design protrude from the surface of the wall. With some examples lines radiate both above and below the horizontal line; all are usually encompassed within a circle.

PHOTO 54 - St Bartholomew's Church, Aldbrough, East Yorkshire. Sundial divided into eight segments with lines radiating above and below the horizontal line; with an Inscription. See: Page 108, Site 1.

With all examples, in the centre of the horizontal line, the intersection of the radiating lines would have a wooden or metal peg or stele – the "gnomon" which would cast a shadow thus indicating the time. The gnomon is now usually missing but the hole in which it was housed is still identifiable. A few sundials have accompanying wording, usually in Old English.

Sundials are usually found externally near the south door of the church, the "lay folk's" door, where church ceremonies were conducted utilising the instructive information contained on or by (where there was an accompanying inscription) the sundial. They may now be located over the apex of the more recently added south porch, or removed from the original position to the south face of the south porch. Sundials may also be found somewhere along the south wall of the nave, often above door height level; the nave wall where they are located may now be enclosed by a later, added, south aisle. They may also be found on the outer south and west walls of a tower.

SCRATCH SUNDIAL

The adjacent illustration identifies the main features likely to be found on a sundial scratched onto the surface of an individual piece of stonework. There is a central hole for the missing gnomon and lines radiate both above and below the horizontal line but there is no encompassing circle – other examples may have such a circle. Although quite common, these sundials can be very indistinct and difficult to identify.

HOLE FOR MISSING GNOMON IN THE CENTRE

For sundials accompanied by wording, see above, PHOTO 54, St Bartholomew's Church, Aldbrough, East Yorkshire; see Page 70, top right, PHOTO 56, St Andrew's Church, Bishopstone, Sussex; see Page 70, middle photograph, PHOTO 57, St Gregory's Minster, Kirkdale, North Yorkshire. For a sundial accompanied by plant decoration, see Page 70, top left, PHOTO 55, Corhampton Church, Hampshire. For a sundial accompanied by human figures, see Page 70, bottom of page, PHOTO 58, St Mathew's Church, Langford, Oxfordshire.

PHOTO 55 – Corhampton Church, Hampshire. Sundial with plant decoration. See: Page 118, Site 35.

PHOTO 56 – St Andrew's Church, Bishopstone, Sussex. Sundial with distinctive calibrations and incised with the Old English name "Eadric" accompanied by a cross. See: Page 111, Site 12.

PHOTO 57 – St Gregory's Minster, Kirkdale, North Yorkshire. Sundial with Old English Inscriptions including references to King Edward the Confessor and Earl Tostig of Northumbria. See: Page 133, Site 72.

PHOTO 58 – St Matthew's Church, Langford, Oxfordshire. Sundial with two standing figures. See: Page 133, Site 73.

An Introduction to Anglo-Saxon Church Architecture &
Anglo-Saxon & Anglo Scandinavian Stone Sculpture   71

ANGLO-SAXON STONE FURNITURE

With a few notable exceptions, such as the Bishop's Chairs at Hexham Abbey in Northumberland (see adjacent PHOTO 59, Hexham Abbey Northumberland), and Beverley Minster in East Yorkshire, only fragments of stone ecclesiastical furniture survive. These fragments may be part of a bishop's chair or clergy bench, with elaborately carved arm supports or finials in the stylised shape of animals or their heads, for example at St Peter's Church, Monkwearmouth, County Durham (Wearside). Usually only vestiges of decoration survive. In addition, part of a reading desk from the monastic refectory survives at Jarrow (Bede's World), County Durham (Tyneside).

PHOTO 59 – Hexham Abbey, Northumberland. Bishop's Chair known as "Frith Stool". See: Page 128, Site 60.

OTHER ANGLO-SAXON STONE FEATURES

i. Decorative panels: possibly part of an altar frontages. See below, PHOTO 60, St Mary and St Hardulph Church, Breedon-on-the-Hill, Leicestershire.

PHOTO 60 - St Mary and St Hardulph Church, Breedon-on-the-Hill, Leicestershire. Panel with abstract and figurative designs (see Pages 88 to 97) including: Round-Headed interlocking archways with haloed Saints below; larger central figure is probably the Virgin Mary. See: Page 113, Site 18.

ii. Architectural decorative friezes with abstract and figurative designs. See below, PHOTO 61, St Mary and St Hardulph Church, Breedon-on-the-Hill, Leicestershire.

PHOTO 61 - St Mary and St Hardulph Church, Breedon-on-the-Hill, Leicestershire. Architectural Freize with "Inhabited Plant-Scroll Design (see Pages 95 to 96). See: Page 113, Site 18.

iii. Wall Panels depicting Christ, the Evangelists, the Apostles, angels, ecclesiastics, animals and birds, as well as plant and abstract designs (see Pages 88 to 97). Some may have decorated altars. Below: top left, PHOTO 62, Lichfield Cathedral, Staffordshire; top centre, PHOTO 63, Bristol Cathedral, Gloucestershire; top right, PHOTO 64, St Margaret's Church, Fletton, Cambridgeshire; and at the bottom of the page, PHOTO 65, St Michael's Church, Winterbourne Steepleton, Dorset.

PHOTO 62 - Lichfield Cathedral Staffordshire.
Panel depicting the Archangel Gabriel - with vestiges of paint. See: Page 134, Site 76.

PHOTO 63 - Bristol Cathedral, Gloucestershire. Panel with representation of Christ, "Harrowing of Hell". See: Page 114, Site 21.

PHOTO 64 - St Margaret's Church, Fletton, Cambridgeshire. Panel depicting Archangel. See: Page 124, Site 49.

PHOTO 65 -St Michael's Church, Winterbourne Steepleton, Dorset. Panel with most of a haloed and winged Angel. See: Page 149, Site 122.

An Introduction to Anglo-Saxon Church Architecture & 73
Anglo-Saxon & Anglo Scandinavian Stone Sculpture

iv. Shrine covers which may be rectangular-shaped with coped tops and box-like. Decorated with abstract and figurative designs (see Pages 88 to 97). See adjacent, PHOTO 66, Peterborough Cathedral, Cambridgeshire.

PHOTO 66 - *Peterborough Cathedral, Cambridgeshire. "Hedda" or "Monks' Stone" - a coped, box-shaped Shrine with abstract and figurative designs. See: Page 140, Site 95.*

v. Holy Roods depicting Crucifixion Scenes, Christ Crucified, Christ in Majesty and Christ Ascending. See below, PHOTO 67 and PHOTO 68, both from Romsey Abbey, Hampshire.

PHOTO 67 - *Romsey Abbey, Hampshire. Rood with Christ Crucified and the Hand of God. See: Page 142, Site 101.*

PHOTO 68 - *Romsey Abbey, Hampshire. Rood with Crucifixion Scene. See: Page 142, Site 101.*

PART 3

ANGLO-SAXON
&
ANGLO-SCANINAVIAN STONE SCULPTURE

An Introduction to Anglo-Saxon Church Architecture & Anglo-Saxon & Anglo Scandinavian Stone Sculpture

ANGLO-SAXON/ANGLO-SCANDINAVIAN CROSSES

Most crosses stood between 36 inches/91 centimetres and 240 inches/609 centimetres tall, varying in shape, size and type of decoration. Often when complete they comprised a crosshead affixed or integral with a cross-shaft below; some were supported by a cross-base or plinth.

Where crosshead, cross-shaft and (where provided) cross-base, were carved out of separate pieces of stone they were joined together by a stone carved mortise (a cavity) and tenon (a projection) jointing, or by lead-filled iron rods inserted in dowel holes. The same method of jointing would also be used to join together sections of a cross-shaft when they were carved from separate pieces of stone.

Figure A illustrates a composite cross with its crosshead (see Pages 79 to 82), cross-shaft (see Pages 82 to 83), and cross-base (see Pages 83 to 84). Also see Pages 88 to 97 for their decoration. Figure B illustrates a similar composite cross showing the mortise and tenon jointing.

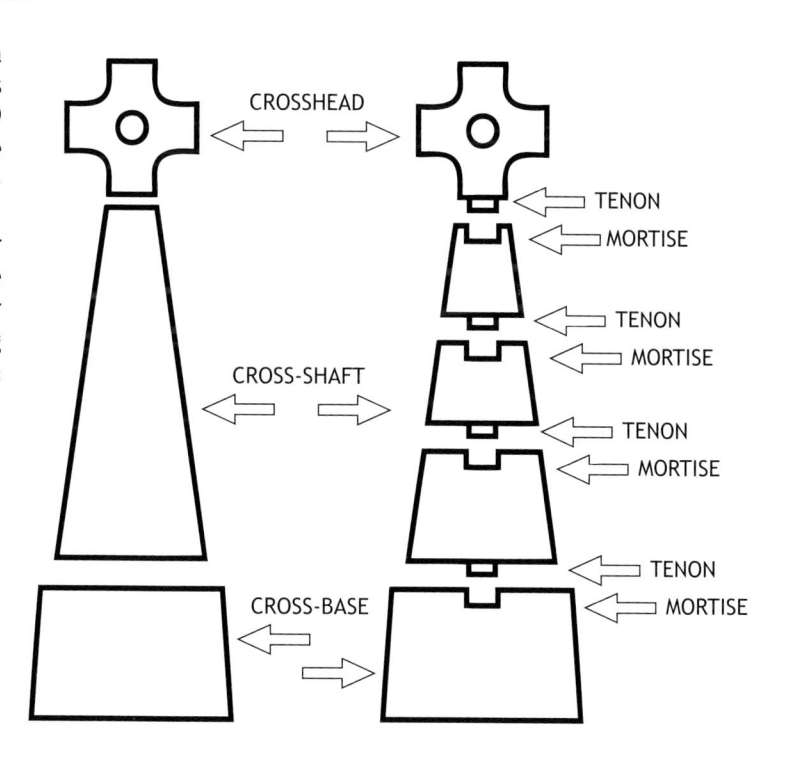

Both wooden and stone crosses were raised as:
1. A focal point for Christian service – a preaching cross, in addition to, or instead of, a church.
2. Places of prayer and contemplation within a monastic community.
3. Memorials to the dead and grave markers including both vertical crosses and recumbent grave covers in a graveyard.
4. Commemorating places in the life of a saint or their funeral route.
5. Boundary markers.
6. Well markers.

PHOTO 69 below on the left from St Paul's Church, Irton, Cumbria, provides an example of an almost complete cross with Free-Arm Crosshead (see Pages 79 to 81), an Angular Cross-Shaft (see Pages 82 to 83), and a Cross-Base (see Pages 83 to 84). Both Crosshead and Cross-Shaft are decorated (see Pages 88 to 97).

PHOTO 70, below on the right from St Mary's Church, Gosforth, Cumbria, provides an example of an almost complete cross with Ring-Head Crosshead (see Pages 80 to 82), a lower Circular and upper Angular Cross-Shaft (see Pages 82 to 83), and a Cross-Base (see Pages 83 to 84). Both Crosshead and Cross-Shaft are decorated (see Pages 88 to 97).

Fragments from Anglo-Saxon and Anglo-Scandinavian crossheads, cross-shafts and cross-bases, grave covers or grave slabs, grave markers, as well as architectural church features such as decorative friezes and wall panels, are sometimes incorporated both internally and externally into the fabric of the church anywhere from ground level to the top of the tower. They can be used as building material for the repair or infilling of walling or used as lintels, or as part of jambs in archways, doorways and windows.

Internally, fragments may be found individually or in groups in wall niches, on window sills and on the floor – particularly in the tower, the west end of the nave or the north or south aisles, beneath and behind benches and pews, and in porches.

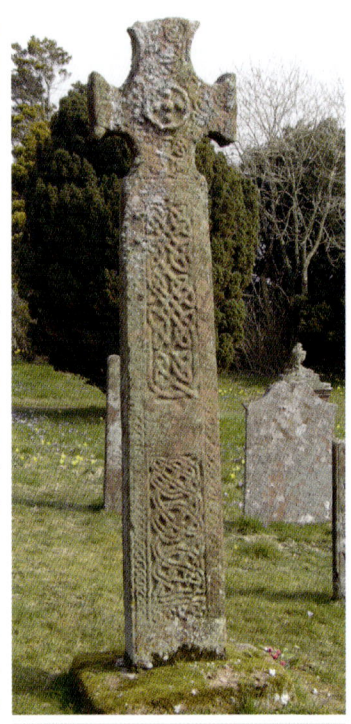

PHOTO 69 - St Paul's Church, Irton, Cumbria. Cross: Free-Arm Crosshead, Angular Cross-Shaft, and Cross-Base. See: Page 131, Site 68.

PHOTO 70 - St Mary's Church, Gosforth, Cumbria. Cross: Ring-Head Crosshead, lower Circular/upper Angular Cross-Shaft with Scenes from Scandinavian Mythology, and Three-Stepped Cross-Base. See: Page 125, Site 52.

Some fragments may also survive in the churchyard even in their original location. Whilst occasionally free-arm crossheads are found almost intact, it is much more common to find that only an arm, or parts of arms and the centre has survived; the survival rate of ring or wheel-head crosses is better. Cross-shafts have invariably been broken into sections - occasionally reunited but not always correctly reassembled – they may have "modern" inserts to assist reconstruction.

CROSSHEADS including FINIALS

Crossheads vary in shape, size and overall dimension. Similarly, the shape, size and dimension of arms, rings and plates also vary. The shape and nature of the juncture and ends of the arms, and the location and stepping of rings, also varies from one example to another.

Crossheads may be constructed from the same section of stonework as the supporting cross-shaft and be integral to it, or constructed from separate sections of stonework and joined to the supporting cross-shaft by mortise and tenon jointing, or joined together by lead-filled iron rods inserted in dowel holes.

The extent and nature of the decoration varies and many will have some form of decoration on both faces, on the rings, and on the ends of each of their arms; some may have decoration on both the top and under sides of the arms and the curves linking the arms together. Examples may have a distinctive central boss. The extent and nature of moulding (see Pages 90 to 91) also varies. The decoration may be abstract or figurative scenes or a combination of both (see Pages 88 to 97). Not all crossheads have moulding and not all are decorated.

Finials are placed on the apex of a roof or gable; they are an architectural decoration. They vary in shape, size and overall dimension and are mostly similar in design to crossheads although usually smaller in overall size. They are less likely to have any moulding or decoration than "normal" crossheads.

"Free-arm" crossheads and "ring-head" crossheads (often referred to as a "wheel-head" crosshead) are the most common; there are also variants known as "plate-ring" and "disc-head" crossheads.

FREE-ARM CROSSHEADS

Free-arm crossheads are those where the stonework comprises a representation of a standard Latin cross with a horizontal line placed across a vertical line. The horizontal arms are supported by centrally-placed vertical arms.

The illustration below and the photographs on Page 80 indicate the diversity of design of free-arm crossheads. The illustration has narrow arms, a right-angle at the juncture of the arms, arms which become fan-shaped and have rounded ends, and no central boss; there is no decoration. See Page 80, top left: PHOTO 71, St Lawrence's Church, Eyam, Derbyshire, the crosshead has wide arms, a curve at the juncture of the arms, square-ended arms, a central boss, and is richly decorated (note: the lower vertical arm is missing). See Page 80, top centre, PHOTO 72, St Mary's Church, Ovingham, Northumberland, the crosshead has wide fan-shaped arms, rounded at the ends, a protruding central boss, and has no decoration.

PHOTO 71 - St Lawrence's Church, Eyam, Derbyshire. Most of a decorated Free-Arm Crosshead - the lower vertical arm is missing. See: Page 124, Site 48. Photograph with permission of Eyam Parish Church.

PHOTO 72 - St Mary's Church. Ovingham, Northumberland. Free-Arm Crosshead. See: Page 140, Site 93.

PHOTO 73 - St Andrew's Church, Middleton, North Yorkshire. Free-Arm Crosshead with "billets". See: Page 136, Site 83.

For the "classic" free-arm crosshead, which is also decorated, see Page 99, left, PHOTO 103, St Michael's Church, Cropthorne Worcestershire.

In addition to the standard four-arm design, some free-arm crossheads have in the juncture of their arms a small equal-size circular plate or roll of stonework which impinges on the angle between each arm and extends into the void between the arms. These plates or rolls are referred to as "billets". See top right, PHOTO 73, St Andrew's Church, Middleton, North Yorkshire.

Other free-arm crossheads may have two additional horizontal arms which are integrated into, and extend from, each side of the top vertical arm giving the overall appearance of what is described as a "hammer-head"; the crosshead appears top heavy. The top two horizontal arms of the crosshead can differ in height and width from the other arms, they can have similar, or much larger or much smaller, dimensions. Unlike most crossheads, the top vertical arm does not extend above the top two horizontal arms; instead it acts as a link between the lower and upper horizontal arms. These hammer-head crossheads are of later, generally eleventh century date, displaying poorer quality workmanship and design. See the adjacent PHOTO 74, St Chad's Church, Middlesmoor, North Yorkshire.

PHOTO 74 - St Chad's Church, Middlesmoor, North Yorkshire. Hammer-Head Crosshead with part of its attached Angular Cross-Shaft. See: Page 135, Site 82.

RING-HEAD CROSSHEADS

A "ring-head" cross is where the four arms of a free-arm crosshead are linked to each other by curved sections of stonework – known as "quadrants" - to give the overall appearance of a ring; they are often also referred to as "wheel-head" crossheads. There are voids between the junctures of the arms of the crosshead and the underside of the quadrants forming the ring.

An Introduction to Anglo-Saxon Church Architecture &   **81**
Anglo-Saxon & Anglo Scandinavian Stone Sculpture

The shapes of the arms of different crossheads can vary greatly; they may be angular, rounded or fan-shaped with square or rounded ends which may or may not extend beyond the "ring". The stonework forming parts of the ring linking the arms can vary in diameter (height) and depth, and placement from one crosshead to the next. Some rings have been placed on top of the face of the free-arm cross. See the adjacent left, PHOTO 75, St Mungo's Church, Dearham, Cumbria.

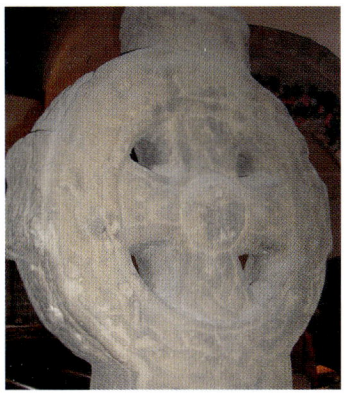

PHOTO 75 - *St Mungo's Church, Dearham, Cumbria. Ring-Head Crosshead. See: Page 118, Site 38.*

PHOTO 76 - *St Andrew's Church, Middleton, North Yorkshire. Ring-Head Crosshead with a central ring bordered by a narrower ring. See: Page 136, Site 83.*

With some examples the quadrants forming the ring comprise a larger, wider, central ring, bordered front and back by a stepped narrower ring. See above right, PHOTO 76, St Andrew's Church, Middleton, North Yorkshire.

PLATE OR PLATE-RING CROSSHEADS
On some examples the ring may comprise solid stonework from the spaces between the junctures of the arms to near or at the top of the ring; these may be termed "plate" or "plate-ring" crossheads. There are a number of variations of these crossheads the more common of which can be identified as either a solid plate quartered and overlaid by a cross (see below left, PHOTO 77, St Giles Church, Chollerton, Northumberland, or a solid circular cross whose arms are narrowly separated in length but at whose juncture there are circular-shaped "eyelets" which may or may not surround a void (see adjacent right, PHOTO 78, Whithorn Priory Museum, Wigtownshire). As with all other crossheads these have wide variations of all features and decoration.

PHOTO 77 – *St Giles Church, Chollerton, Northumberland. Plate-Ring Crossheads and parts of two Cross-Shafts. The Crosshead at right angles to the wall clearly displays the depth of the "plate" forming the lower and upper quadrants on each side of one of it's horizontal arms. See Page 116, Site 29.*

PHOTO 78 - *Whithorn Priory Museum, Wigtownshire. Plate-Ring Crosshead. See: Page 147, Site 117.*

DISC-HEAD CROSSHEADS

Disc-Head Crossheads are usually identified by their large circumference and lack of depth. The band of moulding (see Pages 90 to 91) around the edges continues around the "eyelets" between the junctions of the arms, often highlighting the eyelets. The eyelets can surround voids, a sunken section of stonework, or a very large round pellet-like feature. They have similarities in design with Plate or Plate-Ring Crossheads (see Page 81). Disc-head crossheads are concentrated in Wigtownshire and date from the tenth and eleventh centuries. See the adjacent PHOTO 79, Whithorn Priory Museum, Wigtownshire.

PHOTO 79 - Whithorn Priory Museum, Wigtownshire. Disc-Head Crosshead. See: Page 147, Site 117.

CROSS-SHAFTS

Cross-shafts may have been constructed from the same section of stonework as the crosshead and be integral to it, or, constructed from separate sections of stonework and joined to the crosshead by mortise and tenon jointing, or by lead-filled iron rods inserted in dowel holes. The same method of jointing would also be used to join together sections of a cross-shaft when they were carved from separate pieces of stone.

In shape cross-shafts are usually angular with four sides or circular; both variants can taper from the ground/bottom to top. See Page 78, PHOTO 69, St Paul's Church, Irton, Cumbria, and Page 78, PHOTO 70, St Mary's Church, Gosforth, Cumbria.

Some may have a circular lower part and angular upper part with the join between the two shapes separated by distinctive pendulous swag(s), and/or, by distinctive collar(s). Whether angular or circular, other examples may have a single, or more than one, "collar" projecting around all four sides or the circumference; the extent of the projection of the collar(s) will vary from one example to another. See adjacent PHOTO 80, St Bridget's Church, Beckermet, Cumbria.

Decoratively the sides of angular cross-shafts are often subdivided into vertical panels by moulding (see Pages 90 to 91) which may be plain, rolled or decorated. Moulding is also common down the vertical edges of a cross-shaft even when the sides are not sub-divided into panels. Angular cross-shafts usually have two opposite "faces" wider than the other two narrower sides. It is often on these faces that the decoration (see Pages 88 to 97) is more elaborate. Decoration on circular cross-shafts is similar to angular cross-shafts with panels continuing horizontally around the circumference.

PHOTO 80 - St Bridget's Church, Beckermet, Cumbria. Most of a Cross-Shaft with pendulous Swags and Collars separating a Circular lower part from an upper (incomplete) Angular part. See: Page 110, Site 7.

With some cross-shafts there may be no decoration on the lower parts of all four sides - for example, 16 inches/40 centimetres up from the bottom. The reason for this omission may be an indication that the cross-shaft is intended to be embedded directly into the ground.

An Introduction to Anglo-Saxon Church Architecture &   **83**
Anglo-Saxon & Anglo Scandinavian Stone Sculpture

The lower part and the upper part of some angular cross-shafts may be sub-divided by one or more "collars" which project around all four sides. See below on the left, PHOTO 81, St Mary's Church, Newent Gloucestershire – a single "collar". See below on the right, PHOTO 82, S Mary's Church, Rockcliffe, Cumbria – two "collars".

PHOTO 81 – St Mary's Church, Newent, Gloucestershire. Part of Collared, Angular Cross-Shaft decorated with Adam and Eve. See: Page 138, Site 87.

PHOTO 82 – St Mary's Church, Rockcliffe, Cumbria. Cross with Ring-Head Crosshead, Angular Cross-Shaft with two Collars, and Cross-Base. See: Page 142, Site 100.

CROSS-BASES

Cross-bases are usually provided for cross-shafts which are taller and physically more substantial examples; there are exceptions and not all crosses are supported by cross-bases. Where they are provided the top surface has a mortise carved out ready to receive the tenon from the cross-shaft above. Some examples may have lead-filled iron rods inserted in dowel holes to join the cross-shaft to the cross-base but these are difficult to identify. Other examples may have a central socket with a "hole" straight through the cross-base so that the cross-shaft rested on the ground – smaller pebble-like stones would have been used to pack-in the cross-shaft to ensure stability.

The adjacent illustration identifies the main features likely to be found on a three-stepped flat cross-base with the mortise ready to receive the tenon from the cross-shaft above.

In shape, a cross-base can be a rectangular or tapering block. It can be low and flat or of some height and width. Cross-bases may stand directly on the ground: some may be stepped. Others may be supported by separate, more recent (not Anglo-Saxon/ Anglo-Scandinavian) plinths, some of these may also be stepped. See adjacent left, PHOTO 83, St Wilfrid's Church, Halton, Lancashire.

Particularly with the lower, flatter cross-bases which are multi-stepped, the distinction between the steps may not be readily apparent due to weathering and/or damage. Additionally, the lower steps may be hidden by the surrounding undergrowth, soil accumulation, or ground subsidence.

PHOTO 83 - St Wilfrid's Church, Halton, Lancashire. Reconstructed Cross with Three-Stepped Cross-Base tapering from bottom to top. Part of Angular Cross-Shaft. See: Page 127, Site 57.

PHOTO 84 - Walton Cross, Hartshead, West Yorkshire. Tall Cross-Base with Stepped Base and Socket for insertion of Cross-Shaft. See: Page 128, Site 59.

On some cross-bases moulding (see Pages 90 to 91) is common along both the vertical and horizontal edges of all four sides. The moulding forms panels which may contain decoration (see Pages 88 to 97). See top right, PHOTO 84, Walton Cross, Hartshead, West Yorkshire.

ANGLO-SAXON/ANGLO-SCANDINAVIAN GRAVE MARKERS - "GRAVE SLABS"

Grave Markers - including Pillow and Name Stones, Grave Covers and Grave Slabs. They vary in size, shape and decoration. Grave Markers, including Pillow and Name Stones, either stood vertically or were laid on top of the grave. Grave Covers and Grave Slabs were usually laid flat over the grave - "recumbent". Graves were sometimes covered by horizontal slabs with vertical slabs at the head and foot.

GRAVE MARKERS
There are a number of examples where a grave is marked with a vertical stone inserted directly into the ground. Many are only incised on one - "front" - side with a distinctive cross; there is usually no inscription or any other markings or decoration. Even where they depict what might otherwise be termed a Plate-Ring Crosshead they are usually flat-headed with vertical sides which may or may not expand in size to provide a firm base to assist when they were directly embedded into the ground. See top of Page 85, PHOTO 85 and PHOTO 86, both from St Oswald's Church, Lythe, North Yorkshire - note the lower vertical arms of these grave markers extend further than shown in the photographs.

An Introduction to Anglo-Saxon Church Architecture &   **85**
Anglo-Saxon & Anglo Scandinavian Stone Sculpture

PHOTO 85 – . St Oswald's Church, Lythe, North Yorkshire. Grave Marker incised with a triangular- armed crosshead; the arms are separated from each other by deep grooves. See: Page 135, Site 80.

PHOTO 86 – St Oswald's Church, Lythe, North Yorkshire. Grave Marker incised with a triangular-armed crosshead with a distinctive circular centre; the fan-shaped arms are separated from each other by wide grooves. See: Page 135, Site 80.

However, some grave markers were far more elaborate. They may be round-headed with decoration and/or an inscription both around the curved head and the "front" face. See below on the left, PHOTO 87, St Andrew's Church, Bolam, Northumberland, and, below on the right, PHOTO 88, All Hallows Church, Whitchurch, Hampshire.

PHOTO 87 - St Andrew's Church, Bolam, Northumberland. Round-Headed Grave Marker incised with a Free-Arm Cross. See: Page 111, Site 13.

PHOTO 88 - All Hallows Church, Whitchurch, Hampshire. Round-Headed Grave Marker with Flat Moulding, Roll Moulding, and incomplete Stepped-Pattern Moulding – see Pages 90 to 91. Half-figure of Christ in a recess with His right arm giving a blessing and His left arm holding a book. Inscription interpreted as: "Here rests the body of Frioburga buried into peace". See: Page 147, Site 116.

PILLOW STONES AND NAME STONES

Pillow Stones and Name Stones are usually small, square, flat-headed or round-headed, with square bases. They were laid flat (recumbent) on the grave. Only the top face is decorated, usually with the lettering each side of the vertical arms of a cross which may have "expanded" (lengthened) arms. On occasions the lettering may be in runes. The centre of the cross and the ends of the arms may be angular, circular or stepped. Name Stones tend to be larger in size than Pillow Stones. Despite their name Pillow Stones were placed on a grave, not used to support the head of the deceased. See below left, PHOTO 89, St Hilda's Church, Hartlepool, County Durham.

PHOTO 89 - St Hilda's Church, Hartlepool, County Durham. Name-Stone Grave Marker incised with a Free-Arm Cross within a border with the symbols "alpha" and "omega" -the symbols for Christ as the beginning and the end - and the name of the nun "Hildithryth in runes. See: Page 127, Site 58.

PHOTO 90 - St Peter's Church, Monkwearmouth, Sunderland, County Durham. Grave Cover with large square-armed Free-Arm Cross in relief. Inscription: "Here in the tomb rests Herebericht the priest in the body". See: Page 144, Site 109.

GRAVE COVERS AND GRAVE SLABS

These are usually of considerable size and recumbent; the top may be flat (see above right, PHOTO 90, St Peter's Church, Monkwearmouth, County Durham) or coped in shape (see Page 102, PHOTO 113, Holy Cross Church, Ramsbury, Wiltshire which has two examples). They can be decorated (see Pages 88 to 97) both on the top face and around the edges supporting it. Often with a cross with expanded arms on the top face but, with some exceptions, many seem now to be missing traces of identifying lettering unlike Pillow or Name Stones.

An Introduction to Anglo-Saxon Church Architecture &
Anglo-Saxon & Anglo Scandinavian Stone Sculpture

HOGBACK GRAVE COVERS OR HOGBACK TOMBSTONES

These are recumbent grave covers in the shape of an elongated house with a convex profile comprising a pitched roof above long side walls; often the roof has a top curved ridge. The overall effect is reminiscent in shape to a hog's back (the metaphor is emphasised by the nature of some of the decoration). See below, bottom left, PHOTO 91, St Oswald's Church, Lythe, North Yorkshire. See below, bottom right, PHOTO 92, St Thomas's Church, Brompton-in-Allertonshire, North Yorkshire.

Many, but not all, have inward-facing stylised bear-like animals at each gable end gnawing at the top ridge and roof. They hold the sloping (pitched) roof and long side walls of the house with their paws. Where there are bear-like animals at each gable end the animals may have ears, be muzzled, and have one, two or three sets of paws.

Other examples do not have these bear-like animals. Instead some may have representations of an inward facing serpent or animal head on the top face of the top ridge only; sometimes the sides of the face may be on the sides of the top ridge, with the top of the animal's head on top of the ridge. Alternatively, examples may have gabled, inwardly-sloping end (gable) panels which may be decorated with, for example, a Crucifixion Scene, animals or an abstract design.

The curving roof ridge may be decorated on its top (face) and adjacent sides. Below the ridge, and along the pitched roof, the hogback may be decorated with rows of tegulations (there are various designs) or abstract designs; the pitched roof often expands in volume at the centre.

Below the pitched roof and along the long side walls, and between the paws of the opposing animals where these occur, there may be panels containing abstract and figurative designs. In the centre of both of the long side walls some examples have an arched niche.

Moulding (see Pages 90 to 91) and decoration (see Pages 88 to 97) is usually similar on both the sides of the top ridge, the pitched roof, the long side walls and, where they occur, both the backs of the bear-like animals at each gable end.

PHOTO 91 – St Oswald's Church, Lythe, North Yorkshire. Part of Hogback Grave Cover with end bear-like animal, part of the top ridge, and part of "wall". See: Page 135, Site 80.

PHOTO 92 – St Thomas's Church, Brompton-in-Allertonshire, North Yorkshire. Hogback Grave Covers with end bear-like Animals. See: Page 115, Site 24.

SARCOPHAGUS

A rare surviving richly-decorated Anglo-Saxon sarcophagus (two-piece stone coffin carved out of solid stone) is to be found in Derby Museum. It is known as "St Alkmund's Sarcophagus" after Alkmund the son of King Alhred of Northumbria who reigned from 765 to 774 and was deposed and went into exile in the Kingdom of the Picts. Alkmund was born in 774 and martyred around 800 in Shropshire. The exact circumstances surrounding his death are unclear. See adjacent, PHOTO 93, Derby Museum & Art Gallery.

PHOTO 93 - Derby Museum and Art Gallery, Derbyshire. "St Alkmund's Sarcophagus". See Page 120, Site 40. Photograph Courtesy of Derby Museums.

ANGLO-SAXON/ANGLO-SCANDINAVIAN DECORATION

The decoration used on crossheads, cross-shafts, finials and grave covers can be roughly dated on the following lines:

1. Late eighth century to early ninth century. These designs are characterised by complex and intricate designs which are symmetrical, well-proportioned and balanced. They include Christian figures and scenes, birds and animals, tree and plant-scroll designs, and a variety of interlace and other abstract designs, all well drawn.

2. Mid ninth century to early tenth century. These designs tend to use less difficult patterns; animals and figures are less well drawn. A general lowering of quality often ascribed to the disruptive impact of the Vikings.

3. Late tenth century to early eleventh century. The designs demonstrate something of a renaissance, approaching, but not reaching, the standard of the late eighth century to early ninth century.

4. Late eleventh century to early twelfth century. The designs show a general degradation, a debasement of designs and of the clarity of animals and figures. The reason is often attributed to the disruptive impact of the Norman Conquest.

   Designs can involve both Christian and Scandinavian mythology sometimes depicting an individual scene or a series of scenes.

Christian subjects usually show Christ, the saints and angels with a dish-like halo around their heads. They include the depiction of:

PHOTO 94 - Market Square, Sandbach, Cheshire. Panel from Angular Cross-Shaft with Crucifixion Scene. Above the head of Christ two circles representing the sun and moon; the symbols of the Four Evangelists, all carrying books, in the quadrants of the cross - Angel (Matthew) upper left, damaged Lion (Mark) upper right, Bull (Luke) lower left, Eagle (John) lower right. Below and flanking the bottom of the Cross, the figures of John (left) and Mary (right). Between John and Mary an Angel forming part of a Nativity scene with a swaddled figure lying on a crib with two animals in profile looking over the crib. See: Page 142, Site 103. Photograph Courtesy of Derby Museums.

- Christ Crucified, sometimes with Mary on the right-hand side of Christ and John the Evangelist on the left. Alternatively, with Stephaton the soldier who offered Christ a sponge soaked in vinegar, or a goblet or cup, and Longinus the soldier

An Introduction to Anglo-Saxon Church Architecture &
Anglo-Saxon & Anglo Scandinavian Stone Sculpture

    who pierced Christ's side with a spear.
- Christ in Majesty or Christ Ascending.
- The "Four Evangelists" (Matthew represented by a winged man or angel; Mark by a winged lion; Luke by a winged ox, bull or calf; and John by an eagle).
- The Apostles, saints, angels and biblical stories and scenes.
- Ordinary priests and monks. Those following the Celtic form of Christianity can usually be identified by a head with the Celtic tonsure (the head is shaved at the front, across the forehead, from ear to ear - the hair covers the rest of the top and the back and sides), and a reliquary or book satchel hanging from his neck, and by both feet pointing the same way sideways.

See Page 88, bottom right, PHOTO 94, Market Square, Sandbach, Cheshire.

Scenes from Scandinavian mythology which refer to the main events in the Völuspá in the Edda, including figures such as Odin, Sigurd the Volsung, Fafnir and Weland the Smith. See adjacent, PHOTO 95, St Mary's Church, Gosforth, Cumbria.

Secular figures are often depicted armed with a sword and a spear. Warriors and huntsmen are sometimes shown seated in a high seat complete with their weapons. Stag or hart hunts are also depicted (see below right, PHOTO 96, St Mary & St Helen's Church, Neston, Cheshire).

Designs can include words and runic inscriptions. Ribbon-shaped animals are often depicted with characteristically long and narrow bodies with features, usually in profile.

PHOTO 95 – St Mary's Church, Gosforth, Cumbria. Details from upper Angular part of Cross-Shaft: Odin and his horse Sleipnir. See: Page 125, Site 52.

However, abstract designs are the most common ranging from simple lines, circles, curves and geometrical shapes, to the more common Interlace Designs and Plant-Scroll Designs, to Scandinavian inspired designs such as "Jellinge" and "Ringerike" – see Pages 96 to 97.

Designs on the same section of stonework do not necessarily involve one subject or type of decoration. Individual people can be interposed between abstract designs, groups of people, scenes, words and runes (see Page 99, PHOTO 104, St Cuthbert's Church, Bewcastle, Cumbria, and Page 101, PHOTO 110, St Michael's Church, Great Urswick, Cumbria).

The stonework was originally brightly painted in garish colours and was often coated with gesso and added pigment to give an appearance of more colours. Ornamentation on some examples included glass and metalwork.

Decoration on different examples of stonework can vary greatly from a deliberately planned to a more erratic and confusing design. Designs commonly used on crossheads, cross-shafts, finials and grave covers are described below.

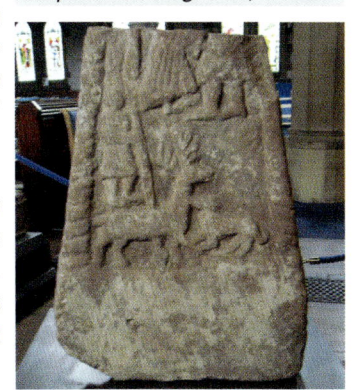

PHOTO 96 – St Mary and St Helen's Church, Neston, Cheshire. Part of Angular Cross-Shaft with Hunting Scene: Huntsman spearing the hart through its back and the hound biting the throat of the hart. Two incomplete human figures above. See: Page 136, Site 85.

MOULDING

Moulding is a continuous section of stonework with defined parallel surface border edges. In relation to the surface of the main stonework it may be integral to, in relief, or sunk. It is often used as a decorative feature to form the boundaries of panels on a cross-shaft or along the edges of all types of decorated stonework likely to be encountered. The width of moulding can vary. Lengths of moulding are usually referred to as "bands".

Moulding can comprise a single narrow or wide band; a pair of narrow or wide adjacent bands, not necessarily of the same width; or two bands, not necessarily of the same width, separated by a groove; or a series of alternating grooves and bands with similar or different widths. The edges of the moulding may be flat, rounded, chamfered or bevelled.

Moulding is often plain containing no decorative patterns within its defined borders. The most common designs are:

1. Flat Moulding. A band having a squared-off cross-section. See Page 94, top left, PHOTO 98, St Mary's & All Saints Church, Nassington, Northamptonshire, and Page 99, right, PHOTO 104, St Cuthbert's Church, Bewcastle, Cumbria,

2. Grooved Moulding. This is where two bands of narrow or wide flat moulding are separated by a groove. It may also comprise a series of alternating grooves and flat bands with similar or different widths. See Page 143, Site 105, All Saints Church & Conyers Chapel, Sockburn, County Durham.

3. Roll Moulding. A roll-shaped band comprising a three-quarter circle in its cross section. Occasionally, roll moulding may be described as "torus moulding" when referring to a design used on a column base. See Page 101, right, PHOTO 111, St Andrew's Church, Bishop Auckland, County Durham.

Moulding can contain decorative patterns within the defined borders. The most common designs are:

1. Cable-Pattern Moulding. A band consisting of a series of distinctive thick diagonal lines in relief which take on a distended curved shape. The cable pattern itself provides the decoration. Sometimes cable-pattern moulding is referred to as "rope-work design". See Page 93, PHOTO 97, St Andrew's Church, Burton Pedwardine, Lincolnshire, and, Page 101, right, PHOTO 111, St Andrew's Church, Bishop Auckland, County Durham.

    The illustration below provides an indication of the design.

2. Key-Pattern Moulding. A band consisting of a row of distinctive alternating key-shapes placed together in a regular pattern. See Page 122, Site 44, Durham Cathedral, County Durham - The Monks' Dormitory.

An Introduction to Anglo-Saxon Church Architecture &   91
Anglo-Saxon & Anglo Scandinavian Stone Sculpture

The illustration below provides an indication of the design. On this example, but not all such designs, the main keys are framed by an additional line of decoration.

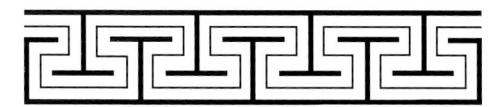

Note: Key-Patterns may also be used to provide decoration for an entire panel on a crosshead, cross-shaft or grave cover.

3. Stepped-Pattern Moulding. A band consisting of a row of distinctive steps placed together in a regular pattern whose central feature is noticeably thicker than its attached extensions. Some examples have the totality of the "steps" at a distinctive angle; others link the top and bottom of the steps to form a zigzag pattern. See Page 122, Site 44, The Monks' Dormitory, Durham Cathedral, County Durham.

The illustration below provides an indication of the design with the central black line feature thicker than the attached extensions.

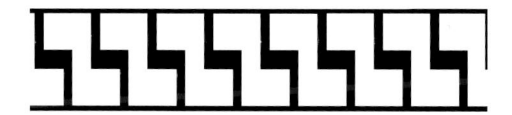

Note: Stepped-Patterns may also be used to provide decoration for an entire panel on a crosshead, cross-shaft or grave cover.

4. Pellet Moulding. A band consisting of a row of small rounded sometimes elongated shapes in relief. In addition to their use in moulding pellets may also be used singly, in groups, or separately in numbers. See Page 143, Site 105, All Saints Church & Conyers Chapel, Sockburn, County Durham.

Other Patterns – less common:

5. Chevron-Pattern Moulding. A band consisting of a row of "V" shapes, one under another, in an upright, curving or inverted sequence. See Page 140, Site 97, Holy Cross Church, Ramsbury, Wiltshire.

6. Baluster Shaft Moulding. A band consisting of a representation of a row of baluster shafts, usually, one under another in an upright sequence. See Page 116, PHOTO 121, St Peter's Church, Codford St Peter, Wiltshire.

INTERLACE DESIGN
Interlace design is a generic description for designs commonly called "Knot-Work Design", "Ring-Knot Design", "Ring-Chain Design" or "Ring-Twist Design", "Plait-Work Design" and "Stopped Plait-Work Design", "Scroll-Design" and "Spiral-Scroll Design". Other, less common descriptions include "Basket-Plait Design" or "Basket-Ware Design", "Cats-Cradle Design", "Gridiron Design", "Strap-Work Design", "Zigzag Design". These, and similar descriptions, either reflect the technical complexities of the construction of the design, or the physical resemblance of the design in total.

The designs consist of a pattern of ribbon-like strands intricately entwined and woven together constantly passing over and under each other. It may include strands which change direction and turn back on themselves to avoid crossing the strands below and above. Some designs may also include strands with an incised groove running in the centre running parallel to its long borders.

Within the design the patterns can be asymmetric or symmetric containing curved and pointed loops, U-bends, V-bends, circles, concentric circles, and spirals. The patterns may be linked together by curving or angular ribbon-like strands, and ribbon-like strands which themselves form a diagonal pattern. Some designs may include pairs of ribbon-like strands mirroring each other. The same patterns may be repeated in the overall width and length, on other occasions the design may contain a number of different patterns. The complexity of the design varies from one example to another.

The designs often have identifiable ends – "terminals" within the panel in which they are contained; these may be achieved by crossing and/or alternating ribbon-like strands, or by joining with a solid bar.

The two adjacent illustrations provide examples of what is often described as a "simple" interlace pattern; both have square-ended bar terminals. The illustration on the right has a groove in the centre of the ribbon.

Sometimes the ribbon-like strands may incorporate animal features. For example, a strand may form the body of a snake-like/serpent-like animal with one end of the strand terminating in the head. Other designs may include humans, animals or birds and consequently are described as "Inhabited Interlace Design", "Inhabited Knot-Work Design", "Inhabited Plant-Scroll Design", "Inhabited Vine-Scroll Design", etc.

Distinctive characteristics of other variations of interlace design may be summarised:

1. Basket-Plait Design or Basket-Ware Design represents the appearance of plaited wickerwork.

2. Cats-Cradle Design consists of a series of ribbon-like strands intricately entwined, producing an elaborate symmetrical pattern.

3. Gridiron Design consists of parallel ribbon-like strands running in squared-off horizontal and vertical directions to pass over and under each other.

4. Knot-Work Design entwines a pattern of ribbon-like strands, usually wider and more angular than those found in a "simple" interlace design involving entwined ribbon-like strands. Some examples display distinctly entwined triangular-shaped knots, often described as "triquetra(s)", representing God the Father, Son and Holy Spirit. Triquetras often decorate the faces of crossheads. Triquetra Design – see adjacent illustration.

An Introduction to Anglo-Saxon Church Architecture &   93
Anglo-Saxon & Anglo Scandinavian Stone Sculpture

5. Plait-Work Design is a pattern of ribbon-like strands which advance towards the base of the design without diverging. Like Interlace Designs the strands are woven together regularly passing over and under each other. Unlike some Interlace Designs the strands do not change direction or turn back on themselves. In addition, often each strand has an incised groove in the centre running parallel to its long borders.

    Mostly in Lincolnshire, but with occasional examples in other counties, plait-work design may incorporate a representation in portrait of a bull's head. A groove separates its head below its horns from the rest of the design. The bull has a square jaw; a pair of incised lines outline a noseband, and further incised lines extend from opposite corners at the top of the noseband to form arcs which cross over the nose and extend into and along the centre of the horns. Holes represent the eyes of the bull, one each side of where the incised arching lines cross on the nose. The horns merge into the ribbon-like strands which form the upper band of plait-work design. The accompanying band of cable-pattern moulding separating the band of plait-work design from the ring-knot (usually – see Page 94, "7") design below temporarily reverts to flat moulding and changes direction to accommodate the shape of the jaw. Note: Not all examples are complete, some do not have eyes or nosebands. See above, PHOTO 97, St Andrew's Church, Burton Pedwardine, Lincolnshire.

    PHOTO 97 - *St Andrew's Church, Burton Pedwardine, Lincolnshire. Grave Cover with Cable-Pattern Moulding, Plait-Work Design incorporating a "Bull's Head", Ring-Knot Design. See: Page 115, Site 25.*

6. Ring-Chain Design or Ring-Twist Design is where ribbon-like strands form a pattern containing an inner and outer pair of concentric circles. These circles are entwined with singular or pairs of distinctly longer, curving or angular and diagonally placed, ribbon-like strands connecting them to similar pairs of concentric circles. See the adjacent illustration on the left; note, it has rounded terminals.

    On other examples, the inner or the outer circles may be divided into semi-circles by angular ribbon-like strands connecting them to other similar circles. See the adjacent illustration on the right; note, it has no distinct terminals. Some examples may have more angular or squared-off components rather than circles. See Page 94, top left, PHOTO 98, St Mary's and All Saints Church, Nassington, Northamptonshire, and Page 99, right, PHOTO 104, St Cuthbert's Church, Bewcastle, Cumbria.

94   *An Introduction to Anglo-Saxon Church Architecture &*
                                Anglo-Saxon & Anglo Scandinavian Stone Sculpture

PHOTO 98 - St Mary's & All Saints Church, Nassington, Northamptonshire. Angular Cross-Shaft with Flat Moulding, Ring-Chain Design (on face to right), Ring-Knot Design (on narrow side to left). See: Page 136, Site 84.

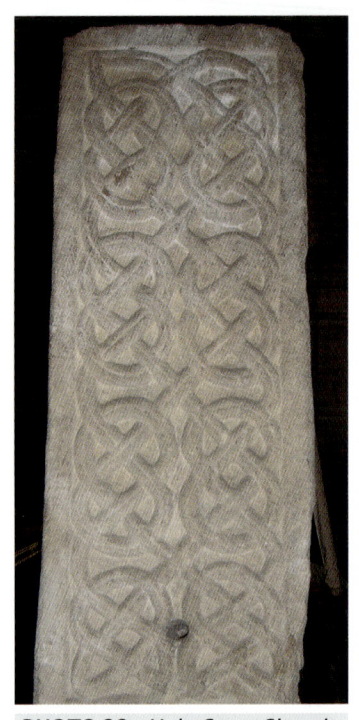

PHOTO 99 - Holy Cross Church, Ramsbury, Wiltshire. Angular Cross-Shaft with Flat Moulding and Ring-Knot Design. See: Page 140, Site 97.

PHOTO 100 - St Mungo's Church, Dearham, Cumbria. Angular Cross-Shaft with Flat Moulding, Pellets, Spiral-Scroll Design. See: Page 118, Site 38.

7. Ring-Knot Design is where a curving pattern of ribbon-like strands form a series of connected circular or angular patterns. Often the circular varieties form a "figure of eight" pattern. Such patterns are entwined with distinctly longer, curving or angular and diagonally-placed, ribbon-like strands connecting them to similar figure of eight or other patterns. Some examples may have more angular or square-like components rather than circles. The illustration on the left provides a representation of the "figure of eight" pattern with angular terminals. See above centre, PHOTO 99, Holy Cross Church, Ramsbury, Wiltshire. The illustration on the right provides a representation of a more angular design; note, it has no terminals.

An Introduction to Anglo-Saxon Church Architecture &
Anglo-Saxon & Anglo Scandinavian Stone Sculpture

8. Scroll Design is where a pattern of ribbon-like strands resembles a circuitous design.

9. Spiral-Scroll Design is where a pattern of ribbon-like strands coil in a cylindrical, conical or helical way. The designs includes strands which may or may not be connected, may form "bands", or may form an idiosyncratic design within a panel containing other designs. See Page 94, top right, PHOTO 100, St Mungo's Church, Dearham, Cumbria.

10. "Stopped" Plait-Work Design is a variation of Plait-Work Design where the individual ribbon-like strands within the design usually have rounded ends and "stop" just before the point where they meet other strands. The strands do not give the appearance of passing over and under each other. In addition, often each strand has an incised groove in the centre running parallel to its long borders. See Page 100, bottom right, PHOTO 108, Whithorn Priory Museum, Wigtownshire.

11. Strap-Work Design is where the ribbon-like strands resemble a flat band or strap.

12. Zigzag Design is where joined, angled ribbon-like strands form a zigzag pattern, at times erratically executed. See Page 143, Site 105, All Saints Church and Conyers Chapel, Sockburn, County Durham.

PLANT DESIGNS

1. Some designs may simply be described as "Plant Design". These involve an individual or collective representation of trees and plants without being part of the more common "Plant-Scroll Design" – see "2" below.

2. Plant-Scroll design can be sub-divided into: "Bush-Scroll", "Tree-Scroll" or "Vine-Scroll". Whichever variant, they resemble a circuitous design representing the branches or trunks of a plant, bush, vine or tree.

The designs vary in shape and complexity and include trees and plants with distinctive and variously styled leaves and buds of different sizes. Often the designs have climbing or trailing vines with fruit laden with variously styled bunches of grapes or berries of different sizes. The trunks of the trees or plants can wind their way alternately between opposite edges of the design or they may be centrally placed with branches extending down from each side.

The adjacent illustration provides an indication of what may be encountered when stonework is described as decorated with "vine-scroll design" (the most common variant). The trunk of the vine winds its way alternately between opposite edges of the design with leaves, buds and a bunch of vine berries at the end of the vine in the centre circle. Buds and leaves sprout from different parts of the trunk. Leaves sprout from part of the trunk to form the terminals. See page 96, PHOTO 101, Hexham Abbey, Northumberland.

Sometimes within or adjacent to the scroll there are stylised animals and/or birds, sometimes humans, with the result that the design is often referred to as "Inhabited Plant-Scroll Design", "Inhabited Bush-Scroll Design", "Inhabited Tree-Scroll Design", or

"Inhabited Vine-Scroll Design".

3. Palmette Design consists of a series of adjacent, narrow-stemmed leaf shapes. Mostly found in Lincolnshire. See Page 52, PHOTO 22, St Michael's Church, Glentworth, Lincolnshire.

OTHER DESIGNS
1. Baluster Design represents baluster shafts – see Glossary. See Page 116, PHOTO 121, Site 30, St Peter's Church, Codford St Peter, Wiltshire. See Page 128, Site 60, Hexham Abbey, Northumberland.

2. Chequer-Board Design represents alternating raised and sunk squares similar to a chequer or chess board. See Page 110, Site 9, St Andrew's Church, Bewcastle, Cumbria.

3. Chevron-Pattern Design. This is a distinctive pattern comprising a series of "V" shapes, one under another, in an upright, curving or inverted sequence. See Page 133, Site 72, St Gregory's Minster, Kirkdale, North Yorkshire.

4. Pellet Design. A moulding or design on which there is a single or row of small rounded, sometimes elongated, shapes in relief. They may form part of a larger design. See Page 94, top right, PHOTO 100, St Mungo's Church, Dearham, Cumbria.

ANGLO-SCANDINAVIAN DECORATION
From around the mid-ninth century onwards some stonework is decorated with Scandinavian inspired designs. These include ribbon-like S-shaped or coiled creatures, or creatures linked or entwined forming a chain. Some of these creatures may be restrained by fetters, but many will be surrounded and entwined with spirals, scrolls and branching and tapering threads of interlace. However, the use of some of these characteristics

PHOTO 101 – Hexham Abbey, Northumberland. Angular Cross-Shaft with: Flat Moulding, Plant-Scroll Design, Roll Moulding. See: Page 128, Site 60.

in Anglo-Saxon and Celtic designs predates the Scandinavian settlements in England. There is frequently a merger of various designs to form a hybrid. In addition Scandinavian inspired designs often include human or mythological figures, some fettered, and some designs depict a scene such as hunting. (See Page 78, right, PHOTO 70, and Page 89, top, PHOTO 95, both from St Mary's Church, Gosforth, Cumbria. See also, Page 103, top, PHOTO 114, St Peter's Church, Heysham, Lancashire. For hunting scene, see Page 89, bottom, PHOTO 96, St Mary and St Helen's Church, Neston, Cheshire.)

As well as stonework these designs decorated jewellery, belt-fittings, metalwork and woodwork. The principal Scandinavian designs which may be found in an Anglo-Scandinavian context in England are identified below.

BORRE DESIGN is distinguished by a symmetrical pattern with concentric circles held together by bands. Animal heads, gripping paws, knot-work and chain work motifs are typical. The design was in use from the mid ninth century to the late tenth century. It was named after the designs on artefacts found in a rich ship burial in Borre, Norway. See Page 100, top centre, PHOTO 106, St Mungo's Church, Dearham, Cumbria.

JELLINGE DESIGN is distinguished by ribbon-like reptilian S-shaped creatures who are fettered. The design was in use in the tenth century. It is named after the animal which decorates a small silver cup found at the royal burial ground in Jellinge in Jutland in Denmark. See Page 113, Site 18, St Mary and St Hardulph Church, Breedon-on-the-Hill, Leicestershire.

RINGERIKE DESIGN is typically distinguished by a large quadruped or bird with extensions from their bodies erupting in fans and taking on a foliate appearance. The design was in use in the late tenth and eleventh centuries. It is named after a group of animal and plant motifs on ornamental slabs found in the Ringerike district in Norway. See Page 139, Site 92, All Saints Church, Otley, West Yorkshire.

RYEDALE DRAGON DESIGN is similar to the Jellinge Design. The Ryedale variation usually comprises a single, bound beast or dragon shown in S-shape with its jaws open. The design features on a number of examples of cross-shafts and grave covers in the Ryedale area in North Yorkshire – hence the name. See Page 136, Site 83, St Andrew's Church, Middleton, North Yorkshire.

URNES DESIGN is distinguished by elongated stylised animals entwined with spiral and scroll strands. The design was in use during the second half of the eleventh century and the first half of the twelfth century. It is named after the wood carvings on Urnes Church in Norway. See Page 134, Site 78, Victoria and Albert (V & A) Museum, London.

EXCELLENT EXAMPLES OF ANGLO-SAXON AND ANGLO-SCANDINAVIAN STONE SCULPTURE

PHOTO 102 - Market Square, Sandbach, Cheshire. Free-Arm Crossheads, Angular Cross-Shafts, and Cross-Bases. Decorated with Scenes including: The Nativity, Adoration of the Magi, Christ's Road to Calvary, Crucifixion Scene with the Evangelists' symbols, Christ committing the Keys of Heaven to Peter and the Book of the New Law to Paul, Transfiguration of Christ on Mount Tabor, The Annunciation, Transfiguration Scene, Adoration of Mary, The Veneration of Christ. Decorated with other scenes including human figures, winged angels, animals, and birds. Decorated with abstract designs including: Cable-Pattern Moulding, Flat Moulding, Interlace Design, Knot-Work Design, Pellets, Ring-Chain Design, Roll Moulding. Inhabited Scroll Design with human, animal and bird, figures. See: Page 142, Site 103.

An Introduction to Anglo-Saxon Church Architecture & Anglo-Saxon & Anglo Scandinavian Stone Sculpture

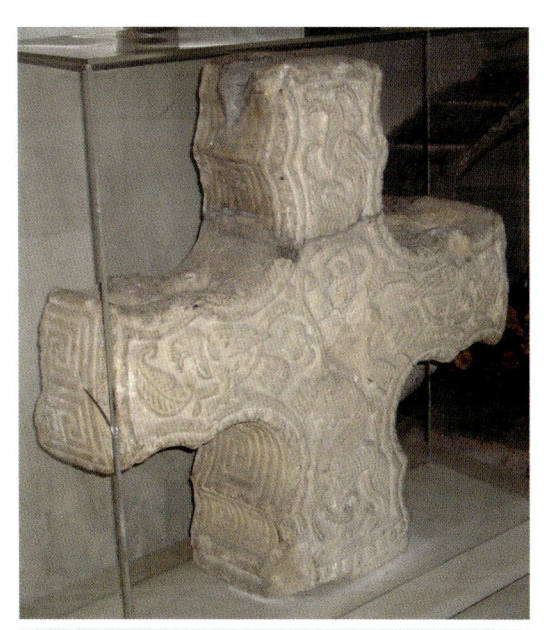

PHOTO 103 – St Michael's Church, Cropthorne, Worcestershire. Free-Arm Crosshead with Cable-Pattern Moulding, Flat Moulding, Rectangular Maze-Like Pattern. Inhabited Plant-Scroll Design with Animals, Birds. See: Page 118, Site 36.

PHOTO 104 - St Cuthbert's Church, Bewcastle, Cumbria. Angular Cross-Shaft with Flat Moulding, Interlace Design, Knot-Work Design, Plant-Scroll Design, Ring-Chain Design, Ring-Knot Design, Roll Moulding. Sundial. Runic Inscriptions interpreted as: "This token of Victory Hwaetred set up in memory"; and another interpreted as the female personal name "Cyneburh". Representations of Christ in Glory, St John the Evangelist with his symbol the eagle, John the Baptist. Animals. See: Page 110, Site 9.

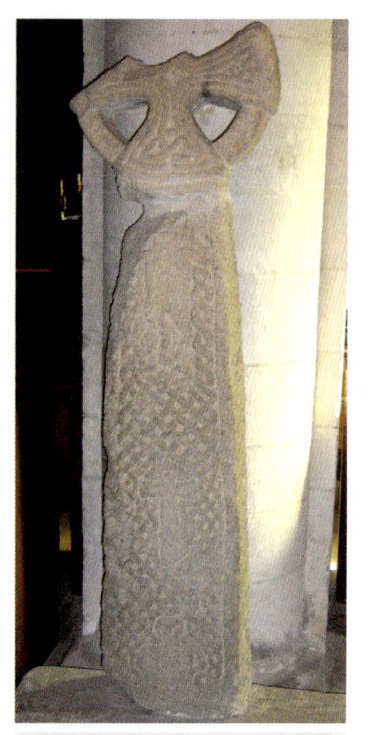

PHOTO 105 - Holy Trinity Church, Stonegrave, North Yorkshire. Incomplete Ring-Head Crosshead with most of its Angular Cross-Shaft with Flat Moulding, Free-Arm Cross with supporting Cross-Shaft with Interlace, Key-Pattern, Knot-Work, and Plait-Work Designs. Seated Human Figure. Celtic or Irish Priest (by the nature of his tonsure). See: Page 144, Site 107.

PHOTO 106 - St Mungo's Church, Dearham, Cumbria. Ring-Head Crosshead and Angular Cross-Shaft with Borre, Key-Pattern, Knot-Work, Pellets, Plait-Work and Roll Moulding. Plant Designs including Yggdrasil - the world tree of Norse mythology. Bird-like creatures. See: Page 118, Site 38.

PHOTO 107 – Whithorn Priory Museum, Wigtownshire. Disc-Head Crosshead with Angular Cross-Shaft with Flat Moulding, Interlace Design. See: Page 147, Site 117.

PHOTO 108 - ADJACENT RIGHT. Whithorn Priory Museum, Wigtownshire. Plate-Ring Crosshead with part of its Angular Cross-Shaft with Cable-Pattern Moulding, Flat Moulding, Grooves, Interlace Design, Knot-Work Design, Stopped Plait-Work Design. Vestiges of Runic Inscription. See: Page 147, Site 117.

An Introduction to Anglo-Saxon Church Architecture &   **101**
Anglo-Saxon & Anglo Scandinavian Stone Sculpture

PHOTO 109 - Ruthwell and Mount Kedar Church, Ruthwell, Dumfriesshire. Panel of Angular Cross-Shaft. Christ in Glory surrounded by extracts from the Scriptures. See: Page 142, Site 102.

PHOTO 110 - St Michael's Church, Great Urswick, Cumbria. Part of Angular Cross-Shaft: Flat Moulding, Knot-Work Design, Roll Moulding. Human Figures. Runic Inscriptions interpreted as: "Tunwini put up this cross in memory of his lord Torhtred. Pray for the soul", and: "Lyl made this". See: Page 127, Site 55.

PHOTO 111 - St Andrew's Church, Bishop Auckland, County Durham. Angular Cross-Shaft: Cable-Pattern Moulding, Roll Moulding. Inhabited Plant-Scroll Design: Archer. In each Scroll an Animal or a Bird. See Page 111. Site 11.

PHOTO 112 - St Mary's Church, Wirksworth, Derbyshire. Coped Grave Cover - the "Wirksworth Stone". A "Tomb Lid" for the seventh century Northumbrian missionary "Betti" with figurative designs including: Christ washing the disciples' feet, Crucifixion Scene, The Blessed Virgin being borne out for burial, Presentation of Christ in the Temple, The Descent into Hell, The Ascension of Christ, The Annunciation, The Mission; there is also Flat Moulding. See: Page 149, Site 123.

PHOTO 113 - Holy Cross Church, Ramsbury, Wiltshire. Parts of two Recumbent Round-Ended and Coped Grave Covers. Grave Cover on right: with a top, raised central ridge which divides and terminates with the heads of animals whose tongues entwine in a knot. It is also decorated with Flat Moulding, Knot-Work Design, Plant-Scroll Design including Pellets, Inhabited Plant-Scroll Design including Animals. Grave Cover on left: with Flat Moulding and Plant-Scroll Design. See: Page 140, Site 97.

An Introduction to Anglo-Saxon Church Architecture & **103**
Anglo-Saxon & Anglo Scandinavian Stone Sculpture

PHOTO 114 - *St Peter's Church, Heysham, Lancashire. Complete Hogback Grave Cover with end bear-like Animals. Decorated with Cable-Pattern Moulding, Tegulations. Scene with Human, Animals, a Snake's Head and Birds. Most probably the scene is from Norse Mythology involving Sigurd or Ragnarök. Alternatively it could be a Biblical scene involving Adam naming the Animals or "The Tree of Life". See: Page 129, Site 61.*

PHOTO 115 – *St Luke's Church, Hickling, Nottinghamshire. Coped Hogback Grave Cover, stylistically unique. A Free-Arm Cross overlying the top ridge and the "roof" on both long sides. Flat Moulding, Interlace Design, Knot-Work Design, Pellets, Ring-Chain Design. Inhabited Interlace Design with Animals. Inhabited Knot-Work Design with Animals. Affronted Animals. Inward-looking heads of bear-like animals on the top ridge with their paws holding the tops of the side walls on each side. See: Page 129, Site 62.*

PHOTO 116 - *St Mary's Church, Gosforth, Cumbria. Hogback Grave Cover known as the "Warrior's Tomb" with a scene depicting two groups of standing warriors. See: Page 125, Site 52.*

PART 4

RECOMMENDED EXEMPLAR SITES

ACCESS TO CHURCHES

Printed details about access to churches in touring guides and local guidebooks are not always reliable. The best way to obtain contact details for a particular church, prior to a visit, is to go to the Church of England web site at www.cofe.anglican.org. Alternatively, use a search engine quoting the name and location of the church and choosing the page entitled "A Church Near You" which will usually provide the initial contact details. Some, but not all, churches will have their own web site but the details provided may not always contain the information required.

Alternatively, consult the current Crockford's Clerical Directory published by Church House Publishing. This Directory includes details of Church of England clergy and identifies the church(es) for which they are responsible. Copies of this Directory can be obtained from Church House, Great Smith Street, London SW1P 3NZ if enquiries of booksellers and public libraries are unsuccessful.

Opening times of the church, and the names and addresses of key holders, are sometimes included in notices on the internal walls of the porch, on the door into the church itself, or on freestanding notice boards outside. Where there are no such notices, local post offices or tourist information offices may be able to assist. Often churches are open on Saturdays and Sundays and on these occasions special arrangements may not be necessary.

RECOMMENDED AND NUMBERED EXAMPLE "SITES" OF ANGLO-SAXON CHURCH ARCHITECTURE AND ANGLO-SAXON/ANGLO-SCANDINAVIAN STONE SCULPTURE

1. Each entry is alphabetically listed and numbered to assist cross-referencing in Parts 2 and 3.

2. Each entry identifies:
   a. Anglo-Saxon church architectural features (externally then internally, and from west to east). Note: All Anglo-Saxon doorways are identified and where they are not at ground level their position is indicated. AND/OR,

   b. Anglo-Saxon and Anglo-Scandinavian sculptured stonework."

1. ALDBROUGH, East Yorkshire – St Bartholomew's Church.
   - Nave, the "Melsa Chapel", and Chancel: Anglo-Saxon Lintel Window Heads can be identified in the fabric; one is decorated with an Animal.
   - Sundial divided into eight segments with lines radiating above and below the horizontal line; in the centre a distinctive hole for the missing gnomon. With an Inscription interpreted as "Ulf ordered the church to be built for himself and for Gunwaru's soul".

2. APPLETON-LE-STREET, North Yorkshire - All Saints Church.
   - Square Tower: Coursed Stone Walling. Side Alternate Quoining. Partially-Blocked Doorway with non-Anglo-Saxon window inserted. Blocked Flat-Headed Door. Blocked Flat-Headed Windows or Doorways at first floor level. Circular Window. Former Nave Roofline. Square String Courses. Between the first and second string courses: Round-Headed Double-Belfry Openings with cylindrical mid-wall shafts. Above the second string course: Round-Headed Double-Belfry Openings with square mid-wall shafts curved and decorated externally – these openings are noticeably smaller than those below.
   - Nave: Coursed Stone Walling. Side Alternate Quoins.

3. BAKEWELL, Derbyshire – All Saints Church.
   - Part of lower vertical Arm from a Free-Arm Cross-Head and most of Angular Cross-Shaft with abstract and figurative designs including: Flat Moulding, Knot-Work Design, Plant-Scroll Design. Scenes including: The Crucifixion. The Annunciation. St Peter. King David with harp. Scenes from Scandinavian mythology including: Inhabited Scroll Design with Odin (incomplete) and his horse Sleipnir. Inhabited Scroll Design with an Animal and the bow and arrow of an Archer (missing).
   - Part of Angular Cross-Shaft with abstract designs including: Flat Moulding, Interlace Design, Ring-Chain Design, Scroll Design.
   - In the South Porch and under an arch on ledges and shelves abutting the West Wall of the North Aisle is displayed one of the largest collections anywhere of assorted sections of stonework from Free-Arm Crossheads, Angular Cross-Shafts, part of a Cross-Shaft with Collar separating Circular Lower Part with Angular Upper Part, and Round-Headed Grave Markers. These are decorated with abstract and figurative designs including: Borre Design (possibly), Cable-Pattern Moulding, Flat Moulding, Interlace Design, Key-Pattern Design, Knot-Work Design, Pellets, Plait-Work Design, Ring-Knot Design, Roll Moulding, Scroll Design, Vine-Scroll Design. Incomplete Christ figure. Complete and Incomplete Haloed figures including winged Angels. Human figures. Animals.

An Introduction to Anglo-Saxon Church Architecture &   **109**
Anglo-Saxon & Anglo Scandinavian Stone Sculpture

4. BARDSEY, West Yorkshire – All Hallows Church.
- Square Tower incorporating earlier Porch: Coursed Rubble Walling. Side Alternate including Megalithic Quoining – the megalithic quoins relate to the earlier porch. Round-Headed Doorways. Roofline of Former Porch. Round-Headed Single-Splayed Windows. Round-Headed Single Belfry Openings – east face at both second and third floor levels. Round-Headed Double Belfry Openings with cylindrical mid-wall shafts – south face at both second and third floor levels. Former Nave Roofline.
- Nave: Coursed Rubble Walling. Side Alternate including Megalithic Quoining. Indications of Blocked Window.
- Architectural Fragment from the undecorated base of an opening with a separate, but integral, section of a Baluster Shaft incised with a Groove.
- Grave Marker incised with a Free-Arm Cross with long lower vertical arm; it could be Anglo-Saxon in origin.

5. BARNACK, Cambridgeshire – St John The Baptist Church.
- Square Tower: Coursed Rubble Walling. Square Single Plinth. Square String Course. Mostly Long and Short Quoining but with some Face Alternate Quoins in the lower Anglo-Saxon stage of the tower. Unusual String Course made up of three courses of stonework; the lower and upper course project from the wall whilst the middle course is recessed. Pilaster-Strips. Round-Headed Doorway with Hood Moulding and Strip-Work, and "Escomb" Jambs. Round-Headed Single-Splayed Window with "Escomb" Jambs; externally, the unusual window head has the semi-circle of the window and the "frame" of the stonework outlined with a band of roll moulding with most of the space in between hollowed out and containing two birds in relief confronting each other. Round and Triangular-Headed Single-Splayed Windows with "Escomb" Jambs. Round-Headed Single-Splayed Windows (one a 1936 copy). Narrow Round-Headed Window. Triangular-Headed Doorway at second stage. Flat-Headed Doorway with "Escomb" Jambs below the Roofline of earlier nave – the top half is now visible externally, the lower half internally. Triangular-Headed Single Belfry Openings with, set back in the depth of the opening and across the width, stone fretwork in a surrounding frame containing a design resembling Ring-Chain Design on the north and south sides, and containing a design with four long, vertical spaces in two pairs resembling panels in a door on the west and east sides. (The third stage of the tower and the spire were added in the thirteenth century.) Three separate panels of stonework each decorated with a band of Roll Moulding forming a complete panel containing Plant-Scroll Design. The Plant-Scroll Design is surmounted on the south side by a farmyard cock in profile to the left, and on the west side by a Bird in profile to the left with its wings half extended – its head is mostly missing but its beak is turned to the right. The north side by a Bird which appears to be feeding on the plants on which it stands and is integral to the Plant-Scroll Design, rather than on top like those on the other two sides. Circular Stone incised with a Sundial and leaf decoration above. Prokrossos. Tower Arch with Hood Moulding and Strip-Work and Two-Stepped Plinth - the imposts continue along the west wall of the nave providing a Moulded String Course. Triangular-Headed seat-like recess outlined with Strip-Work. Small, square-shaped Niches.
- Nave: Coursed Rubble Walling. Mostly Face Alternate Quoins but with Long and Short Quoins higher up. Six Stones forming part of an arch which may be Anglo-Saxon with vestiges of walling above.
- Panel outlined with a band of Flat Moulding containing a seated representation of Christ in Majesty in relief – it could be Anglo-Saxon in origin.
- Part of Angular Cross-Shaft with abstract designs including: Knot-Work Design, Ring-Knot Design, Roll Moulding.

6. BARTON-UPON-HUMBER, Lincolnshire – St Peter's Church.
- Western Annexe/Baptistry: Random Rubble Walling. Vestiges of Square Plinth. "Cut-Back" Long and Short Quoining. Indications of Blocked Round-Headed Doorway. Round-Headed Double-Splayed Windows. Circular Double-Splayed Windows; one with window frame.
- Square Tower: Random Rubble Walling. Coursed Stone Walling. Square Plinth. "Cut-Back" Long and Short Quoining. Side Alternate Quoining. Round-Headed and Triangular-Headed Pilaster-Strips in Long and Short Fashion. Square String Courses. Round-Headed Doorway with "Escomb" Jambs, Hood Moulding and Strip-Work. Blocked Triangular-Headed Doorway with "Escomb" Jambs, Hood Moulding and Strip-Work. Round-Headed Double Windows with "Escomb" jambs, decorated mid-wall baluster shafts and Hood Moulding. Triangular-Headed Double Openings with "Escomb" Jambs, decorated mid-wall baluster shafts, Hood Moulding and Strip-Work; west opening is blocked and incomplete, east opening has Human Head Label-Stops. Round-Headed Double Belfry Openings with cylindrical and square-shaped decorated mid-wall shafts. Tower Arches with "Escomb" Jambs, Hood Moulding and Strip-Work. Round-Headed Doorways with "Escomb Jambs" formerly providing access between upper stages of nave, chancel and western annex. Roofline of earlier nave.
- Panel with head of figure interpreted as Christ in Majesty or a Crucifixion Scene.
- Current Nave: Indications of former Chancel walling on east face of Tower. Position of foundations of Chancel walling and altar indicated on floor of nave.

7. BECKERMET, Cumbria - St Bridget's Church.
- Part of Anglo-Scandinavian Cross-Shaft and its associated Cross-Base with Socket. Cross-Shaft with "Collar" separating the two differently-shaped parts; Circular Lower Part (square with rounded corners) with an Angular Upper Part with swag. The Cross-Shaft is decorated with abstract designs including: Cable-Pattern Moulding, Pellets, Roll Moulding, Stopped Plait-Work Design.
- Part of Anglo-Scandinavian Cross-Shaft and its associated Cross-Base with Socket. Cross-Shaft with "Collar" separating the two differently-shaped parts; Circular Lower Part with an Angular Upper Part with swag. The Cross-Shaft is decorated with abstract designs including: Cable-Pattern Moulding, Flat Moulding, Grooved Moulding, Plant-Scroll Design. Incomplete Inscription: subject of debate for centuries - mostly unintelligible and there is even uncertainty as to the language.

8. BEVERLEY, East Yorkshire – Minster.
- Bishop's Chair.

9. BEWCASTLE, Cumbria – St Cuthbert's Church.
- Almost complete Angular Cross-Shaft with abstract and figurative designs including: Chequer-Pattern Design, Flat Moulding, Interlace Design, Knot-Work Design, Plant-Scroll Design, Ring-Chain Design, Ring-Knot Design, Roll Moulding. Inhabited Vine-Scroll Design with Animals and Birds. Sundial. Runic Inscriptions: two identifying Jesus Christ; another incomplete interpreted as "This token of Victory Hwaetred…set up in memory"; and another interpreted as "the female personal name "Cyneburh". Representations of Christ in Glory, St John the Evangelist with his symbol the eagle, John the Baptist. Animals. Cross-Base (no decoration survives).
- Other stonework (not good examples): Part of a font (no decoration survives). Parts of Grave Covers with incised Cross – including Crosshead, part of Cross-Shaft and one with part of stepped Base.

10. BILLINGHAM, County Durham – St Cuthbert's Church.
- Square Tower: Coursed Stone Walling. Side Alternate Quoining. Single-Splayed Window with round head externally and square head internally. Round-Headed Doorway with Hood

An Introduction to Anglo-Saxon Church Architecture & Anglo-Saxon & Anglo Scandinavian Stone Sculpture

Moulding and Strip-Work at former second floor level for external access. Square String Course. Round-Headed Double-Belfry Openings with rectangular and circular mid-wall shafts, Hood Moulding, Strip-Work, and Tympanum with round and octagonal star-shaped Sound Holes.
- Nave: Coursed Stone Walling. Side Alternate Quoining. Round-Headed Doorway with Tympanum – the lintels are particularly large.
- Parts of Angular Cross-Shafts with abstract and figurative designs which are all very weathered and some very faint with only slight vestiges remaining of: Flat Moulding, Interlace Design, Pellets, Plait-Work Design, Plant-Scroll Design, Stepped-Pattern Design. Inhabited Scroll Design with Man and two Birds. Birds.
- Parts of Grave Markers with abstract and figurative designs including: Flat Moulding, representations of Free-Arm Crosses.

11. BISHOP AUCKLAND – SOUTH CHURCH, County Durham – St Andrew's Church.
- Reconstructed Cross – Free-Arm Crosshead, Angular Cross-Shaft and Cross-Base with abstract and figurative designs including: Cable-Pattern Moulding, Pellets, Roll Moulding. Crucifixion Scene with haloed figures (one probably female) and Inscription whose interpretation is a matter of debate. Haloed winged Angels – one female. Haloed Figures – one is probably female. Inhabited Plant Scroll Designs with an Archer, parts of Human bodies, Animals and Birds.
- Part of Grave Cover with abstract designs including: Grooved Moulding, Pellets, Plait-Work Design, Roll Moulding outlining a Cross.
- Part of Grave Marker with abstract designs including: Flat Moulding, Key-Pattern Design, Stepped-Pattern Design, Zigzag-Pattern Design.

12. BISHOPSTONE, Sussex – St Andrew's Church.
- Nave: Random Rubble Walling. Long and Short Quoins. Blocked Round-Headed Single-Splayed Windows.
- South Porch (former Portico): Random Rubble Walling. Long and Short Quoins. Round-Headed Stone with incised parallel Grooves forming a border and the lower curvature of a Sundial with similarly distinct incised Grooves providing the calibrations – every third Groove is bisected to form a cross; also incised is the Old English name "Eadric" accompanied by a Free-Arm Cross, (the gnomon is not Anglo-Saxon).

PHOTO 117 – Site 11. St Andrew's Church, Bishop Auckland, County Durham. Reconstructed Cross-Shaft.

13. BOLAM, Northumberland – St Andrew's Church.
- Square Tower: Coursed Stone Walling including some Herringbone Masonry. Side Alternate Quoining. Vestiges and Complete Round-Headed Single-Splayed Windows. Square String Course. Round-Headed Double Belfry Openings with cylindrical mid-wall shafts. Triangular-Headed Single Belfry Openings – one is Round-Headed.
- Nave: Coursed Stone Walling. String Course. Reused Anglo-Saxon Columns for Doorway. Side Alternate Quoining.
- Imposts or Fragments from Friezes with abstract designs including: Cable-Pattern Moulding used to produce a Herringbone Pattern Design, Design akin to a St Andrew's cross,

Roll Moulding.
- Grave Cover with abstract designs including: Design akin to a St Andrew's cross, Flat Moulding, Incised Diagonal and Vertical Lines.
- Round-Headed Grave Marker incised with abstract designs including: Flat Moulding, Free-Arm Cross.

14. BOSHAM, Sussex – Holy Trinity Church.
- Square Tower: Coursed Rubble Walling. Chamfered String Courses. Long and Short Quoining including the "Sussex" variation. Some surviving parts and vestiges of Double-Belfry Openings with "Escomb" Jambs. In the west at the top stage Saxo-Norman Double-Belfry Opening with a cylindrical mid-wall shaft. Restored Tower Arch with "Escomb" Jambs. Triangular-Headed Doorway at first floor level. Small Rectangular-Shaped Opening. Round-Headed Doorway at second floor level.
- Nave: Coursed Rubble Walling. Vestiges of Long and Short Quoining.
- Chancel: Coursed Rubble Walling with vestiges of Herringbone Masonry. Saxo-Norman Chancel Arch. Blocked Round-Headed Opening or Doorway above the Chancel Arch. Blocked Small Square-Shaped Opening. Part of Round-Headed Single-Splayed Window. Vestiges of Blocked Round-Headed Doorway or Opening.
- Fragment from a Decorated Frieze or Impost with a representation of a stepped capital and a Foliate Design.

15. BRADFORD-ON-AVON, Wiltshire - St Laurence Church. Complete Restored Anglo-Saxon Church.
- Nave, Chancel and Side-Chapel or Porch – south porch now demolished: Ashlar Walling. Square Single Plinth. "Cut-Back" Side Alternate Quoining. Round-Headed Doorways with Strip-Work. Pilaster-Strips. Square String Courses. Round-Headed Blind-Arch Arcading between two Square String Courses. Round-Headed Double-Splayed Windows. Chancel Arch with Strip-Work.
- Two Panels depicting flying Angels.
- Part of an Angular Cross-Shaft with abstract and figurative designs, Plait-Work Design including: Flat Moulding, Knot-Work Design, Pellets, Interlace Design.
- Three separate pieces from same panel whose purpose is a matter of debate. They are decorated with abstract designs including: Flat Moulding, Free-Arm Crosses enclosed within a serrated Diamond-Pattern Design, Knot-Work Design.

16. BRADWELL-ON-SEA, Essex – St Peter-On-The-Wall Church. Restored Cruciform Church.
- Restored Nave: Coursed Rubble Walling including re-used Roman Stonework, Bricks and Tiles. A mixture of Side Alternate and Long and Short Quoining; including Megalithic Quoins. Projecting small buttress-like Pillars – sometimes referred to as "Pilaster Buttresses" - rising up to a level in line with the sills of the windows. Flat-Headed Single-Splayed Windows with wooden lintels – one blocked and only vestiges surviving. Flat-Headed Doorway with wooden lintel with slight indications on each side of attached walling of former western Porch. Round-Headed Single-Splayed Window. Vestiges of Blocked Doorway from Nave to South Portico with indications of an "Escomb" Jamb. Parts of the Jambs and Arches of the blocked Chancel Arch utilising distinctive Roman tiles – what remains of the Arches indicate by their curvature that there may have been a series of arches rather than a single arch to bridge the intervening space.
- Apsidal Chancel: Vestiges of Coursed Rubble Walling including re-used Roman Stonework, Bricks and Tiles but mostly with the foundations outlined in cement. Fragment of western Jamb of Doorway from Chancel to North Portico.

- Porticos: Foundations outlined in cement.

17. BREAMORE, Hampshire – St Mary's Church.
- Nave: Random Rubble Walling of Flints. Long and Short Quoining. Pilaster-Strips. Round-Headed Double-Splayed Windows – one blocked. Jambs of Blocked Doorway. Roofline of former North Portico. Indications of former western annex. On the south wall above the south door now within the porch, a defaced Rood with Crucifixion Scene with the Virgin and St John; with paint. One letter "G" from an Inscription on the external west wall of the nave.
- Central Square Tower with two receding pyramidal roofs separated by vertical walling: Random Rubble Walling with Flints. Long and Short Quoining. Round-Headed Double-Splayed Windows – one blocked. Vestiges of Round-Headed Double-Splayed Windows now replaced with flat-headed fifteenth century adaptations. Part of Roofline of former Chancel.
- South Portico: Random Rubble Walling with Flints. Long and Short Quoining. Round-Headed Double-Splayed Windows – one partly replaced by a thirteenth century window. Round-Headed Doorway with incomplete Inscription on Arch whose interpretation is debated "Here the agreement which....reveals...."; decorated Imposts.
- Rebuilt Chancel: Random Rubble Walling of Flints. The letters "DE" and part of probably "S" from an incomplete Inscription above Chancel Arch.

PHOTO 118 – Site 17. St Mary's Church, Breamore, Hampshire. Round-Headed Doorway with Inscription.

18. BREEDON-ON-THE-HILL, Leicestershire – St Mary and St Hardulph Church.
- Friezes with abstract and figurative designs including: Flat Moulding, Interlace Design, Key-Pattern Design, Ring-Chain Design, Ring-Knot Design, Roll Moulding, Shell Design involving a series of interlocking shells, Vine-Scroll Design. Inhabited Plant-Scroll Design with Humans, including Warriors both Horsemen and unmounted. Inhabited Plant-Scroll Design with Animals and Birds.
- Panels with abstract and figurative designs including: Flat Moulding, Roll Moulding. Round-Headed interlocking Archways with haloed Saints below; the central, separate, and much larger figure is probably a representation of the Virgin Mary. Angel known as "The Breedon Angel" - with Archway. Two Human Figures each swinging a censer connected to the frame of the panel. A haloed Figure giving a blessing. Representation of a Lion.
- Parts of Angular Cross-Shafts with abstract and figurative designs including: Cable-Pattern Design, Flat Moulding, Interlace Design, Ring-Chain Design, Ring-Knot Design, Roll Moulding. Two Scenes, one depicting Adam and Eve with the tree and serpent, the other depicting two figures - one with a drinking horn. A Halo – the accompanying head is defaced. "Jellinge-Style" Animals.

19. BRIGHAM, Cumbria – St Bridget's Church.
- Part of Free-Arm Crossheads and a Hammer-Head Crosshead with abstract and figurative designs including: Flat Moulding, Interlace Design, Knot-Work Design, Pellets, Roll Moulding. Human figure and Human head. Possibly a Snake.

- Parts of Angular Cross-Shafts with abstract and figurative designs including: Flat Moulding, Interlace Design, Knot-Work Design, Pellet, Plait-Work Design, Plant-Scroll Design, Ring-Chain Design, Roll Moulding. Animal.
- Part of Hogback Grave Cover with abstract designs including: Roll Moulding, Scroll Design, Tegulations.
- Most of Cross-Base with abstract and figurative designs including: Cable-Pattern Moulding, Interlace Design, Roll Moulding, Scroll Design. Animals.

PHOTO 119 - Site 19. St Bridget's Church, Brigham, Cumbria. Most of Free-Arm Crosshead with Human Figure with Scroll Design, Interlace Design, Roll Moulding.

20. BRIGSTOCK, Northamptonshire - St Andrew's Church.
- Stair-Turret: Coursed Rubble Walling. Square Single Plinth. Flat-Headed Double-Splayed Windows.
- Square Tower: Coursed Rubble Walling. Square Single Plinth. Long and Short Quoining. Round Headed Single-Splayed and Double Splayed Windows. Triangular-Headed Doorway with "Escomb" Jambs. Flat-Headed Doorway. Blocked Flat-Headed Doorway at first floor level. Tower Arch with "Escomb" Jambs and Strip-Work.
- Nave: Coursed Rubble Walling. Square Single Plinth. Long and Short Quoining. Blocked Incomplete Single-Splayed Window. Square String Course.

21. BRISTOL, Gloucestershire - St Augustine's Cathedral.
- Panel outlined with a band of Flat Moulding (incomplete) containing a standing representation of Christ in relief known as "The Harrowing of Hell". As well as Christ there are at least two smaller human figures (one mostly incomplete) below His lower hand with below His feet the snout, upper jaw of an animal within whose gaping mouth is another smaller bound animal with distinctive head and open jaw.

22. BRITFORD, Wiltshire - St Peter's Church.
- Nave: Rubble Walling including Flints, reused Roman Bricks and Tiles.
- Archway into the former Northern Portico reusing Roman Bricks with stone blocks alternating sunken and level panels in the centre of the soffit of the arch and in the centre of the jambs; Hood Moulding and Strip-Work. The Eastern Jamb of the Archway is decorated with Knot-Work Design, Plant-Scroll Design; the Western Jamb has only a single panel decorated with Knot-Work Design.
- Archway into the former Southern Portico with Hood Moulding and Strip-Work: the arch reuses Roman tiles.
- Restored Round-Headed Doorway.

23. BRIXWORTH, Northamptonshire - All Saints Church.
- Stair Turret: Random Rubble Walling including reused Roman Bricks and Tiles, Herringbone Masonry. Flat-Headed Single-Splayed Windows. Spiral Stairway with Steps formed

PHOTO 120 - Site 22. St Peter's Church, Britford, Wiltshire. Archway.

An Introduction to Anglo-Saxon Church Architecture &
Anglo-Saxon & Anglo Scandinavian Stone Sculpture

separately from the Newel and with the treads supported by barrel-vaulting. First Floor Round-Headed Doorway into tower cut through former window of western porch.
- Square Tower incorporating earlier Porch: Random Rubble Walling including reused Roman Bricks and Tiles, Herringbone Masonry. Round-Headed Doorways. Blocked Round-Headed Doorway. Fragments of walling from former Narthexes. Round-Headed and Flat-Headed Single-Splayed Windows.
- Nave: Random Rubble Walling including reused Roman Bricks and Tiles. Blocked Round-Headed Arches formerly leading to Porticos now with Round-Headed Windows inserted; one has been used for the current south door. Round-Headed Clerestory Windows. Round-Headed Doorway. At first floor level Blocked Round-Headed Doorway. Round-Headed Triple Window with bulbous-shaped mid-wall shafts. Former Roofline. Vestiges of Walls and Archways dividing the Nave from what is referred to as the Presbytery.
- Presbytery – a continuation of the Nave and between the easternmost porticos: Random Rubble Walling including reused Roman Bricks and Tiles. Blocked Round-Headed Doorway. Blocked Round-Headed Window. Vestiges of Arches – the remains of the Arches (and by known excavation) indicate by their curvature that there were three arches bridging the intervening space separating the Presbytery from the Nave.
- Apsidal Chancel: Chancel Arch. Round-Headed Single-Splayed Windows. Pilaster-Strips. Blocked Round-Headed Doorways into Ambulatory.
- External (Sunken) Ambulatory. Random Rubble Walling including Recesses for Relics.
- Part of an Angular Cross-Shaft comprising most of a Panel framed by Flat Moulding enclosing the figure of an eagle – the symbol of St John the Evangelist.
- Part of an Angular Cross-Shaft with abstract and figurative designs including: Cable-Pattern Moulding. Animals.
- The "Brixworth Relic" thought to contain the throat bone of the West Saxon St Boniface, the eighth century missionary to the Frankish Empire and Patron Saint of Germany.

24. BROMPTON-IN-ALLERTONSHIRE, North Yorkshire – St Thomas's Church.
- Three complete and two incomplete Hogback Grave Covers with abstract and figurative designs including: Cable-Pattern Moulding, Flat Moulding, Interlace Design, Knot-Work Design, Pellets, Plait-Work Design, Ring-Chain Design, Stepped-Pattern Design, Tegulations. Complete and vestiges of end bear-like Animals.
- Plate-Ring Crosshead with part of its attached Angular Cross-Shaft with abstract designs including: Incised Diagonal Cross, Flat Moulding, Knot-Work Design, Pellets, Plait-Work Design.
- Most of Plate-Ring Crosshead with its attached Angular Cross-Shaft with abstract designs including: Flat Moulding, Pellets, Knot-Work Design, Plait-Work Design.
- Part of Angular Cross-Shaft known as the "Cock Shaft" with abstract and figurative designs including: Cable-Pattern Moulding, Flat Moulding, Plant-Scroll Design, Human Figure with wings. Haloed Ecclesiastics. Animals. Birds.
- Incomplete Ring-Head and Plate-Ring Crossheads and incomplete Angular Cross-Shafts with abstract designs including: Flat Moulding, Knot-Work Design, Pellets, Plait-Work Design, Ring-Knot Design, Scroll Design.

25. BURTON PEDWARDINE, Lincolnshire – St Andrew's Church.
- Incomplete Angular Cross-Shaft with abstract designs including: Flat Moulding, Plait-Work Design.
- Incomplete Grave Covers with abstract and figurative designs including: Cable-Pattern Moulding, Flat Moulding, Interlace Design, Knot-Work Design, Plait-Work Design, Ring-Knot Design. Part of a Cross. Plait-Work Design including "Bull's Head".

26. BYWELL, Northumberland – St Andrew's Church.
- Square Tower: Coursed Rubble Walling. Side Alternate Quoining. Round-Headed Single-Splayed Windows. Square String Courses. Round-Headed Doorway with Hood Moulding and Strip-Work at second floor level just below the belfry-stage. Round-Headed Double-Belfry Openings with cylindrical mid-wall shafts: with Hood Moulding, Strip-Work and Circular Sound Holes.
- Nave: Coursed Rubble Walling. Side Alternate Quoining.
- Impost with Chequer-Pattern Design and Grooved Moulding.
- Part of an Angular Cross-Shaft with abstract designs including: Flat Moulding, Key-Pattern design, Pellets, Ring-Chain Design, Designs providing a swag-like design on one face and a triangular-shaped design on the other face. Part of an Animal.

27. CAMBRIDGE, Cambridgeshire – St Bene't's Church.
- Square Tower: Random Rubble Walling. Square Single Plinth. Square String Courses. "Cut-Back" Long and Short Quoining. Slight vestiges of Round-Headed Window. Round-Headed Double-Belfry Openings with mid-wall baluster shafts. Round Sound Holes. Above the Belfry Openings, a centrally placed Pilaster Strip above the centre which possibly originally extended to a gable supporting a "Rhenish-Helm" Roof. Tower-Arch with: Hood Moulding ending with crouching animals confronting each other across the width of the arch; imposts continuing along the west wall of the nave providing a Moulded String Course; Strip-Work and "Escomb" Jambs. Round-Headed Doorway with "Escomb" Jambs at first floor level.
- Nave: Random Rubble Walling. Long and Short Quoining.

28. CHESTER-LE-STREET, County Durham – Anker's House Museum – part of St Mary and St Cuthbert's Church.
- Complete and incomplete Cross-Bases with abstract and figurative designs including: Columns with Capitals, Flat Moulding, Interlace Design, Knot-Work Design, Standing Cross. Crucifixion Scene. Human Figures. Animals.
- Part of an arm from a Free-Arm Crosshead and Parts of Angular Cross-Shafts decorated with abstract and figurative designs including: Cable-Pattern Moulding, Flat Moulding, Grooved Moulding, Interlace Design, Key-Pattern Design, Knot-Work Design, Plait-Work Design, Plant-Scroll Design, Ring-Knot Design. Mounted Warrior. Animals. Inscription – "Eadmund".

29. CHOLLERTON, Northumberland - St Giles Church.
- One complete and two incomplete Plate-Ring Crossheads and parts of two Cross-Shafts.

30. CODFORD ST PETER, Wiltshire – St Peter's Church.
- Part of Angular Cross-shaft (possibly part of an architectural feature) with abstract and figurative designs including: Representations of Baluster Shafts as Moulding, Plant-Scroll Design, Roll Moulding, Stepped-Pattern Design. Inhabited Plant-Scroll Design with Human Figure.

PHOTO 121 - Site 30. St Peter's Church, Codford St Peter, Wiltshire. Angular Cross-Shaft/Architectural Feature.

An Introduction to Anglo-Saxon Church Architecture &
Anglo-Saxon & Anglo Scandinavian Stone Sculpture

31. COLCHESTER, Essex – Holy Trinity Church.
- Square Tower: Random Rubble Walling including reused Roman Bricks and Tiles. Re-used Roman Brick Double Plinth. Wholly faced with reused Roman Brick and Tile: Quoining. Triangular-Headed Doorway with Hood Moulding and Strip-Work. Double-Splayed Round-Headed Windows. Square String Courses. Round-Headed Doorway at the top of the first stage. Blocked Round-Headed Windows. Differently sized sets of Round-Headed Single Belfry Openings – the lower set is ornamented by an Arcade of Round-Headed Pilasters. Tower Arch with Hood Moulding and Strip-Work.

32. COLLINGHAM, West Yorkshire – St Oswald's Church.
- Nave: Coursed Rubble Walling. Side Alternate including Megalithic Quoining.
- Two parts of a Cross-Shaft joined together with a circular lower part and an angular upper part. Known as the "Apostles' Cross" with figurative and abstract designs including: Archways, Cable-Pattern Moulding, Flat Moulding, Plant-Scroll Design. Haloed Figures including possibly Christ, the Virgin Mary with the Christ Child – (most are thought to represent the Apostles).
- Two parts of an Angular Cross-Shaft joined together and known as the "Aerswith Cross" with abstract and figurative designs including: Flat Moulding, Interlace Design, Knot-Work Design, Plant-Scroll Design. Animals including Confronting Animals. Incomplete Runic Inscription whose translation is a matter of debate but has been interpreted as "Aerswith".
- Parts of Angular Cross-Shafts with abstract designs including: Flat Moulding, Interlace Design, Key-Pattern Design, Line Design, Plait-Work Design, Plant-Scroll Design, Stepped-Pattern Design.
- Part of an Arm from a Free-Arm Crosshead with abstract designs including: Flat Moulding, Knot-Work Design, Ring-Knot Design, Roll Moulding.

33. COLYTON, Devon – St Andrew's Church.
- Angled Cross-Shaft, Cross-Base and reconstructed Free-Arm Crosshead with abstract and figurative designs including: Basket-Plait Design, Plant-Scroll Design, Ring-Knot Design, Roll Moulding. Inhabited Plant-Scroll Design with Animals and a Bird.

34. CORBRIDGE, Northumberland – St Andrew's Church.
- "The King's Oven" – east side of the structure in the churchyard: Large Side Alternate Quoins in the northeast and southeast corners could be Anglo-Saxon in origin.
- Buildings extending west and north of Square Tower: Vestiges of Square and Chamfered Double Plinth and Coursed Rubble Walling.
- Square Tower incorporating earlier Porch. Coursed Rubble Walling including reused Roman Stonework. Square Single Plinth. Side Alternate including Megalithic Quoining. Blocked Round-Headed Doorway with "Escomb" Jambs and Hood Moulding. Square String Course. Round-Headed Single-Splayed Window. Round-Headed Single-Splayed Window which may have been a Doorway. Indications former Nave Roofline. Vestiges of a Blocked Doorway or Window below gable of Roofline before battlements added. Tower Arch built of reused Roman Stonework.

PHOTO 122 – Site 33. *St Andrew's Church, Colyton, Devon. Angled Cross-Shaft with Ring-Knot Design.*

- Nave: Coursed Rubble Walling including reused Roman Stonework. Buttress-like Stonework providing indication of higher nave walls and higher former nave roofline. Vestiges of Round-Headed Windows. Vestiges of foundations of north wall and associated flooring beside it.
- Part of a Grave Marker incised with a Free-Arm Cross within a circle and part of another.
- Part of a Grave Marker incised with an Inscription interpreted as representing "here lies Eric".
- Plate-Ring Crosshead Finial with incised concentric Circles – some with indentations in the centre, Design akin to a St Andrew's Cross, and Lines.

35. CORHAMPTON, Hampshire – Church (No Dedication).
- Nave: Restored, lightly plastered, Flint Walling. Square Single Plinth. Long and Short Quoining. Pilaster-Strips, some with vestiges of decoration on the bases. Part of Square String Course. Blocked Doorway (now window) with Strip-Work and decorated Imposts and Bases (weathered). Restored Bell-Cote Double Opening. Possible Saxo-Norman font. Sundial with foliate decoration.
- Chancel: Restored, lightly plastered, Flint Walling. Square Single Plinth. Pilaster-Strips, some with vestiges of decoration on the bases. Chancel Arch with "Escomb" Jambs, Hood Moulding and Strip-Work (damaged). Possible Anglo-Saxon Altar Stone.

36. CROPTHORNE, Worcestershire – St Michael's Church.
- Virtually complete Free-Arm Crosshead with abstract and figurative designs including: Cable-Pattern Moulding, Flat Moulding, Rectangular Maze-like Pattern. Inhabited Plant-Scroll Design with Animals, Birds.

37. DAGLINGWORTH, Gloucestershire – Church of the Holy Rood.
- Nave: Random Rubble Walling. Chamfered Single Plinth. "Cut-Back" Long and Short Quoining. Chamfered String Course. Round-Headed (externally)/Flat-Headed (internally) Doorway with Imposts with two bands of Cable-Pattern Design forming what is described as "wheat-ear" decoration. Sundial framed by a circular band of Roll Moulding.
- Porch: Re-Use of Anglo-Saxon material including Round-Headed Doorway with chamfered Imposts incised with a narrow groove, and with "Escomb" Jambs.
- Rebuilt Chancel: Random Rubble Walling. "Cut-Back" Long and Short Quoining. Chancel Arch rebuilt but retains Imposts decorated with Pellets.
- Two Carved Panels with Crucifixion scenes; one with Christ only, the other with Christ with the figures of Roman soldiers – the cup/sponge-bearer Stephaton and the spear-bearer Longinus. Carved Panel with Christ in Majesty - sitting. Carved Panel with St Peter holding the Key to Heaven.

38. DEARHAM, Cumbria – St Mungo's Church.
- Most of Cross comprising Ring-Head Crosshead and Angular Cross-Shaft with abstract and figurative designs including: Borre Design, Key-Pattern Design, Knot-Work Design, Pellets, Plait-Work Design, Roll Moulding. Plant Design including Yggdrasil –

PHOTO 123 – Site 37. Church of the Holy Rood, Daglingworth, Gloucestershire. Panel with Crucifixion scene.

An Introduction to Anglo-Saxon Church Architecture &   **119**
Anglo-Saxon & Anglo Scandinavian Stone Sculpture

the world tree of Norse mythology. Bird-like creatures.
- Part of Angular Cross-Shaft with abstract and figurative designs including Flat Moulding, Pellets, Spiral-Scroll Design, Stopped Plait-Work Design. Scene depicting legend of St Kenneth – horse and rider, human figure, baby and bird-like creature.
- Part of Hammer-Head Crosshead with abstract designs including: Roll Moulding, Spiral-Scroll Design, Pellets.

39. DEERHURST, Gloucestershire – St Mary's Church. Incorporating former monastic church.
- Tower incorporating earlier Porch: Coursed Rubble Walling including Herringbone Masonry. Lower stages with Rubble Quoining and upper stages with Face Alternate Quoining reflecting different building periods. Surviving Arch from a Round-Headed Doorway with Hood Moulding. Restored Round-Headed Doorway with two original Animal Head Label-Stops at the terminals of the hood moulding on the east face. At second floor level, Round-Headed (externally)/Flat-Headed (internally) Doorway with the Hood Moulding (unusually outlining the rectangular shape of the lintel rather than the arch of the doorway) and with very weathered Animal Head Label-Stops; the doorway now functions as both doorway and window. Open and Blocked Single-Splayed and Double-Splayed Flat-Headed Windows – one now converted to a doorway. Round-Headed Aumbries. At third floor level, Round-Headed (internally)/Flat-Headed (externally) Doorway – part above existing nave roofline but below former Anglo-Saxon nave Roofline. Incomplete, differently shaped, Animal Head Prokrossi. Indications of present Belfry Opening inserted into earlier Anglo-Saxon opening. Strip-Work outlining a Round-Headed Panel made smooth for painting the detail of a representation of a haloed Virgin holding up an oval-shaped shield on which was painted a depiction of Christ; there is a row of recessed, stepped free-arm crosses along the base of the panel.
- Nave: Coursed Rubble Walling including Herringbone Masonry. Round-Headed Doorway with Hood Moulding on the west face. Parts of moulded Corbels at first floor level supporting former western gallery. At first floor level, Blocked Round-Headed (east face)/Flat-Headed (west face) Doorway. Triangular-Shaped Windows or Squints. Parts of Stepped String Course with varied mouldings. Double Triangular-Headed Opening with Hood Moulding, Stepped Imposts, Jambs and Mid-Wall Square-Shaped Shaft decorated with fluted columns, Chamfered Bases (north opening has had the chamfering cut back when it was enlarged to become a doorway). Rectangular Panel prepared for possibly painted Inscription or decoration. Large horizontal stone providing indications of sill of doorway. Aisles, incorporating former North and South Porticos which themselves had further Porticos added, including those flanking the Chancel: Coursed Rubble Walling including Herringbone Masonry.
- South Aisle: Blocked Round-Headed Archway. Round-Headed (externally)/Flat-Headed (internally) Doorway with Hood Moulding and with Animal Head Label-Stops; it is now blocked and reused as a window. Incomplete Animal Head Prokrossos. Part of West Wall of Portico: Round-Headed Single-Splayed Window. Jamb and Lintel from a Flat-Headed

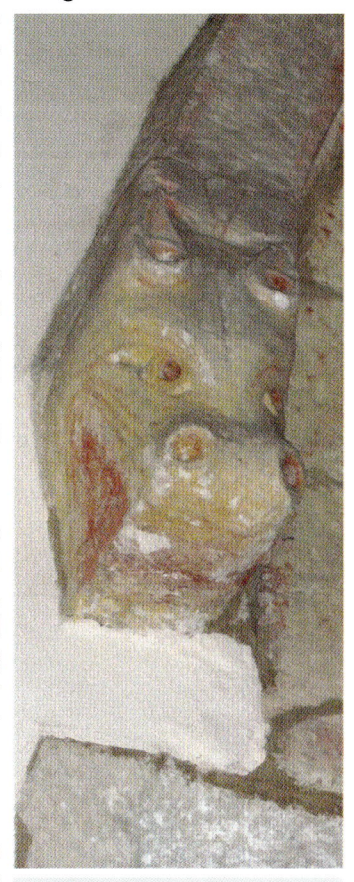

PHOTO 124 – Site 39. St Mary's Church, Deerhurst, Gloucestershire. Label Stop including original paint.

Doorway at first floor level. Vestiges of Square String Course.
- North Aisle: Blocked Flat-Headed Doorway. Flat-Headed Aumbries. Font and Stem (the Stem is probably part of a Round Cross-Shaft) with abstract and figurative designs including: Flat Moulding, Interlace Design, Plant-Scroll Design, Roll Moulding. Spiral-Scroll Design including Ribbon-Shaped Animals.
- Present Chancel formerly part of the Central Crossing separating the nave from the chancel and providing access to the Porticos on the North and South sides: Coursed Rubble Walling with Herringbone Masonry. Chamfered Double Plinth. Blocked Chancel Arch with decorated capitals with a design likened to the stern of an Anglo-Saxon ship; the design can be seen on both sides of the intervening blocking wall. This blocked Chancel Arch also has Hood Moulding with Animal Head Label-Stops; the north, left-hand, Label-Stop has some of its original painted design. Parts of moulded Corbels at first floor level supporting former eastern gallery. Triangular-Headed Panels: left-hand (north) panel is framed with a band akin to Flat Moulding with very slight indications of a painted haloed standing figure; the other right-hand (south) panel is almost entirely lacking in decoration; there are slight indications of probably two horizontal lines. Blocked Triangular-Headed Doorway providing ground floor access to one of the former northern porticos. Its triangular head reuses part of a Grave Cover with vestiges of Interlace Design. Blocked Flat-Headed Doorways providing ground floor access to former north and south Porticos. Round-Headed Openings providing access to former Porticos at first floor level (confirmation that Porticos could be more than one storey). Externally, large horizontal stone providing indications of sill of Window or Doorway below the present east Window.
- Ruined Polygonal-Shaped Apse: Some Coursed Rubble Walling and Foundations. Pilaster-Strips. Part of Square String Course. Strip-Work forming a Triangular-Headed Arch above the String Course. Within this one surviving arch is part of a Panel framed with Flat Moulding enclosing the haloed (incomplete) head and distinctive hair of an Angel in portrait with some of its left wing (on the right) and vestiges of its right wing (on the left).

40. DERBY, Derbyshire – Museum and Art Gallery.
- St Alkmund's (martyred son of King Alhred of Northumbria) Sarcophagus with abstract designs including Flat Moulding, Interlace Designs, Ring-Chain Design, Roll Moulding.
- Parts of Angular Cross-Shafts known as "St Alkmund's Cross" and "The Repton Stone" with abstract and figurative Designs including: Flat Moulding, Ring-Chain Design, Roll Moulding, Scroll Design. Three of the four Evangelists. A mounted warrior on horseback possibly depicting King Aethelbard of Mercia. "The Mouth of Hell" depicting a monster with a human head devouring human bodies. Animals. Birds.
- Almost complete Grave Cover and part of another Grave Cover with abstract designs including: Flat Moulding, Ring-Chain Design, Roll Moulding, Scroll Design.
- Part of a Hogback Grave Cover with Ring-Chain Design incorporating an animal into the design.

41. DEWSBURY, West Yorkshire – The Minster Church of All Saints.
- Coursed Stone Walling including a Quoin.
- Arm from a Free-Arm Crosshead with abstract and figurative designs including: Cable-Pattern Moulding, Angel. Human Figure. Possible Animals.

PHOTO 125 – Site 40. Derby Museum & Art Gallery, Derbyshire. "The Repton Stone". Photograph Courtesy of Derby Museums.

An Introduction to Anglo-Saxon Church Architecture &
Anglo-Saxon & Anglo Scandinavian Stone Sculpture

- Part of a Free-Arm Crosshead with Cable-Pattern Moulding and Flat Moulding.
- Part of the central section of a Crosshead with Boss and Interlace Design.
- Three Fragments possibly from the same Circular Cross-Shaft with abstract and figurative designs including: Cable-Pattern Moulding, Christ giving a Blessing with an Inscription above with the abbreviated Latin name for Jesus Christ. Human Figures some below and some standing on Arches.
- Part of an Angular Cross-Shaft with abstract and figurative designs including: Archway, Cable-Pattern Moulding, Plant-Scroll Design. Seated figure of the Virgin and Child. Feet of Human Figures.
- Part of an Angular Cross-Shaft with abstract and figurative designs including: Cable Pattern Moulding, Christ flanked by the figures of the Virgin and St John with representations of water jars; an Inscription interpreted as referring to the Miracle of turning water into wine. Christ with representations of the Loaves and Fishes with a "crowd" of people represented by six Human Heads; an Inscription interpreted as referring to the Miracle of the Loaves and Fishes.
- Part of an Angular Cross-Shaft with abstract and figurative designs including: Cable-Pattern Moulding, Flat Moulding, Interlace Design, Plant-Scroll Design. Christ Crucified. Possibly the Virgin and Child.
- Parts of an Angular Cross-Shaft with abstract designs including: Plant-Scroll Design, Roll Moulding. Human Figure.
- Part of a Cross-Base with abstract designs including:
  Representations of Baluster Shafts as Moulding, Plant-Scroll Design, Roll Moulding.
- House-shaped Grave Cover resembling an upturned boat with abstract designs including: Representations of Baluster Shafts as Moulding, Flat Moulding, Free-Arm Cross in relief, Line Design, Plant-Scroll design, Tegulations.

42. DOLTON, Devon – Church of St Edmund King and Martyr.
- Two Parts of Angled Cross-Shaft reused as a font, the upper part upside down and used as a font bowl, the lower part – the right way up – used as the base. Abstract and figurative designs including: Flat Moulding, Knot-Work Design, Ring-Knot Design, Roll Moulding. Inhabited Knot-Work Design with: Human Head with two reptile-like animals extending from its nostrils; entwined Animals; winged Animals with affronted heads.

PHOTO 126 – Site 42. Church of St Edmund King and Martyr, Dolton, Devon. Cross-Shaft reused as font.

43. DOVER, Kent – St Mary-In-The-Castle Church. Restored Cruciform Church.
- Nave: Coursed Rubble Walling with Flints and some reused Roman Bricks and Tiles. Square Single Plinth. Side Alternate Quoining – a mixture of reused Roman tiles and some dressed and megalithic stones. Vestiges of former western Doorway. Blocked Round-Headed Doorway providing access to first floor gallery. Large Round-Headed Double-Splayed Windows with reused Roman tiles. Flat-Headed Double-Splayed Windows with reused Roman tiles.
- Central Square Tower: Coursed Rubble Walling with Flints and some reused Roman Bricks and Tiles. Square Single Plinth. Side Alternate Quoining – a mixture of reused Roman tiles and some dressed stones. Double-Splayed Circular Windows with reused Roman tiles. Pairs of Round-Headed Single Belfry Openings. Arches with Hood Moulding and Strip-Work. Blocked Round-Headed Doorways formerly providing access between upper stages of nave, tower and chancel.

- Transepts: Coursed Rubble Walling with Flints and some reused Roman Bricks and Tiles. Square Single Plinth. Side Alternate Quoining – a mixture of reused Roman tiles and some dressed stones. Flat-Headed Double-Splayed Window.
- Chancel: Coursed Rubble Walling with Flints and some reused Roman Bricks and Tiles. Square Single Plinth. Side Alternate Quoining – a mixture of reused Roman tiles and some dressed stones. Vestiges of Blocked Doorway.
- Coped Grave Cover broken in three, with abstract designs including: Flat Moulding, Incised Straight and Diagonal Lines, incomplete rows of Straight and Curving Indentations with abstract designs.
- Part of Baluster with incomplete bands of Roll Moulding and Grooves.

44. DURHAM CATHEDRAL, County Durham – The Monk's Dormitory.
- Incomplete and parts of Free-Arm, Plate-Ring and Ring-Head Crossheads with both abstract and figurative designs including: Flat Moulding, Grooved Moulding, Interlace Design, Knot-Work Design, Pellets, Plait-Work Design, Plant Design, Ring-Chain Design, Ring-Knot Design, Roll Moulding, Scroll Design. Crucifixion Scenes. "Lamb of God". Baptismal Scene. Winged Angels. Haloed Figures. Human Figures. Animals. Birds.
- Incomplete and parts of Angular Cross-Shafts with both abstract and figurative designs including: Cable-Pattern Moulding, Flat Moulding, Grooved Moulding, Interlace Design, Key-Pattern Design, Knot-Work Design, Pellets, Plait-Work Design, Plant-Scroll Design, Roll Moulding, Ring-Chain Design, Ring-Knot Design, Scroll Design, Spiral-Scroll Design, Vine-Scroll Design. Haloed Figures. Horseman. Human Figures. Winged Human Figures. Animals. Birds. Inscription translated as "Pray for Heriberecht set up (this cross) a monument after (in memory of) his brothers".
- Incomplete Grave Covers, including Hogbacks, with abstract and figurative designs including: Cable-Pattern Moulding, an incomplete Crosshead and Cross-Shaft, incised Cross, Flat Moulding, Herringbone Design, Interlace Design, Key-Pattern Design, Pellets, Plait-Work Design, Plant Design, Ring-Knot Design, Roll Moulding, Scroll Design, Stepped-Pattern Design, Tegulations. Winged Figures. Animals. End bear-like Animals. Inscription interpreted as "Alrihic set up".
- Complete Grave Marker with incised lines and Inscription the female name "Beorhtgyd".
- Part of a Cross-Base with Flat Moulding, Interlace Design, Key-Pattern Design.
- Architectural Fragments including: Impost with Cable-Pattern Moulding, Chequer-Pattern Design, Flat Moulding, Scroll Design - some with abstract decoration.
- Fragments of Wall Panels with abstract and figurative designs including: Roll Moulding, Scroll Design, Vine-Scroll Design. Inhabited Plant-Scroll Design with an Archer.
- Parts of Friezes with abstract designs including: Flat Moulding, Representations of Balusters some with Cable-Pattern Moulding and some placed in Herringbone fashion.
- Balusters with sets of narrow and wide grooves alternating with plain bands of stonework.

PHOTO 127 - Site 43. St Mary-in-the-Castle Church, Dover, Kent. Central Tower.

- Casts of Ruthwell Cross, Dumfriesshire; Bewcastle Cross, Cumbria; "Acca's Cross", Hexham, Northumberland.

45. EARLS BARTON, Northamptonshire – All Saints Church.
- Square Tower: Coursed Rubble Walling. Square Single Plinth. Long and Short Quoining; uniquely the entirety of each stone protrudes from the surface of the walls – they are not "Cut-Back". Pilaster-Strips. Chamfered (between ground and first stages) and Square (between the three upper stages) String Courses. Round-Headed Doorway with "Escomb" Jambs and Strip-Work. Restored Round-Headed Single-Splayed Window. On the south face, Round-Headed (externally)/Flat-Headed (internally) Double-Splayed Double Windows with: each head decorated with moulding enclosing a free-arm cross in relief; jambs externally ornamented with baluster shafts; and mid-wall shafts formed of slabs of stonework ornamented both externally and internally (west window only) with baluster shafts. On the west face, the heads of Round-Headed Double-Splayed Windows presumed similar to those on the south face. Circular Stone Slab with Free-Arm Cross in relief. At Second Stage, Round-Headed Doorways with Strip-Work; one is partially blocked and another, beneath the former Roofline of the nave, has been restored. Strip-Work providing interlinked semi-circular and diamond-shaped arcading. Triangular-Headed Windows. Round-Headed Belfry Openings each with five (rare, if not unique) lights separated by slabs of stonework which are externally ornamented with baluster shafts: the opening on the east face additionally has circular openings similar to sound-holes.

46. EDINBURGH, Lothian - National Museum of Scotland.
- Parts of Angular Cross-Shafts with abstract and figurative designs including: Cable-Pattern Moulding, Flat Moulding, Interlace Design, Key-Pattern Design, Knot-Work Design, Pellets, Ring-Chain Design, Roll Moulding, Spiral-Scroll Design, Stopped Plait-Work, Vine-Scroll Design. Scenes depicting a building - on one face a gable-headed structure - with representations of Round-Headed Archways/Doorways with haloed Figures, Human heads, the Sun, the Moon, Round-Headed Window, Panel for an Inscription. Lower part of body, legs and feet of Christ with pairs of Human Figures, the figure of David playing his harp. Lower part of body, legs and feet of Christ with Human Figures, hooded Human Figures. Inhabited Interlace Design with Birds. Inhabited Vine-Scroll Design with Animals and Birds. Inhabited Ring-Chain Design with an Animal. Animals.
- Parts of Free-Arm, Plate-Ring, and Disc-Head Crossheads with Parts of their attached Angular Cross-Shafts with abstract designs including: Flat Moulding, Interlace Design, Knot-Work Design, Ring-Knot Design, Roll Moulding, Stopped Plait-Work Design. Incised Crosses with crossheads and cross-shafts.
- An Arm from a Free-Arm Crosshead with Flat Moulding and Interlace Design.
- Parts of Cross Slabs with abstract and figurative designs including: Free-Arm Crosses and their Angular Cross-Shafts in relief; one with a Billet Free-Arm Crosshead. Flat Moulding, Interlace Design, Key-Pattern Design, Knot-Work Design, Roll Moulding, Scroll Design, Spiral-Scroll Design. Rider with drinking horn. Runic Inscription which has been interpreted as "In memory of Þorgerðr Steinarsdóttir is the cross raised". Animals.
- Section of Slate incised with part of a Free-Arm Crosshead with an incomplete Runic Inscription.
- Triangular-Headed Stone known as the "Aberlemno Stone" ("Aberlemno 2"). One face is decorated with a Billet Free-Arm Crosshead and supporting Cross-Shaft with designs including: Key-Pattern Design, Knot-Work Design, Scroll Design. The other face is decorated with fighting mounted and unmounted warriors. It probably represents the battle in AD 685 of Nechtansmere where the forces of King Bridei of the Picts defeated the forces of King Ecgfrith of Northumbria – Ecgfrith was killed.

47. ESCOMB, County Durham – Church. Complete Anglo-Saxon Church with Nave and Chancel and Foundations of former Annexes.
- Nave: Coursed Walling. Side Alternate Quoining. Round and Flat-Headed Single-Splayed Windows including grooves for Shutters. Flat-Headed Doorway. Roofline of former western Annex. Consecration Cross. Sundial with Cable-Pattern Design and a Serpent. Prokrossos. Font possibly Anglo-Saxon.
- Chancel: Coursed Walling. Side Alternate Quoining. Derivative "Escomb" Jambs supporting Chancel Arch. Consecration Cross. Blocked Flat-Headed Doorway with vestiges of decoration.
- Foundations of Annexes extending from: west end of nave and north of the chancel.
- Parts of Angular Cross-Shafts with abstract and figurative designs including: Cable-Pattern Moulding, Plant-Scroll Design, Roll Moulding. Inhabited Plant-Scroll Design with Animals and a Bird.
- Part of possible pillar with abstract designs including: Flat Moulding, Interlace Design, Roll Moulding.
- Part of a Ring-Head Crosshead incised with a large Cross.
- Grave Marker with Flat Moulding, Roll Moulding, and incised with a Standing Cross in relief.

48. EYAM, Derbyshire – St Lawrence's Church.
- Most of Free-Arm Crosshead and its associated Angular Cross-Shaft decorated with abstract and figurative designs including: Plant-Scroll Design, Ring-Chain Design, Ring-Knot Design, Roll Moulding, Scroll Design. Mary with Christ Child – the top of Mary's head is missing. Angels.
- Tub-Shaped font tapering from bottom to top. It is decorated in relief with Interlocking Arches with shared Columns, Imposts and Bases, similar to those of a Chancel or Tower Arch in an Anglo-Saxon Church. There is a broad band of Flat Moulding around the top and bottom of the circumference.

49. FLETTON, Cambridgeshire – St Margaret's Church.
- Two Wall Panels framed with a band of Roll Moulding forming a complete panel containing standing, but with legs slightly bent, haloed figures in portrait, one turned to the left, and the other to the right. The figure on the left is thought to represent the Archangel Michael (carrying a cross-shaped sword), the figure on the right has not been confidently identified – could it be the Archangel Gabriel holding his horn/trumpet in his right hand, or the Archangel Raphael holding a bottle or flask in his right hand?
- Seven sections of stonework from a decorated frieze now placed together decorated with both abstract and figurative designs including: Plant-Scroll Design, Roll Moulding. Inhabited Scroll Design with Haloed Half-Figures of Saints and Angels (with wings) in portrait – some with the heads turned to the

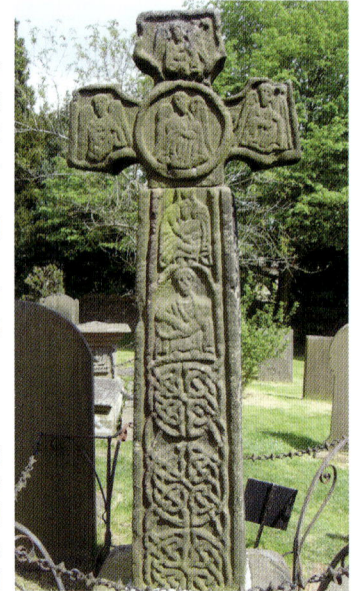

PHOTO 128 - Site 48. St Lawrence's Church, Eyam, Derbyshire. Free-Arm Crosshead and Angular Cross-Shaft. Photograph with permission of Eyam Parish Church.

PHOTO 129 - *Site 49. St Margaret's Church, Fletton, Cambridgeshire. Part of Frieze.*

left or right. Standing, but bending Human figure (possibly representing Samson) between two columns. Bird-like creatures.
- Part of an Angular, Collared Cross-Shaft, with abstract and figurative designs including: Cable-Pattern Moulding, Inhabited Plant Scroll Design including addorsed birds, animals. Lower part of Ring-Head Crosshead attached to Cross-Shaft. Other separate sections of stonework from this Cross-Shaft are stored inside the church.

50. FORNCETT ST PETER, Norfolk – St Peter's Church.
- Round Tower: Coursed Rubble Walling with Flints. One row of eight and another row of three Circular Double-Splayed Windows. Triangular and Round-Headed (one restored) Double-Belfry Openings with cylindrical mid-wall shafts. Round-Headed Single-Splayed Windows – sometimes described as "Circular Sound Holes". Round-Headed Doorway (interior is original). Roofline of former nave. Tower Arch.
- Nave: Coursed Rubble Walling with Flints.
- Chancel: Coursed Rubble Walling with Flints. Slight vestiges of probable blocked Double-Splayed Window.

51. GLENTWORTH, Lincolnshire – St Michael's Church.
- Square Tower: Coursed Rubble Walling. Side Alternate Quoining. Square String Courses. Round-Headed "Key-Hole" Single-Splayed Windows – one with Hood Moulding decorated with Palmette Design. Blocked Doorway. Round-Headed Double-Belfry Openings with octagonal, cylindrical and bulbous shaped mid-wall shafts with decorated capitals. The west belfry opening at one time had a bell hung between the mid-wall shaft and the left-hand (north) jamb. Round-Headed Tower Arch. First floor level, Blocked Flat-Headed Doorway.
- Grave Marker decorated with a Free-Arm Cross and abstract designs including: Cable-Pattern Moulding, Chevron-Pattern Design.

52. GOSFORTH, Cumbria - St Mary's Church.
- Cross: Ring-Head Crosshead with abstract designs including; Cable-Pattern Moulding, Knot-Work Design, Plait-Work Design, Roll Moulding. Lower Circular/Upper Angular Cross-Shaft with abstract and figurative designs including: Cable-Pattern Moulding, Knot-Work Design, Plait-Work Design, Ring-Chain Design, Roll Moulding. Various scenes are represented including: Christ Crucified with Longinus and Mary Magdalene. From Norse Mythology: Odin and his horse Sleipnir, the hart Eikthyrnir, Fenris the wolf, Garm the wolf, Heimdall, Loki, Mímir, Sigyn, Surt, Vithar, as well as the heads of wolf-like animals and serpents, and indistinct representations of the sun and moon. The scenes tell of the main events referred to in the Völuspá in the Edda. 1. Chaos and creation; 2. The wars of the gods and giants; 3. Ragnarök and the attack on the gods; 4. The new world with Vithar slaying Fenris the wolf and the promise of the rebirth of Baldr (another of Odin's sons), here identified with Christ. Three-Stepped Cross-Base – no decoration survives.
- Most of Hogback Grave Cover known as the "Warrior's Tomb" with abstract and figurative designs including: Flat Moulding, Interlace Design, Plait-Work Design, Ring-Knot Design, Tegulations. Human figure, Serpent-like and other Animals. A scene depicting two groups of standing warriors.
- Most of Hogback Grave Cover known as the "Saints Tomb" with abstract and figurative designs including: Flat Moulding, Cable-Pattern Moulding, Diamond-Pattern Design, Knot-Work Design, Plait-Work Design, Roll Moulding. Serpent-like and other Animals. Human figures, Crucifixion Scenes.
- Part of Ring-Head Crosshead with abstract designs including: Cable-Pattern Moulding, Flat Moulding, Plait-Work Design, Ring-Chain Design, Roll Moulding. Almost complete Ring-Head

Crosshead with tenon (to fit into the mortise of a cross-shaft), and with abstract designs including: Cable-Pattern Design, Knot-Work Design, Plait-Work Design, Roll Moulding.
- Part of Angular Cross-Shaft or Frieze with figurative designs including; Flat Moulding, Plait-Work Design. From Norse Mythology: Animal, Serpent and the "Fishing Scene" depicting Thor, Hymir, a boat, fish, a circular ring and possibly part of the Midgard World Serpent (now indistinct).
- Part of a Cross-Shaft reshaped and reused to support a sundial – not Anglo-Scandinavian (no decoration survives).

53. GREAT DUNHAM, Norfolk – St Andrew's Church.
- Nave: Random Rubble Walling with Flints including some reused Roman brick and tile. Blocked Triangular-Headed Doorway with Strip-Work. Complete Round-Headed Double-Splayed Window and vestiges of Round-Headed Double-Splayed Windows (Roman bricks and tiles aid identification of what remains of their heads). Incomplete rows of Round-Headed Sunken Blind Arcading separated by Pilaster-Strips; some with decorated Imposts.
- Central Square Tower (not Cruciform): Random Rubble Walling with Flints including some reused Roman brick and tile. Long and Short Quoining. Round-Headed Double-Splayed Windows. Round-Headed Double-Belfry Openings with cylindrical mid-wall shafts. Circular Double-Splayed Windows – sometimes described as "Circular Sound Holes". Blocked Round-Headed Doorways providing access to nave and chancel at first floor level – now surviving only internally. Tower Arches with decorated Imposts; two faces with Hood Moulding, one additionally with vestiges of Strip-Work. Roofline of former chancel.

PHOTO 130 – Site 53. St Andrew's Church, Great Dunham, Norfolk. Tower Arches.

54. GREAT PAXTON, Cambridgeshire – Holy Trinity Church.
- Nave: Random Rubble Walling. Round-Headed Arches with plain plinths, moulded bases, piers comprising four half-round shafts, bulbous capitals and imposts; the eastern arch has an eastern "Escomb" Jamb. Chamfered String Courses.
- Clerestory: Random Rubble Walling. Complete and Incomplete (Blocked) Double-Splayed Windows.
- Former Crossing: Northern Archway with tall, plain bases, "Escomb" Jambs incorporating piers comprising four half-round shafts separated by roll moulding, bulbous capitals and imposts. Strip-Work. Southern Archway has only parts of the jambs surviving. Chancel Arch with tall plain plinths, Jambs with moulded bases supporting piers comprising six curving shafts, no capitals, but with imposts which may also be Anglo-Saxon in origin.

PHOTO 131 – Site 54. Holy Trinity Church, Great Paxton, Cambridgeshire. Clerestory.

An Introduction to Anglo-Saxon Church Architecture & **127**
Anglo-Saxon & Anglo Scandinavian Stone Sculpture

55. GREAT URSWICK, Cumbria – St Michael's Church.
- Part of Angular Cross-Shaft with abstract and figurative designs including: Flat Moulding, Interlace Design, Knot-Work Design, Roll Moulding, Inhabited Plant-Scroll Design with animals and possibly birds. Human Figures. Runic Inscriptions interpreted as "Tunwini put up this cross in memory of his lord Torhtred" and "Lyl made this".
- Fragment of Crosshead and Angular Cross-Shaft with abstract designs including: Interlace Design, Ring-Knot Design, Roll Moulding, Stepped-Pattern Design.

56. HADSTOCK, Essex – St Botolph's Church. Cruciform Church.
- Nave: Coursed Rubble Walling of Flints with some Roman material and Herringbone Masonry. Square Single Plinth. Vestiges of Side Alternate Quoining. Round-Headed Double-Splayed Windows with Oak Frames – one is blocked. Rebuilt Round-Headed Doorway with decorated Hood Moulding, Imposts and Capitals. Door dated dendrochronologically to 1034-1042. (The west door in the nave may also be Anglo-Saxon in origin.)
- Transepts: Coursed Rubble Walling. Vestiges of Side Alternate Quoining. Restored Capitals and Imposts with decoration, Jambs, Bases and Square Stepped Double Plinths – the upper two stepped chamfered stages of the plinth are a later addition.

PHOTO 132 – Site 56. St Botolph's Church, Hadstock, Essex. Round-Headed Doorway with Anglo-Saxon wooden Door.

57. HALTON, Lancashire – St Wilfrid's Church.
- Reconstructed Cross in Churchyard comprising Crosshead, Cross-Shaft and Cross-Base.
- Original parts of Free-Arm Crosshead: Basket-Plait Design, Cable-Pattern Moulding, Knot-Work Design, Pellets, Design akin to a St Andrew's cross.
- Original parts of Angular Cross-Shaft with abstract and figurative designs including: Cable-Pattern Moulding, Flat Moulding, Knot-Work Design, Pellets, Plant-Scroll Design, Ring-Knot Design, Scroll Design. Various standing, seated and squatting Human figures – possibly including an Angel; what some of the scenes depicted represent is a matter of debate. Symbols of The Evangelists with haloed half-figures of Humans, birds and animals. Scenes from Norse Mythology including: Sigurd's ability to understand the language of birds, Sigurd sucking his thumb, the decapitation of Reginn the Smith, Reginn the Smith with a raised hammer working on a sword, the horse Grani. Animals. Birds.
- Original Three-Stepped Cross-Base, tapering bottom to top, with no surviving decoration.
- Reconstructed parts of Angular Cross-Shaft cemented onto the internal north wall of the church tower with abstract and figurative designs including: Cable-Pattern Moulding, Interlace Design, Knot-Work Design, Plant-Scroll Design. Seated haloed figure of Christ figure above an Angel holding an open book with crouching figure below – a Judgement Scene. Scene depicting "Harrowing of Hell". Haloed and non-haloed Figures. Inhabited Vine-Scroll Design with an Archer and Bird.
- Reconstructed parts of Angular Cross-Shaft cemented onto the internal south wall of the church tower with abstract and figurative designs including: Cable-Pattern Moulding, Flat Moulding, Knot-Work Design, Pellets, Plant-Scroll Design, Roll Moulding. Flock of Animals.

58. HARTLEPOOL, County Durham – St Hilda's Church.
- "Name-Stone" Grave Marker incised with a Free-Arm Cross within a border with the symbols "alpha" and "omega" – the symbols for Christ as the beginning and the end – and the name

of the nun "Hildithryth" in runes.
- Grave Markers or Finials in the form of Plate-Ring Crosshead.

59. HARTSHEAD, West Yorkshire – Walton Cross.
- Cross-Base with a stepped base and Socket for insertion of Cross-Shaft. It is decorated with abstract and figurative designs including: Cable-Pattern Moulding, Flat Moulding, Interlace Design, Knot-Work Design, Plait-Work Design, Roll Moulding. Inhabited Bush-Scroll Design with Birds. Inhabited Scroll Design with winged Animals.

60. HEXHAM, Northumberland – Abbey.
- Nave: Vestiges of Coursed Rubble including reused Roman Stonework. Vestiges of Flooring and Foundations.
- Crypt: Ashlar Walling including reused Roman Stonework – some with decoration and some covered with vestiges of coloured Plasterwork. Round-Headed Archways (Doorways). Barrel-Vaulted Chambers. Triangular-Headed Chambers. Niches. Flat-Headed Passages. Stairs. Ventilation Shaft.
- Chancel (below floor): St Peter's Church, comprising eastern part of nave and apsidal chancel: Coursed Rubble Walling. Possible site of Grave of St Acca.

PHOTO 133 – Site 60. Hexham Abbey, Northumberland. Incomplete Frieze with Running Animal.

- Bishop's Chair known as "Frith Stool" with Incised Lines and Knot-Work Design.
- Font Bowl – a reused base of a Roman Pillar.
- Fragments forming an incomplete Holy Rood.
- Reconstructed part of Free-Arm Crosshead and part of its attached Angular Cross-Shaft known as "Acca's Cross" with abstract designs including: Pellets, Plant-Scroll, Roll Moulding Design. Incomplete Inscriptions – the letters are difficult to confidently identify.
- Part of an Angular Cross-Shaft known as the "Spittal Cross" with abstract and figurative designs including: Flat Moulding, Plant-Scroll Design, Roll Moulding. Crucifixion Scene with Roman soldiers - the cup/sponge-bearer Stephaton and the spear-bearer Longinus. Possible Inscriptions.
- Parts of Free-Arm Crossheads and vestiges and parts of Angular Cross-Shafts (some attached) with abstract designs including: Flat Moulding, Interlace Design, Knot-Work Design, Plait-Work Design, Plant-Scroll Design, Ring-Chain, Ring-Knot Design, Roll Moulding. Animals.
- Part of an Angular Cross-Base with abstract designs including: Interlace Design, Plant-Scroll Design, Roll Moulding, Scroll Design.
- Part of a Round-Headed Grave Marker with a Free-Arm Cross with fan-shaped arms within an incised circle and an Inscription thought to represent the name "Tondwine".
- Part of a Round-Headed Grave Marker with in relief a Free-Arm Cross with a long lower vertical arm.
- Part of Grave Marker with a Free-Arm Cross with long lower vertical arm with a Plant Design between each of the junctions of the arms.
- One Complete and Parts of Grave Covers, including part of Hogback Grave Cover and a Grave Cover similar in shape to a Hogback (neither have bear-like end animals), with abstract designs including: representation of a Chalice, Flat Moulding, Free-Arm Cross within a Circle at each end separated by Round-Headed Arcade. Free-Arm Cross with long lower vertical arm. Free-Arm Cross with Angular Cross-Shaft and Angular Cross-Base, Incised Circles, Plait-

*An Introduction to Anglo-Saxon Church Architecture &
Anglo-Saxon & Anglo Scandinavian Stone Sculpture*

Work Design, Roll Moulding.
- Part of Panel with abstract designs including: Flat Moulding, Roll Moulding. Inhabited Vine-Scroll Design with parts of Human Figures, an Animal and a Bird.
- Parts of Imposts or Friezes or String Courses with abstract and figurative designs including: Representations of Baluster Shafts, Cable-Pattern Moulding, Chamfered Moulding, Chequer-Pattern Design, Circular and Diamond Design, Flat Moulding, Herringbone-Pattern Moulding, Interlace Design, Pellets, Roll Moulding, Scroll Design, "Torus" Roll Moulding. Incomplete running Animals. Coiled Animal. Part of a Fish-like Creature.
- Incomplete Circular Columns and a Half-Circular Column.

61. HEYSHAM, Lancashire – St Peter's Church.
- Nave: Coursed Rubble Walling. Face Alternate Quoining. Blocked Round-Headed Doorway. Possibly Blocked Flat-Headed Doorway leading to the first floor of a former Annex.
- Chancel: Imposts with Cable-Pattern Moulding of possible Anglo-Saxon origin.
- Complete Hogback Grave Cover including end bear-like animals. Abstract and figurative designs including: Cable-Pattern Moulding, Tegulations. Scenes with Humans, Animals, Birds, a Snake's head or large Fish most probably from Norse Mythology involving Sigurd and Ragnarök. Alternatively, the scenes could be Christian representing "Adam naming the Animals" or the "Tree of Life".
- Possible plinth with Cable-Pattern Moulding (not connected with hogback grave cover).
- In Churchyard: Reconstructed Coursed Rubble Walling including Round-Headed Doorway with indications of "Escomb" Jambs.
- Part of Angular Cross-Shaft with abstract and figurative designs including: Cable-Pattern Moulding, Knot-Work Design, Plait-Work Design, Plant-Scroll Design, Roll Moulding. Seated haloed figure, possibly Christ in Glory. Scenes depicting a building - on one face probably a mausoleum - with representations of Round-Headed Archways/Doorways with haloed Figure/haloed swathed Figure. Round-Headed Windows each containing a Human head and neck. Round-Headed Niches containing Human figures.
- Grave Cover with representation of a Hammerhead Crosshead with Angular Cross-Shaft.
- Damaged three-stepped Cross-Base with indications of Socket for insertion of Cross-Shaft (no decoration survives).
- Part of Cross-Shaft with Plant-Scroll Design reused as quoin.

62. HICKLING, Nottinghamshire – St Luke's Church.
- Virtually complete, coped Hogback Grave Cover; stylistically unique. Abstract and figurative designs including: A Free-Arm Cross overlying the top ridge and the "roof" on both long sides. Flat Moulding, Interlace Design, Knot-Work Design, Pellets, Ring-Chain Design. Inhabited Interlace Design with Animals. Inhabited Knot-Work Design with Animals. Affronted Animals. Inward-looking heads of strange bear-like Animals on the top ridge with their paws holding the tops of the side walls on each side.

63. HOLY ISLAND (LINDISFARNE), Northumberland – The Priory Museum.
- Virtually complete Ring-Head Crosshead with Flat Moulding and a Groove on the Free-Arm – the "Ring" has no decoration.
- Incomplete Angular Cross-Shafts with abstract and figurative designs including: Diagonal Cross, Flat Moulding, Grooved Moulding, Interlace Design, Key-Pattern Design, Plait-Work Design, Ring-Knot Design, Roll Moulding. A scene which may represent Christ in the day of Judgement with the central haloed figure of Christ with four other figures who may include representations of the Archangels. Scene with two Human Figures separated by a central column. Inhabited Interlace Designs with Ribbon Animals. Incomplete Animals.

- Most of Round-Headed Grave Marker known as "The Viking Raiders Stone" – it may commemorate the attack on Lindisfarne in 793 AD or a similar attack at a later date. One face is decorated with a scene which may represent the Day of Judgement: a Free-Arm Cross around which are representations the Sun and Moon, two "Human" Hands, two Human Figures who may be praying. The other face is decorated with a scene which may represent a Viking attack: a procession of Human Warriors carrying Axes and Swords above their heads. There is a band of Flat Moulding around the edges of both faces.
- Parts of and almost complete Round-Headed Grave Markers or Name Stones with Single or Parallel Lines forming a Panel containing a Free-Arm Cross with arms emerging from a centre circle; one has a border edge of Interlace Design and Roll Moulding and another has a Free-Arm Cross within the centre circle. The Centre Circle is surrounded by Concentric Circles from which emerge sets of Parallel Lines providing the arms for the Free-Arm Cross which have Cup-Like or Concentric Circles Ends – some with vestiges of Knot-Work Design. Some have both a Runic and a Latin Inscription. Some are so incomplete it is not now possible to identify the personal name represented. Those that can be translated include the female name "Osgyth" and the male names: "Aedberecht", "Beanna", "Coina" or "Coena", "Ethelhard".
- Part of a Grave Cover with a Free-Arm Cross in relief with Flat Moulding and Knot-Work Design, with Flat Moulding around the edge of the Grave Cover.

64. HOUGH-ON-THE-HILL, Lincolnshire - All Saints Church.
- Stair Turret. Coursed Rubble Walling. Round-Headed, Pentagonal, Circular and Diamond-Shaped Single-Splayed Windows – some with Roll Moulding. Spiral Stairway with Steps formed separately from the Newel.
- Square Tower: Coursed Rubble Walling. Vestiges of Square Double Plinth. Square String Courses. Face Alternate Quoining. Single-Splayed Flat-Headed Windows. Round-Headed Single-Splayed Windows – one altered at a later non-Anglo-Saxon date. Round-Headed Doorway altered at a later non-Anglo-Saxon date. Flat-Headed Doorway. At first floor level Flat-Headed Doorway with "Escomb" jambs. Second floor, Triangular-Headed Doorways, one with "Escomb" Jambs, one blocked. Faint indications of Roofline of former Nave.
- Nave: Coursed Rubble Walling. Incomplete Long and Short Quoining. Slight vestiges of Square Double Plinth.
- Incomplete Architectural Frieze/String Course with abstract and figurative designs including: Representations of Balusters, Cable-Pattern Moulding, Interlace Design, Roll Moulding. Possibly part of an animal.
- Grave Cover with incised Free-Arm Cross.

PHOTO 134 - Site 64. All Saints Church, Hough-on-the-Hill, Lincolnshire. Stair Turret. Interior, Round-Headed Single-Splayed Window.

65. HOVINGHAM, North Yorkshire – All Saints Church.
- Square Tower: Coursed Stone Walling including Herringbone Masonry: Side Alternate Quoining (including window and door heads reused as quoins). Round-Headed Doorway. Flat-Headed Windows. Square String Courses. Round-Headed Double-Splayed Window. Round-Headed Double-Belfry Openings with square mid-wall shafts which are curved externally. Tower Arch. Flat-Headed Doorway with "Escomb" Jambs at first floor level.
- Externally, incorporated into the fabric of the tower it is possible to identify: a Free-Arm Crosshead with no surviving decoration; and, a Plate-Head Crosshead and part of its Angular

An Introduction to Anglo-Saxon Church Architecture &   **131**
Anglo-Saxon & Anglo Scandinavian Stone Sculpture

- Cross-Shaft both with abstract and figurative designs including: Flat Moulding, Interlace Design, Roll Moulding. Birds (crosshead) and Humans (cross-shaft).
- Nave: Coursed Stone Walling. Side Alternate Quoining.
- Shrine, reused as reredos, with abstract and figurative designs including: Flat Moulding, Inhabited Plant-Scroll Design with birds. Weathered and damaged scenes depicting under an Arcade: The Annunciation, The Visitation, The Circumcision of St John the Baptist or the Presentation at the Temple, Joseph, Angels (one facing inwards at each end).
- A Free-Arm Crosshead and part of its Angular Cross-Shaft both with abstract and figurative designs including: Flat Moulding, Knot-Work Design incorporating Animals.
- Two sections from the same Angular Cross-Shaft with abstract design including: Flat Moulding, Plant-Scroll Design.

66. HOWE, Norfolk - St Mary's Church.
- Round Tower: Random Rubble Walling with Flints. Round-Headed Double-Splayed Windows. Circular Double-Splayed Windows. Blocked Round-Headed Doorway now with modern window inserted. Tower Arch. Blocked Flat-Headed Doorway formerly providing access to upper storey.
- Nave: Random Rubble Walling with Flints. Rubble Quoining of Flints, Bricks and Stone. Double-Splayed Round-Headed Window - slight indications of others.

67. ILKLEY, West Yorkshire – All Saints Church.
- Parts of Free-Arm Crosshead with abstract and figurative designs including: Flat Moulding, Roll Moulding. Possible winged Figure with halo representing the symbol of St Matthew the Evangelist. Inhabited Plant-Scroll Design with Birds.
- Angular Cross-Shaft with abstract and figurative designs including: Plant-Scroll Design, Roll Moulding, Spiral Scroll Design. Haloed Figure probably Christ in Majesty. Representations of the Four Evangelists with their Heads replaced by their Symbols: the Eagle - St John; the Bull – St Luke; the Lion – St Mark; a Human – St Matthew. Animals including Confronting Animals. Inhabited Plant-Scroll Design with an Animal.
- Incomplete Angular Cross-Shaft with abstract and figurative designs including: Cable-Pattern Moulding, Flat Moulding, Plant-Scroll Design. Inhabited Plant-Scroll Design with a scene depicting Adam and Eve. Inhabited Plant-Scroll Design with Confronting Animals. Inhabited Plant-Scroll Design with Addorsed Animals. Inhabited Plant-Scroll Design with an Animal. Inhabited Plant-Scroll Design with Confronting Birds. Inhabited Plant-Scroll Design with Bird.
- Incomplete Cross-Shaft, possibly with a circular lower part and an angular upper part, with abstract and figurative designs including: Flat Moulding, Pellets, Roll Moulding. Haloed Human Figure. Inhabited Interlace, probably Plant-Scroll, Designs with Animals.
- Roman Altars re-used as Lintel Window-Heads.

PHOTO 135 – Site 67. All Saints Church, Ilkley, West Yorkshire. Inhabited Plant-Scroll Design with addorsed Animals.

68. IRTON, Cumbria – St Paul's Church.
- Cross: Free-Arm Crosshead with abstract designs including: Cable-Pattern Moulding, Interlace Design, Knot-Work Design, Pellets, Roll Moulding, Inhabited Plant-Scroll Design with Animals. Human figures. Angular Cross-Shaft with abstract designs: including: Chequer-Pattern Design, Interlace Design, Key-Pattern Design, Knot-Work Design, Pellets, Plant-Scroll Design,

Roll Moulding, Spiral-Scroll Design. Inscription (now unreadable). Cross-Base (no decoration survives).

69. JARROW, County Durham – St Paul's Church.
- Square Tower incorporating earlier Porch: Coursed Stone Walling. Side Alternate Quoining. Double-Splayed Windows – one now a doorway, the other with Hood Moulding with decoration below. Blocked Round-Headed Doorway at first floor level giving access to the Western Gallery. Triangular Headed Doorway at third storey level. Round-Headed Double Belfry Openings with cylindrical mid-wall shafts. Former Roof Line. Dedication Stone.
- Nave: Some Foundations visible under glass cover.
- Chancel: Coursed Stone Walling. Square Single Plinth. Side Alternate including Megalithic Quoining. Blocked Round-Headed Doorway. Vestiges of Doorway Round-Headed (internally)/Flat-Headed (externally). Vestiges of Round-Headed Doorway at first floor level giving external access to the Western Gallery. Round-Headed Single-Splayed Windows. Indications of earlier Walling and earlier Chancel Arch.
- Evidence of Saxo-Norman workmanship in surviving walling from Monastery Buildings.
- Incomplete Angular Cross-Shafts decorated with abstract and figurative designs including: Flat Moulding, Interlace Design, Plant-Scroll Design, Roll Moulding. Inhabited Plant-Scroll Design with Animals.
- Incomplete Grave Cover known as the "Jarrow Cross" with Inscription interpreted as "In this unique sign life is returned to the world".
- Balusters with sets of narrow and wide grooves alternating with plain bands of stonework.
- Incomplete Friezes decorated with both abstract and figurative designs including: Representations of Balusters, Flat Moulding, Roll Moulding. Inhabited Plant-Scroll Design with the figure of a Hunter, the head of a Woman, an incomplete Animal. Inhabited Tree-Scroll Design with Birds known as "The Tree of Life".
- Part of what may have been a Lamp with part of an incomplete Inscription.

70. JEDBURGH, Roxburghshire/Scottish Borders – Abbey, Visitor Centre.
- Parts of Free-Arm Crossheads and Angular Cross-Shafts with abstract and figurative designs including: Flat Moulding, Interlace Design, Key-Pattern Design, Knot-Work Design, Roll Moulding.
- Parts of an Angular Cross-Shaft later reused as building stone with abstract and figurative designs including: Cable-Pattern Moulding, Interlace Design, Roll Moulding. Haloed Figure. Incomplete Human Figures confronting each other possibly representing Adam and Eve. Human Figures. Inhabited Scroll Design with Animals and Birds.
- Panel with figurative designs including: Christ in Majesty. Human Figures.
- Part and two fragments of a Shrine with abstract and figurative designs including: Flat Moulding, Knot-Work Design. Inhabited Vine-Scroll Design with Animals and Birds.

71. KIRK HAMMERTON, North Yorkshire – St John The Baptist Church.
- Square Tower: Coursed Stone Walling. Square Double Plinth. Side Alternate Quoining. Round-Headed Doorway. Flat-Headed Single-Splayed Windows. Square String Course. Round-Headed Double Belfry Openings with cylindrical mid-wall shaft. Tower Arch with Megalithic Jambs. Vestiges of a Blocked Flat-Headed Doorway at first floor level.
- Nave: Coursed Stone Walling. Square Single Plinth. Side Alternate Quoining. Restored Doorway with Hood Moulding and Strip-Work. Vestiges of Blocked Round-Headed Doorway with Hood Moulding and Strip-Work.
- Chancel: Coursed Stone Walling. Square Single Plinth. Side Alternate Quoining. Restored Chancel Arch. Vestiges of Blocked Round-Headed Single-Splayed Window.

An Introduction to Anglo-Saxon Church Architecture &   **133**
Anglo-Saxon & Anglo Scandinavian Stone Sculpture

72. KIRKDALE, North Yorkshire – St Gregory's Minster.
- Nave: Coursed Stone Walling. Side Alternate Quoining. Round-Headed Doorway with "Escomb" Jambs. Chancel Arch Jambs. Moulded String Course.
- Sundial with three Inscriptions in Old English translated as: 1. "Orm, the son of Gamel, bought St Gregory's church when it was utterly ruined and collapsed and he had it rebuilt from the foundations in honour of Christ and St Gregory, in the days of King Edward the king and in the days of Earl Tosti". 2. "And Hawarth made me and Brand the priest". 3. "This is the day's sun-marker at every hour". Incised Free-Arm Crosses act as prefixes to each Inscription and after "Eorl"; they also appear on most of the divisions on the sundial itself.
- Incomplete Free-Arm and Hammerhead Crossheads and Angular Cross-Shafts (one may be part of a Hogback Grave Cover) mostly with indistinct abstract and figurative designs including: Flat Moulding, Incised Free-Arm Crosshead, Interlace Design, Knot-Work Design, Pellets, Spiral Scroll-Design, Stopped Plait-Work Design, S-shaped addorsed Animals. Incomplete Animal. Crucifixion Scene. Damaged Human Head and shoulder.
- Grave Cover with abstract designs including: a Crosshead and Cross-Shaft with damaged base. Flat Moulding, Plant-Scroll Design.
- Grave Cover in two pieces with Chevron-Pattern Design, Flat Moulding, Interlace Design including "rings", Pellets, Ring-Knot Design, Zigzag-Pattern Design.

73. LANGFORD, Oxfordshire – St Matthew's Church.
- Central Square Tower (no indication of porticos or transepts): Random Rubble Walling. Square Single Plinth. "Cut-Back" Face Alternate Quoining. Square String Courses. Pilaster-Strips including one interrupted by a Sundial with two standing Human Figures reaching up to hold the semi-circular dial on which the divisions of time were incised – the hole for missing gnomon can be identified. Round-Headed Double-Splayed Windows. Unusually wide ashlar Round-Headed Single Belfry Openings in pairs with semi-circular moulding around the window heads, jambs and the central pier separating the two openings; with decoration. Tower Arches - one with Hood Moulding and Strip-Work. Flat-Headed Doorway with "Escomb" Jambs at first floor level providing access between tower and nave. Blocked Flat-Headed Doorway at first floor level providing access between tower and chancel - former Roofline above.
- Holy Rood with Crucifixion Scene – Christ with the Virgin Mary and St John.
- Incomplete Holy Rood – the Head is missing.

PHOTO 136 – Site 73. St Matthew's Church, Langford, Oxfordshire. Holy Rood.

74. LAUGHTON-EN-LE-MORTHEN, South Yorkshire – All Saints Church.
- Former Portico: Coursed Stone Walling. Square Triple Plinth. "Cut-Back" Long and Short Quoining. Blocked Round-Headed Doorway with Hood Moulding and Strip-Work (a smaller later, non-Anglo-Saxon, doorway has been inserted).
- Chancel: Reuse of Anglo-Saxon material in some of the walling.

PHOTO 137 - Site 74. All Saints Church, Laughton-en-le-Morthen, South Yorkshire. Former Portico. Round-Headed Doorway.

75. LEDSHAM, West Yorkshire – All Saints Church.
- Square Tower incorporating earlier Porch: Coursed Stone Walling. Round-Headed Single-Splayed Windows. Roofline of former Porch. Round-Headed (externally)/Flat-Headed (internally) Doorway with Decorated Imposts, Hood Moulding and Strip-Work (all decoration restored in 1871). The Imposts are decorated with Flat Moulding and a Scroll Design – some of the stonework and decoration is original. The Hood Moulding and Strip-Work are decorated with Flat Moulding and Plant Scroll Design. However the two blocks of stone on the ground at the base of the Strip-Work are original and retain some slight vestiges of decoration: on the right-hand (east) side a Plant Design within a circle, and on the left-hand (west) side a Plant-Scroll Design.
- Nave: Coursed Stone Walling. Side Alternate including Megalithic Quoining. Incomplete Blocked Round-Headed Windows. Complete Blocked Round-Headed Window.
- Chancel: Restored Chancel Arch with restored, decorated Imposts with Flat Moulding, Pellets and a Plant Design.
- Portico/South Porch: Coursed Stone Walling. Side Alternate including Megalithic Quoining. Incomplete Blocked Flat-Headed (externally)/Round-Headed (internally) Doorway which reached from ground to first floor level.
- Parts of Angular Cross-Shafts or Decorated Friezes with abstract designs including: Plant-Scroll Design, Roll Moulding. Inhabited Plant-Scroll Design with Addorsed Birds.

76. LICHFIELD, Staffordshire – Cathedral.
- Most of a Panel probably from the Shrine of St Cedd; it formed part of a scene of what is presumed to be "The Annunciation". Abstract and figurative designs including: Flat Moulding and Plant Design. The Archangel Gabriel with vestiges of paint.

77. LITTLE BARDFIELD, Essex – St Katherine's Church.
- Square Flint Tower: Coursed Rubble Walling with Flints. Part of Square Single Plinth. Rubble Quoining with Flints. Square String Courses. Indications of Blocked Doorway. Single Round-Headed Windows – some are blocked - including sets of two in pairs similar to double-belfry openings and separated by a thin mid-wall shaft.
- Nave: Coursed Rubble Walling of Flints. Part of Square Single Plinth. Round-Headed Double-Splayed Window, possibly vestiges of another.

78. LONDON - Victoria and Albert Museum
- Reconstructed Cross from Easby, North Yorkshire, comprising part of Crosshead and much of the Cross-Shaft with abstract and figurative designs including: Cable-Pattern Moulding, Interlace Design, Plant-Scroll Design, Roll Moulding. Inhabited Plant-Scroll Design including Animals and Birds. Scenes including: Christ in Majesty, the risen Christ between two Apostles, groups of the Apostles.
- Resin Casts of Crosses from: Bewcastle, Gosforth and Irton (Cumbria); Ruthwell (Dumfriesshire); Hexham (Northumberland); Wolverhampton (West Midlands). Cast of Shrine known as the "Hedda or Monks' Stone" ("Offa Stone"), Peterborough (Cambridgeshire). Doorway and Pillar from Norwegian Church of Urnes – "Urnes Design".

79. LOWTHER, Cumbria – St Michael's Church.
- Two almost complete and parts of one other Hogback Grave Covers with abstract and figurative designs including: Cable-Pattern Moulding, Interlace Design, Key-Pattern Design, Plant-Scroll Design, Scroll Design, Tegulations. Human figures, Standing Warriors. Bird-like Creature, Serpents, a Fish. Indications of End Bear-like Animals (on one of the grave covers). A representation of a Boat.

An Introduction to Anglo-Saxon Church Architecture &
Anglo-Saxon & Anglo Scandinavian Stone Sculpture

- Parts of Grave Covers with abstract designs including: Cable-Pattern Moulding, Flat Moulding, Interlace Design, Key-Pattern Design, Pellets, Ring-Knot Design, Roll Moulding, Stepped Pattern Design. Head of an Animal.
- Part of Free-Arm Crosshead (no decoration survives).

80. LYTHE, North Yorkshire – St Oswald's Church.
- Part of a Door Jamb from earlier Anglo-Saxon Church with Interlace Design and Roll Moulding.
- Part of Free-Arm Crosshead with abstract and figurative designs including: Flat Moulding, Interlace Design, Knot-Work Design. Human Head.
- Most of a Ring-Head Crosshead without surviving decoration.
- Part of an Angular Cross-Shaft known as "The Wrestlers" with abstract and figurative designs including: Flat Moulding, Interlace Design. Pair of Human Figures "wrestling". S-shaped Animal.
- Parts of Angular Cross-Shafts with abstract designs including: Flat Moulding, Key-Pattern Design, Plait-Work Design, Roll Moulding, Stepped Pattern Design.
- Complete and Incomplete Grave Markers incised with distinctive Triangular-Armed Plate Crosshead with long lower vertical arms for insertion into the ground; a variation of Plate-Ring type Crossheads. On each example, deep Grooves outline the shape of a Free-Arm Cross whose lower vertical arm (where it survives) continues until reaching the base of the Grave Marker. They are not decorated.
- Incomplete Grave Markers each incised with a different variety of Free-Arm Cross.
- Complete, but mostly parts of, Hogback Grave Covers with abstract and figurative designs including: Flat Moulding, Grooved Moulding, Interlace Design, Plait-Work Design, Roll Moulding, Stepped-Pattern Design, Pellets, Tegulations. Incomplete and complete scenes with Humans and Animals. End bear-like Animals. Animal. Birds.
- Nondescript Grave Covers probably Hogbacks.
- Fragment of a Finial with Flat Moulding.

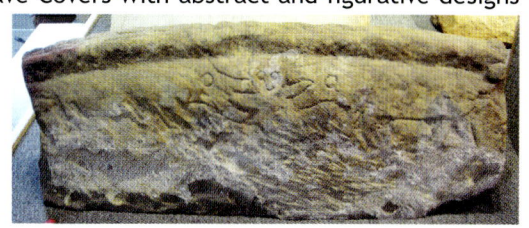

PHOTO 138 - Site 80. St Oswald's Church, Lythe, North Yorkshire. Hogback Grave Cover; scene with Human and Animals.

81. MELBURY BUBB, Dorset - St Mary's Church.
- Part of a Round Cross-Shaft reused as a font with abstract and figurative designs, now upside down, including: Two pairs of large facing Animals in profile. One Pair: a Cat-like Animal with a collar-like feature, open jaws, teeth and tongue, facing a Horse-like Animal whose bending neck and head in portrait holds the neck of a smaller Animal in profile between them. Second Pair: a Lion-like Animal with a mane and plumed tail with its jaws open holding a smaller Animal in profile in front of it, facing a Stag-like Animal with branching antlers with its head turned to look over its back towards another smaller Animal in profile who is touching its rump. All four large Animals and one of the smaller Animals are ensnared in an extended Interlace Design. The larger Animals stand on a band of Flat Moulding. The rectangular design along what is now the upper border may well be an addition when the lining to the font was added at a later date – not A-S. What is now the lower border comprises a row of Square-Shaped Pellets.

82. MIDDLESMOOR, North Yorkshire – St Chad's Church.
- Hammer-Head Crosshead with part of its attached Angular Cross-Shaft with abstract designs including: Incised Lines, Scroll Design.
- Font with later, non-Anglo-Saxon decoration added.

83. MIDDLETON, North Yorkshire – St Andrew's Church.
- Square Tower: Coursed Rubble Walling. Square Single Plinth. Side Alternate including Megalithic Quoining. Blocked Incomplete Round-Headed Doorway with Strip-Work and vestiges of Hood Moulding, now with later non Anglo-Saxon window inserted. Flat-Headed Single-Splayed Windows. Square String Course.
- Nave: Coursed Rubble Walling. Square and Chamfered Double Plinth. Side Alternate including Megalithic Quoining.
- Free-Arm Cross in relief with Flat Moulding, Interlace Design and a Plant Design.
- Complete Ring-Head Crosshead and its complete attached Angular Cross-Shaft with abstract and figurative designs including: Flat Moulding, Interlace Design, Knot-Work Design, Pellets, Roll Moulding. Hunt Scene with Huntsman, Hart and Hound. "Ryedale Dragon Design" – an S-shaped Ribbon Animal.
- Most of Ring-Head Crosshead and most of its attached Angular Cross-Shaft with abstract and figurative designs including: Flat Moulding, Interlace Design, Knot-Work Design, Lines incised in a Triangular Design, Pellets, Stepped-Pattern Design. Seated Warrior with his weapons. Ribbon Animal.
- Complete Billet-Head Crosshead and its complete attached Angular Cross-Shaft with abstract and figurative designs including: Flat Moulding, Interlace Design, Knot-Work Design, Pellets, Plait-Work Design, Ring-Knot Design, Spiral-Scroll Design.
- Part of Ring-Head Crosshead and part of its attached Angular Cross-Shafts with abstract and figurative designs including: Flat Moulding, Interlace Design, Ring-Knot Design. Head and shoulders of a Human Figure.
- Part of an Angular Cross-Shaft with abstract and figurative designs including: Flat Moulding, Pellets, Plait-Work Design, Roll Moulding. Seated Warrior with his weapons.
- Part of Arm from Crosshead and part of its attached Angular Cross-Shaft with Flat Moulding and Spiral-Scroll Design.
- An Arm from a Ring-Head Crosshead with Flat Moulding and Plait-Work Design.
- Fragments, one with vestiges of a Human Face, the other with Flat Moulding.

PHOTO 139 – Site 83. St Andrew's Church, Middleton, North Yorkshire. Angular Cross-Shaft with seated Warrior and his weapons.

84. NASSINGTON, Northamptonshire – St Mary's and All Saints Church.
- Nave: Coursed Rubble Walling. Slight vestiges of Square Single Plinth. Vestiges of "Cut-Back" Long and Short Quoining. Blocked Triangular-Headed Doorway just below current nave Roofline in the west wall. A blocked Round-Headed Doorway or Window above the tower arch in the west wall of the nave; its exact purpose and origin is a matter of debate.
- Angular Cross-Shaft with abstract and figurative designs including: Flat Moulding, Plant-Scroll Design, Ring-Chain Design, Ring-Knot Design. Crucifixion Scene with Christ with the sun and moon above, Roman soldiers - the cup/sponge-bearer Stephaton and the spear-bearer Longinus. Incomplete Figure possibly representing the Ascension.

85. NESTON, Cheshire – St Mary and St Helen's Church.
- Parts of Ring-Head Crossheads and Angular Cross-Shafts with abstract and figurative designs including: Cable-Pattern Moulding, Interlace Design, Knot-Work Design, Ring-Chain Design,

An Introduction to Anglo-Saxon Church Architecture &   **137**
Anglo-Saxon & Anglo Scandinavian Stone Sculpture

Stepped-Pattern Design. The figure of a Priest, a winged Angel, individual Human Figures, Human Figures fighting each other (possibly David slaying Goliath), Horsemen, Animals - including a Hunting Scene.

86. NEWCASTLE-UPON-TYNE, Northumberland – Great North (Hancock) Museum.
- Most of a Free-Arm Crosshead and Part of a separate section of its Angular Cross-Shaft. The Free-Arm Crosshead is decorated with abstract and figurative designs including: Flat Moulding, Interlace Design, Plant Design, Roll Moulding. Incomplete Crucifixion Scene with part of the Haloed Head of Christ who has an outstretched Arm and a Hand with large nail embedded; Winged Angel gripping Christ's halo. Human Figure without legs or feet. Head of an Angel or Human Figure. Flying Winged Figure. The Angular Cross-Shaft is decorated with abstract and figurative designs including: Flat Moulding, Roll Moulding. Scene depicting Christ in Majesty under an Arch with a Plant Design. Inhabited Spiral-Scroll Design with an incomplete Animal. Two Miracles with Christ healing of a Blind Man and the healing of a Woman. Representation of eighteen people in galleried rows; incrementally greater amounts of the heads and faces are depicted in descending order.
- Part of an Angular Cross-Shaft with vestiges of the lower arm from its attached Free-Arm Crosshead with abstract designs including: Flat Moulding and Interlace Design.
- Most of an Arm from a Free-Arm Crosshead with abstract designs including: Central Deep Groove, Roll Moulding, Zigzag-Pattern Design.
- Part of a Two-Collared Angular Cross-Shaft with the lower collar now forming a plinth. It is decorated with abstract and figurative designs including: Large Protruding Pellets, Plant-Scroll Design, Roll Moulding. Inhabited Plant-Scroll Design with affronted Animals and confronting Birds.

PHOTO 140 – Site 86. Great North (Hancock) Museum, Newcastle-upon-Tyne, Northumberland. Angular Cross-Shaft with scene depicting Christ in Majesty.

- Part of an Angular Cross-Shaft with abstract and figurative designs and inscriptions including: Flat Moulding, Interlace Design, Key-Pattern Design, Ring-Knot Design. Incomplete Crucifixion Scene with Roman soldiers - the cup/sponge-bearer Stephaton and the spear-bearer Longinus; two further incomplete Human Figures and representations of the Sun and Moon. Inscription in Lettering and Runes translated as "Myredah made me". Incomplete Inscription in Lettering which cannot now be interpreted.
- Part of an Angular Cross-Shaft with abstract designs including: Roll Moulding, Plant-Scroll Design. Inhabited Plant-Scroll Design with an Animal.
- Part of a decorated Architectural Panel, or possibly part of an Angular Cross-Shaft, with abstract designs including: Flat Moulding. Inhabited Interlace Design with incomplete entwined S-shaped Animals.
- Incomplete Memorial Stone with abstract designs and inscription including: Cable-Pattern Moulding, Flat Moulding, Plait-Work. Inscriptions in both Old English and Runes have been translated together as reading "In memory of Hroethbert, a monument of the uncle, pray for his soul".
- A Complete Flat-Headed Grave Marker or Name Stone with a Flat-Topped, Raised Border forming a Panel containing a Free-Arm Cross with arms emerging from a centre circle; the ends of the arms are cup-shaped. It is incised with a Latin Inscription translated as "Pray for Vermund" (male name) and "Pray for Torhtsuid" (female name).
- An almost complete Flat-Headed Grave Markers or Name Stone incised with a line providing

a border and forming a Panel containing an incised Free-Arm Cross with arms emerging from a centre circle; the ends of the arms are cup-shaped. It is incised with a Runic inscription translated as the female name "Hildgyth".
- Part of a Grave Marker with a representation of a row of Balusters, Roll Moulding, and an Incomplete Inscription in Latin "Berchti Edveri Ccrvcem" too incomplete to translate into anything meaningful.
- Incomplete Round-Headed Grave Markers with abstract designs including: Free-Arm Cross, Interlace Design, Knot-Work Design, Ring-Knot Design, Roll Moulding.

87. NEWENT, Gloucestershire – St Mary's Church.
- Part of Angular, Collared, Cross-Shaft with abstract and figurative designs including: Tree-Scroll Design, Roll Moulding. Scenes depicting: Adam and Eve with the Serpent and the Tree of Knowledge; David and Goliath; one complete, two incomplete Human Figures and an Animal, probably representing Abraham sacrificing Isaac; Inhabited Interlace Design including an Animal, Inhabited Plant-Scroll Design including two Birds looking away from each other, possibly representing the riches of Creation in the Garden of Eden. Round-Headed Arcading some with weathered figures surviving including: a man, a figure with wings, possibly a bird.
- Grave Covers each incised with a free-arm cross with fan-shaped arms surrounded by a band of Flat Moulding.
- Copy of possible Portable Altar later reused as a Pillow Stone known as "The Newent Stone". It is decorated with: a Crucifixion Scene including a number of Human figures. A scene depicting a central Human figure surrounded by smaller Human figures with the name "Eadric" carved above one of them. The four narrow-edges have inscriptions: "Matheus", "Marcus", "Lucas" and "Iohannes" – the four Gospel writers - and "Eadric".

88. NEWTON-BY-CASTLE ACRE, Norfolk – St Mary's and All Saints Church. (Former) Cruciform Church.
- Nave: Random Rubble Walling with Flints. Slight indications of Blocked Doorway.
- Square Tower: Random Rubble Walling with Flints. Side Alternate Quoining. Blocked Triangular-Headed Doorways formerly providing access between upper stages of nave, tower and chancel. Round-Headed Double-Splayed Window. Triangular-Headed Double Belfry Openings with cylindrical and rubble mid-wall shafts. Tower Arch. Indications of former South Transept comprising: internally, an unusually-shaped and aligned archway within which is now the south window; externally, uneven face of walling up to nave wall height.
- Chancel: Random Rubble Walling with Flints. Part of Window-Frame with rebate which has four separate "holes"; the rebate was for a shutter.

89. NORTON, County Durham – St Mary The Virgin Church.
- Square Tower: Coursed Walling. Round-Headed Arches with Hood Moulding opening to Transepts. Flat-Headed Doorway for access to upper gallery. Triangular-Headed Windows - formerly Doorways which gave access from a gallery within the tower between the second floor of the nave, transepts and chancel. Round Headed Single-Splayed Windows. Side Alternate including Megalithic Quoining. Former Roofline.
- Transepts: Coursed Walling.
- Nave and Chancel: Vestiges of Coursed Walling.
- Parts of Angular Cross-Shafts decorated with abstract designs including: Diamond-shaped Design, Flat Moulding, Ring-Knot Design, Roll Moulding.

An Introduction to Anglo-Saxon Church Architecture &   **139**
Anglo-Saxon & Anglo Scandinavian Stone Sculpture

90. NUNBURNHOLME, East Yorkshire - St James Church.
- Incorrectly reconstructed incomplete Angular Cross-Shaft with nearly complete and incomplete panels containing abstract and figurative designs; the top has a mortise.
- Top Half including: Flat Moulding, Pellets, Plant Design. Heads, Wings, and Arms of Angels with Hands grasping the top of an Archway under which a seated Warrior. Heads, Wings and Arms of Angels with Hands grasping the top of an Archway under which is a hooded Monk or Nun. Confronting Wyverns (part eagle, part snake) above an Archway under which is a representation of the Virgin and Child. Heads, Wings and Arms of Angels with Hands grasping the top of Arch similar to the halo of the figure – a Saint - under the Archway below; between the arch and the archway is an S-shaped Animal.
- Bottom Half including: Flat Moulding. Incomplete seated Human Figure with a Centaur and an adjacent human head. Interlace Design entwining two Animals. Crucifixion Scene with a Headless Christ with a headless Bird (Angel) on each shoulder and with Christ's hands clasping the Heads of two smaller Human Figures of Roman soldiers - the cup/sponge-bearer Stephaton and the spear-bearer Longinus below. A representation of a Mass with a Priest (part of his head is missing) with a chalice and host and below a feast with two sitting confronting Figures from Norse Mythology - Sigurđ and the animal-headed Reginn the smith.

91. ORPINGTON, Kent – All Saints Church.
- Incomplete Sundial with abstract designs including: Cable-Pattern Moulding, Roll Moulding. Four Inscriptions: two inscriptions have been taken together and translated as "(This dial shows) to him who knows how to seek, how (better) to reckon and keep (the time)"; the third "OR....VM" has been interpreted as possibly "Or(alogi)vm" or "Or(alog)vm" ; the fourth inscription is in Runes and provides no obvious textural reading.

92. OTLEY, West Yorkshire – All Saints Church.
- Three sections of stonework from the same Incomplete Angular Cross-Shaft known as the "Evangelist Cross" with abstract and figurative designs including: Archways, Plant-Scroll Design, Roll Moulding. Inhabited Plant-Scroll Design with representations of some of the Evangelists and an Angel. Inhabited Plant-Scroll Design with Animals and Birds. Unused flat areas for Inscriptions.
- Incomplete Angular Cross-Shaft known as the "Dragon Cross" with abstract and figurative designs including: Cable-Pattern Moulding, Interlace Design, Roll Moulding. Inhabited Plant-Scroll Design with Haloed Figures. Inhabited Plant-Scroll Design with Bird-like Animal - the Dragon or Wyvern (part eagle, part snake). Inhabited Interlace Design with Animals.
- Incomplete Angular Cross-Shafts with abstract and figurative designs including: Interlace Design, Knot-Work Design, Plait-Work Design, Plant-Scroll Design, Roll Moulding. Inhabited Interlace Design with Animals.
- Half-Barrel-Shaped Cross-Base with Socket for insertion of Cross-Shaft. It is incised with Panels within which are Free-Arms Crosses with long lower vertical arms.
- Grave Cover incised with Lines and Spiral-Scroll Design.
- Incomplete Grave Marker incised with V-shaped Lines and Ringerike Design.

PHOTO 141 - Site 92. All Saints Church, Otley, West Yorkshire. "Dragon Cross".

93. OVINGHAM, Northumberland – St Mary The Virgin Church.
- Square Tower: Coursed Rubble Walling. Side Alternate Quoins. Square String Course. Double Belfry Openings with cylindrical mid-wall shafts and Strip-Work. Circular Sound Holes. Round-Headed Single-Splayed Windows. Round-Headed Doorways – one in the south wall near the top of the first stage and the other in the east wall at first floor level. Vestiges of Tower Arch.
- Nave: Coursed Rubble Walling. Vestiges of Side Alternate Quoins.
- Parts of Angular Cross-Shafts with abstract and figurative designs including: Cable-Pattern Moulding, Interlace Design, Knot-Work Design, Pellets, Roll Moulding, Stepped-Pattern Design. Incomplete Human Figure with possibly a Bird on its shoulder under an Arch with a Scroll Design. Possible a Hunting Scene with incomplete Human Figures one holding an Animal, or a scene from Norse Mythology – Ragnarök - with Loki, the wolf Fenris and Heimdall with his horn.
- "The Goose Fair Cross" – Crosshead on a reconstructed Cross Shaft and Cross-Base – both not Anglo-Saxon. (Now separated from Churchyard.)

94. OXFORD, Oxfordshire – St Michael's Church.
- Square Tower: Random Rubble Walling. Long and Short and Rubble Quoining (also modern ashlar insertions). Blocked Round-Headed Doorway. Second floor Round-Headed Doorway. Round-Headed Double-Splayed Windows – the west has later been enlarged to the size of a doorway. Round-Headed Double Belfry Openings with mid-wall baluster shafts on both the second and third floors. Round Sound Holes.

95. PETERBOROUGH, Cambridgeshire – Cathedral Church of St Peter, St Paul and St Andrew.
- Coursed Rubble Walling: visible in vaults beneath the floor of the present nave and south transept, comprising: several courses of stonework forming most of the former North and South Transepts and some of the joining North and South walls of the Chancel.
- Parts of Angular Cross-Shafts with abstract and figurative designs including: Flat Moulding, Interlace Design.
- "Hedda" or "Monks' Stone". A coped, box-shaped Shrine with abstract and figurative designs including: Roll Moulding, Plant-Scroll Design. Inhabited Plant-Scroll design including, standing haloed figures in portrait representing Jesus and Mary and the Apostles.
- A Panel. A band of Roll Moulding forming an almost complete panel containing two standing figures separated by a central column which they both clasp with one hand – their legs nearer to the central column are angled and bend towards it.
- Architectural Features including fragments from: Jambs of Arches, Imposts, String Courses, Columns, Pilaster Strip, Mid-Wall Frame from a Double-Splayed Window, and a large section of a lintel for a doorway decorated with Strip-Work.

96. POTTERNE, Wiltshire – St Mary's Church.
- Font with incised lines bordering a Latin Inscription from Psalm 42.2: "As the hart panteth after the fountains of water; so my soul panteth after thee, O God. (added) Amen".
- Grave Marker with a Free-Arm Cross with a base all in relief.

97. RAMSBURY, Wiltshire – Holy Cross Church.
- Parts of Angular Cross-Shafts reconstructed in a non-Anglo-Saxon column. These are decorated with abstract and figurative designs including: Chevron-Pattern Design, Flat Moulding, Ring-Chain Design, Ring-Knot Design. Inhabited Plant-Scroll Design with Animals. Inhabited Interlace Design with Animals. Dowel holes to connect to adjoining section of Cross-Shaft.

- Fragments of Angular Cross-Shafts with abstract and figurative designs including: Knot-Work Design, Roll Moulding. Inhabited Interlace Design with entwined Animals two of whose bodies are incised with Herringbone Pattern Design, and one whose body is incised with a row of Pellets. Possible vestiges of representation of Human hair or clothing.
- Part of Recumbent Round-Ended and Coped Grave Cover with a top, raised Central Ridge which divides and terminates with the heads of Animals whose tongues entwine in a knot. It is decorated with abstract and figurative designs including: Flat Moulding, Knot-Work Design, Plant-Scroll Design - including Pellets. Inhabited Plant-Scroll Design including Animals.
- Part of Recumbent Round-Ended and Coped Grave Cover with Flat Moulding and Plant-Scroll Design.
- Part of a Grave Cover with a Free-Arm Cross in relief including an "Agnus Dei" (Lamb of God).
- (Foundations of possible Anglo-Saxon Cathedral underlying and overlapping present chancel; its precise extent is a matter of conjecture – nothing is now visible.)

98. REPTON, Derbyshire – St Wystan's Church.
- Nave incorporating Central Crossing and Transepts overlying former Porticos: Coursed Rubble Walling. Fragments of Flooring on top of which are the Bases and fragments of the Columns which once supported the arches separating the central space from the transepts. Moulded String Course.
- Chancel: Coursed Rubble Walling. Chamfered String Course. Pilaster-Strips. Above Chancel Arch, a Blocked Flat-Headed Doorway has an "Escomb" Jamb" and is now separated by walling from northern "Escomb Jamb" which together originally formed a much larger Opening comprising more than one arch.
- Crypt: Ashlar Walling. Megalithic "Square" Quoining. Square Stepped Triple Plinth. Vestiges of Windows. Decorated Columns with bases and decorated Capitals. Stepped and Square String Courses. Pilasters. Vaulted Roof.
- Parts of Columns with Capitals removed from those which once supported the arches separating the central space from the transepts (their bases and stumps survive in situ).
- Lintels from Round-Headed Windows and probably a Doorway.
- Part of an Angular Cross-Shaft with abstract and figurative designs including: Cable-Pattern Moulding, Plait-Work Design. Plant-Scroll Design. Roll Moulding. Human Figures.

99. RIPON, North Yorkshire - Cathedral.
- Crypt: Ashlar Walling including reused Roman Stonework with layers of Plasterwork. Round-Headed Archways (Doorways). Barrel-Vaulted Chambers. Niches. Flat-Headed Passages. Stairs. Ventilation Shaft. Reused Grave Cover with incomplete Free-Arm Cross in relief with long lower vertical arm.
- North Transept: Lengths of a Frieze or Imposts with abstract designs including: Flat Moulding, Interlace Design, Ring-Chain Design, Spiral-Scroll Design.
- Cathedral Treasury: Architectural Feature or Item of Furniture with abstract designs including: Cable-Pattern Moulding, Flat Moulding, Interlace Design, Plant Design, Roll Moulding, Zigzag-Pattern Design.
- Cathedral Treasury: Incomplete Free-Arm Crosshead decorated with abstract and figurative designs including: Flat Moulding, Knot-Work Design. From Norse Mythology, part of a scene in which the figure of Sigurd (sucking his thumb) roasts and eats the heart of the dragon Fafnir. (This item is not currently displayed.)
- Chapel of Resurrection: Reused Base of a Pillar.

100. ROCKCLIFFE, Cumbria – St Mary's Church.
- Almost complete Cross with Ring-Head Crosshead, Angular Cross-Shaft with two "collars", and Cross-Base. The Ring-Head Crosshead and Angular Cross-Shaft are decorated with abstract and figurative designs including: Interlace Design, Roll Moulding. Animals. Note: weathering makes the identification of decoration difficult.

101. ROMSEY, Hampshire - Abbey.
- Rood with Crucified Christ and the Hand of God.
- Rood Panel with Crucifixion Scene – Christ, winged Angels each holding a sceptre (one is incomplete), the Virgin Mary, St John, with Roman soldiers - the cup-sponge-bearer Stephaton and the spear-bearer Longinus. An extended Plant-like Design.

102. RUTHWELL, Dumfriesshire (& Galloway) – Ruthwell and Mount Kedar Church.
- Almost complete Cross comprising Crosshead, Cross-Shaft and Cross-Base – but with some stonework dating from the nineteenth century reconstruction.
- Free-Arm Crosshead with figurative and abstract designs including: Flat Moulding. A representation of St Mathew the Evangelist with his symbol the winged angel, a large Eagle – the symbol of Christ's Resurrection and Ascension, St John the Evangelist with his symbol the eagle. An Archer. Latin Inscription thought to be the opening words of the Fourth Gospel.
- Angular Cross-Shaft with abstract and figurative designs including: Flat Moulding. Inhabited Vine-Scroll Design with animals and birds. Scenes depicting: The Flight from Egypt, The hermit Saints Paul and Anthony, Christ in Glory, John the Baptist, The Annunciation, Christ healing the man born blind, Christ with Mary Magdalene washing His feet, The Visitation of Mary. Inscriptions in Latin and Runes including the "Dream of the Rood" by the seventh century poet Caedmon of Whitby, North Yorkshire.
- Cross-Base abstract and figurative designs including: Vine-Scroll Design and a Crucifixion Scene.

103. SANDBACH, Cheshire – Market Square.
- Two Reconstructed Crosses comprising parts of lower vertical arms of Free-Arm Crossheads, most of Angular Cross-Shafts, and most of Cross-Bases (no decoration survives on the cross-bases).
- Crossheads and Cross-Shafts with abstract and figurative scenes and designs. Scenes including: The Nativity, Adoration of the Magi, Christ's Road to Calvary, Crucifixion Scene with the Evangelists' symbols, Christ committing the Keys of Heaven to Peter and the Book of the New Law to Paul, Transfiguration of Christ on Mount Tabor, The Annunciation, Transfiguration Scene, Adoration of Mary, The Veneration of Christ, Other figurative designs within the scenes include human figures – individually and in groups, winged angels and animals, animals, and birds. Abstract designs include: Cable-Pattern Moulding, Flat Moulding, Interlace Design, Knot-Work Design, Pellets, Ring-Chain Design, Roll Moulding. Inhabited Scroll Design with human, animal and bird figures.
- [In the churchyard of St Mary's Church nearby there are five other very weathered sections of stonework from Cross-Shafts (whether these formed part of the Crosses in the Market Square is a matter of conjecture) and Grave Covers with indistinct abstract and figurative designs including: Cable-Pattern Moulding, Flat Moulding, Interlace Design. Human figures (possibly the meeting of St Paul and St Anthony). Animals.]

An Introduction to Anglo-Saxon Church Architecture &
Anglo-Saxon & Anglo Scandinavian Stone Sculpture

104. SHELFORD, Nottinghamshire – St Peter and St Paul's Church.
- Part of Cross-Shaft with abstract and figurative designs including: Flat Moulding, Pellet Moulding, Ring-Knot Design. The Virgin and Child. Winged Angels.

105. SOCKBURN, County Durham – All Saint's Church and Conyers Chapel.
- Vestiges of Coursed Rubble Walling. Side Alternate including Megalithic Quoining.
- Nearly complete and incomplete parts of Free-Arm and Ring-Head Crossheads with abstract and figurative designs including: Flat Moulding, Grooved Moulding, Plait-Work Design, Plant-Scroll Design, Ring-Chain Design. Parts of Human bodies.
- Incomplete Angular Cross-Shafts with abstract and figurative designs including: Baluster Shaft Moulding, Cable-Pattern Moulding, Flat Moulding, Grooved Moulding, Interlace Design, Knot-Work Design, Pellets, Plait-Work Design, Ring-Chain Design, Ring-Knot Design, Roll Moulding, Spiral Design. Figures of Warriors, Horseman, Male and Female Human Figures. Animals. Bird.
- Nearly complete and incomplete Grave Covers including Hogbacks with abstract and figurative designs including: Incised Cross, Diamond-Pattern, Flat Moulding, Grooved Moulding, Interlace Design, Key-Pattern Design, Pellets, Plait-Work Design. Ring-Chain Design, Roll Moulding, Tegulations, Zigzag-Pattern Design. Human Figures, including female (incomplete). Horsemen. Animals including serpent-headed animals, end bear-like animals. Bird.

PHOTO 142 – Site 104, St Peter and St Paul's Church, Shelford, Nottinghamshire. Part of Angular Cross-Shaft with Virgin and Child.

106. SOMPTING, Sussex – St Mary The Virgin Church.
- Square Tower: Random Rubble Walling with Flints. "Cut-Back" Long and Short Quoining. Blocked Round-Headed Doorway. Square String Course with a decorative design similar to pairs of teeth (some rather square-shaped) extending alternately from the top and bottom of the string course towards the centre. Pilaster-Strips; those in the upper stage include capitals decorated with Plant-Scroll Design and Roll Moulding. Round-Headed Double-Splayed Windows. Triangular-Headed Windows; internally, at first floor level on the north side of the tower, the base of the mid-wall shaft is decorated with a human head. Round-Headed Double-Belfry Openings with cylindrical mid-wall shafts – the north opening has capitals decorated with Plant-Scroll Design and Roll Moulding. Triangular-Headed Single Belfry Openings. Tower Arch with decorated capitals and imposts. "Rhenish Helm" Roof.
- Nave: Random Rubble Walling with Flints. Part of a Blocked Round-Headed Double-Splayed Window.
- Reused parts of String Course with Plant Designs.
- Parts of Frieze with Roll Moulding, Plant-Scroll Design and Inhabited Plant-Scroll Design with an Animal. One face of part of the frieze has had Christ in Majesty added in the twelfth century.
- Panel with haloed figure below an arch – it was altered in the twelfth century and the identity of the figure is a matter of debate.
- Fragment with Flat Moulding and Plant-Scroll Design.

107. STONEGRAVE, North Yorkshire – Minster (Holy Trinity Church).
- Restored Church whose Square Tower and Nave may contain some Saxo-Norman fabric. In the Tower: an incomplete Blocked Round-Headed Doorway – now with window inserted, a Round-Headed Single-Splayed Window, and a Round-Headed Doorway could possibly be Saxo-Norman in origin.
- Incomplete Ring-Head Crosshead with most of its Angular Cross-Shaft with abstract and figurative designs including: Flat Moulding, Free-Arm Cross with supporting Cross-Shaft, Interlace Design, Key-Pattern Design, Knot-Work Design, Plait-Work Design. Seated Human Figure. Representations of a priest whose tonsure indicates as following the Celtic or Irish practices of Christianity.
- Parts of Angular Cross-Shafts with abstract and figurative designs including: Flat Moulding, Incised Lines, Interlace Design, Knot-Work Design, Pellets, Plait-Work Design, Ring-Knot Design. Incomplete Human Figure and part of another Human Head.
- Parts of a Cross-Base with abstract and figurative designs including: Cable-Pattern Moulding, Flat Moulding, Plait-Work Design. Animal with Bird on its back. Animal.
- Part of Grave Cover with abstract and figurative designs including: Flat and possibly Roll Moulding, Plait-Work Design. Hunting Scene with Archer and Stag.

108. STOW-IN-LINDSEY, Lincolnshire – St Mary's Church. Cruciform Church.
- Nave: Part of Grave Cover with abstract designs including: Cable-Pattern Moulding, Ring-Knot Design. Part of Grave Marker with Cable-Pattern Moulding.
- Stair Turret, not Anglo-Saxon. Window Frames are similar to those of Anglo-Saxon origin in the Stair Turret at All Saints Church, Hough-on-the-Hill, Lincolnshire.
- Central Crossing: Coursed Rubble Walling. Three-Stepped Plinth with two upper chamfered courses. The current floor level is that of the Anglo-Saxon church. "Cut-Back" Side Alternate Quoining with some Quoins laid in Face Alternate fashion; also a few Megalithic Quoins. Round-Headed Arches with Hood Moulding; the west face of the western arch the Hood Moulding decorated with Palmette Design. Jambs of the Arches are complemented on their "outer" west, south, east and north faces by double rows of adjacent but separate Pilaster Strips; the ones nearer to the jambs are "half round", and the outer ones are "half-square". The top of the Pilaster Strips terminate in Imposts supporting the arches and hood moulding. The bases of the Pilasters terminate in Bulbous Corbels which are above the original Five-Stepped Plinth – one flat course now integral with floor, with four chamfered courses above. Incised on stonework is a representations of a Viking longship - believed to be the earliest such representation in England.
- Transepts: Coursed Rubble Walling. Three-Stepped Plinth with two upper chamfered courses. Side Alternate Quoining, some Quoins laid in Face Alternate Fashion. North Transept has "Cut-Back" Side Alternate Quoining. Round-Headed Doorway with "Escomb" Jambs. Round-Headed Single-Splayed Window with "long and short" jambs, also with Hood Moulding decorated with Palmette Design. Incomplete Flat-Headed Single-Splayed Window with "Escomb" Jambs. Incomplete Flat-Headed Window with "Escomb" Jamb.

109. SUNDERLAND – MONKWEARMOUTH, County Durham – St Peter's Church.
- Square Tower incorporating earlier Porch: Coursed Rubble Walling. Side Alternate including Megalithic Quoining. Round-Headed Archway with unique Decorated Jambs including Baluster Shafts. Round-Headed Doorways with "Escomb" Jambs. Barrel-Vaulted Roof. Square String Courses – one decorated with vestiges of animals, possibly human figures, and Cable-Pattern Moulding. Blocked Flat-Headed Doorway providing external access to upper storey of former porch. Blocked Flat-Headed Window. Roofline of Former Porch. Vestiges of a Statue. Flat and Round-Headed Single-Splayed Windows – one with decorated moulding.

An Introduction to Anglo-Saxon Church Architecture &   145
Anglo-Saxon & Anglo Scandinavian Stone Sculpture

- Round-Headed Double-Belfry Openings with cylindrical mid-wall shafts, a single lintel covering both openings, Hood Moulding, Strip-Work and blocked Round Sound Holes.
- Nave: Coursed Rubble Walling including vestiges of Herringbone Masonry. Side Alternate including Megalithic Quoining. Chamfered String Course. Restored Round-Headed Doorway. Round-Headed Window converted into doorway. Vestiges of Blocked Round-Headed Doorway and the Sill of another. Round-Headed Single-Splayed Windows now ornamented with Baluster Shafts. Consecration Cross. Roofline of Nave. Part of foundations of North Portico visible under glass cover.
- Some Stonework from Monastic Buildings - not now forming any recognisable entity.
- Part of "Abbot's Seat" and Clergy Bench – with representation of a lion.
- Two Consecration Crosses.
- Almost complete Grave Cover with Flat Moulding, large square-armed Free-Arm Cross in relief. Inscription interpreted as "Here in the tomb rests Herebericht the priest in the body".
- Incomplete Grave Cover in three pieces with Grooved Moulding and a Cross in relief.
- Part of a decorated Shrine with decoration similar to that in the Lindisfarne Gospels – Flat Moulding, Interlace Design, Ring-Chain Design, Roll Moulding, Ribbon-shaped Animal.
- Part of a Frieze with Flat Moulding, two incomplete figures confronting (fighting) each other.
- Incomplete Baluster Shafts – one with vestiges of paint.
- Stonework from decorated exterior Tower String Course – the decoration is now almost impossible to see.
- A Round-Headed Window Head.

PHOTO 143 – Site 109, St Peter's Church, Shelford, Nottinghamshire. Part of Angular Cross-Shaft with Virgin and Child.

PHOTO 144 – Site 109. St Peter's Church, Monkwearmouth, Sunderland, County Durham. Incomplete Baluster Shafts – one with original paint.

110. TASBURGH, Norfolk – St Mary's Church.
- Round Tower: Coursed Rubble Walling with Flints. Round-Headed Single-Splayed Windows. One row of Round-Headed Sunken Blind Arcading separated by wide Pilaster-Strips, with above, another row of Headless (removed in building work in 1385) Sunken Blind Arcading separated by wide Pilasters Strips; the two rows provide an alternating pattern. Tower Arch with later non-Anglo-Saxon doorway inserted. Round-Headed Doorway now reused as a window.
- Nave: Coursed Rubble Walling with Flints. Indications of earlier Roofline.

111. THORNHILL (NEAR DEWSBURY), West Yorkshire – St Michael and All Angels Church.
- Part of the lower vertical Arm from a Free-Arm Crosshead and part of its attached Angular Cross-Shaft with Interlace Designs.
- Part of an Arm from a Free-Arm Crosshead with Flat Moulding, Knot-Work Design and Ring-Knot Design.

- Incomplete Angular Cross-Shaft with abstract designs including: Flat Moulding, Interlace Design. Incomplete Runic Inscription interpreted as "Gilswith raised up, in memory of Berhtswith, a beacon on a hill. Pray for her soul".
- Incomplete Angular Cross-Shaft with abstract designs including: Flat Moulding, Incised Lines, Plant-Scroll Design. Inscription interpreted as "Ethelbercht set up (this memorial) in memory of Ethelwini".
- Incomplete Angular Cross-Shaft with abstract and figurative designs including: Flat Moulding, Incised Lines, vestiges of Plant Design. Inhabited Interlace Design with Animals. Inscription interpreted as "Eadred set up (this monument) in memory of Eateinne (Eadthegn)".
- Parts of Angular Cross-Shafts with abstract designs including: Flat Moulding, Incised Lines, Plant-Scroll Design, Roll Moulding, Stepped-Pattern Design.
- Incomplete Angular Cross-Shaft or Grave Cover with Flat Moulding and incised with an incomplete Inscription interpreted as "in memory of Osberht, a monument".

112. THORNTON STEWARD, North Yorkshire – St Oswald's Church.
- Nave includes the following which may be of Anglo-Saxon origin: Vestiges of Coursed Rubble Walling including Side Alternate Quoins. Vestiges of jambs of Doorway. Vestiges of the arches of Round-Headed Windows. Vestiges of Chancel Arch.
- Incomplete Plate-Ring Crosshead with abstract and figurative designs including: Flat Moulding, Grooved Moulding, Pellets. Crucifixion Scene.
- Part of a Ring-Head Crosshead with abstract and figurative designs including: Flat Moulding. Incomplete Crucifixion Scene. Incomplete seated Christ in Majesty.
- Vestiges of a Ring-Head Crosshead and part of its attached Angular Cross-Shaft with abstract designs including: Flat Moulding and Plait-Work Design.
- Arm with indications of ring from a Ring-Head Crosshead with abstract designs including: Free-Arm Cross, Pellets, Plait-Work Design.
- Fragments of Angular Cross-Shafts with abstract and figurative designs including: Pellets, Spiral-Scroll Design. Human figures.

113. THORPE-NEXT-HADDISCOE, Norfolk – St Matthias Church.
- Round Tower: Coursed Rubble Walling with Flints. Fabric built in a way that indicates four stages to the tower – there are no string courses. Round-Headed Single-Splayed Windows, two with ornamented heads; only two are now not blocked. Prokrossi. Row of Headless (removed by later building work) Sunken Blind Arcading separated by wide Pilaster-Strips. Side Alternate Quoins.
- Nave: Coursed Rubble Walling with Flints. Side Alternate Quoins. Double-Splayed Circular Window – now blocked by tower.

PHOTO 145 – Site 111. St Michael & All Angels Church, Thornhill, West Yorkshire. Angular Cross-Shaft: Flat Moulding, Interlace Design. Runic Inscription.

PHOTO 146 – Site 112. St Oswald's Church, Thornton Steward, North Yorkshire. Ring-Head Crosshead with Christ in Majesty

An Introduction to Anglo-Saxon Church Architecture &   **147**
Anglo-Saxon & Anglo Scandinavian Stone Sculpture

114. THURSLEY, Surrey – St Michael's Church.
- Nave: Round-Headed Single-Splayed Window. Font with incised lines bordering a Herringbone Pattern.
- Chancel: Plastered Walling. Square Single Plinth. Round-Headed Double-Splayed Windows with Oak Mid-Wall Frames. Indications of flooring for upper chamber.

115. WARDEN, Northumberland – St Michael's and All Angels Church.
- Square Tower: Coursed Rubble Walling. Side Alternate and Face Alternate including Megalithic Quoining. Triangular and a Flat-Headed Window. Round-Headed Single-Splayed Windows - one with a head similar in shape to a crosshead. Blocked Round-Headed Doorway at earlier first floor level. Tower Arch using Roman material.
- Nave: Vestiges of Coursed Rubble Walling. Part of Square Single Plinth. Possible indications of the base of the northwest Quoins.
- Grave Cover reusing part of Roman Altar with Cable-Pattern Moulding; extended Triangular-ended Loops combined with Interlace Design, Pellets and Ring-Knot Design. Human Figure.
- Grave Marker reusing part of a Roman Column incised with a Free-Arm Cross within a circle.
- Hammerhead Crosshead with attached Cross-Shaft; the Crosshead is decorated with a Free-Arm Cross in relief and a Pellet off-centre.
- Plate-Ring Grave Marker decorated in relief with Free-Arm Cross with central roundel and fan-shaped arms.
- Part of a Triangular-shaped (coped) Grave Cover with abstract designs including: Tegulations, indications of Roll Moulding.

116. WHITCHURCH, Hampshire – All Hallows Church.
- Round-Headed Grave Marker decorated with abstract and figurative designs including: Incomplete Stepped-Pattern Moulding with Flat Moulding and Roll Moulding, Plant-Scroll Design. Half-figure of Christ in a recess with the right arm giving a blessing and the left arm holding a book. Inscription which has been interpreted as "Here rests the body of Frioburga buried into peace".

117. WHITHORN, Wigtownshire (Dumfriesshire & Galloway) – Priory Museum.
- Pillar Stone Memorials including the "Latinus Stone" with the Latin inscription to Latinus, aged 35, and his daughter, aged 4; and the "Peter Stone" incised with a Free-Arm Cross with fan-shaped arms surrounded by concentric circles and the inscription interpreted as "the place of Peter".
- Slab known as the "Golgotha Stone" representing the central cross of Christ with a cross on each side representing the two thieves "Dismas" and "Gestas". Incised Free-Arm Crosses with a long lower vertical Arm, Roll Moulding.
- Crosshead and nearly all of Cross-Shaft known as "The Monreith Cross" comprising a Disc-Head Crosshead and an Angular Cross-Shaft. The Crosshead is decorated with distinctive Grooves, Pellet-like features in the "eyelets", Roll Moulding. The Cross-shaft is decorated with Ring-Chain Design and Roll Moulding.
- Plate-Ring Crosshead and Part of its attached Angular Cross-Shaft. The Crosshead is decorated with: Cable-Pattern Moulding, Flat Moulding, Grooves, Interlace Design, Pellet-like features in the "eyelets". The Cross-Shaft is decorated with: Cable-Pattern Moulding, Knot-Work Design, Stopped Plait-Work Design. Vestiges of Runic Inscription.
- Part of an Angular Cross-Shaft with abstract and figurative designs including: Diamond-Pattern Design, Flat Moulding, Interlace Design. Two incomplete Haloed Human Figures - saints or ecclesiastics.
- Slabs incised with Crossheads and Cross-Shafts. Complete and Incomplete Crossheads:

Disc-Head Crossheads, Free-Arm Crossheads, Plate-Ring Crosshead, Ring-Head Crosshead. These are decorated with abstract designs including: Flat Moulding, Free-Arm Crosses with fan-shaped arms surrounded by a circle, distinctive Grooves, Interlace Design, Key-Pattern Design, Pellet-like features in the "eyelets", Plait-Work Design, Roll Moulding, Scroll Design. Complete and Incomplete Angular Cross-Shafts. These are decorated with abstract designs including: Flat Moulding, Cable-Pattern Moulding, Flat Moulding, Free-Arm Crosses with fan-shaped arms bordered by a circle, Interlace Design, Key-Pattern Design, Knot-Work Design, Pellet adjacent to a looping strand, Pellets, Plait-Work Design, Ring-Chain Design, Ring-Knot Design, Roll Moulding, Scroll Design, Stepped-Pattern Moulding, Stopped Plait-Work Design. Runic Inscription translated as the female name "Hwitu". Incomplete Runic Inscription including representations for the letters "f", "e", "r", "th". Incomplete lettering.
- Cross-Base and what is described as a "Stone Collar" for securing the base of the shaft; neither is decorated.
- Stone Pillars incised and decorated with abstract and figurative designs including: Linear and Circular Designs, Pellets. Human Figures. Animals.

118. WHITTINGHAM, Northumberland – St Bartholomew's Church.
- Square Tower: Coursed Rubble Walling. Chamfered Single Plinth. Side Alternate and Long and Short Quoining (some in "Sussex" fashion). Tower Arch with restored arch but original imposts and "Escomb" Jambs.
- Nave: Coursed Rubble Walling. Chamfered Single Plinth. Side Alternate and Long and Short Quoining (some in "Sussex" fashion). Incomplete Blocked Opening possibly to a portico.
- Almost complete Free-Arm Crosshead and Cross-Base; neither are decorated.

119. WICKHAM, Berkshire – St Swithun's Church.
- Square Tower: Coursed Rubble Walling with Flints. Long and Short Quoining. Restored Blocked Round-Headed Doorway above ground level for external access. Round-Headed Double-Splayed Windows. Round-Headed Double Belfry Openings with mid-wall baluster shafts (a mid-nineteenth century belfry stage has been added to the top of the tower).

120. WINCHESTER, Hampshire - City Museum.
- Part of Grave Marker with a band of Flat Moulding forming a round-headed panel containing the back of a horizontal human hand holding between its thumb and fingers a free-arm cross with a long lower vertical arm; the cross is at an acute angle.
- Part of Grave Marker with architectural decoration including: interlocked round-headed arches with decorated capitals and bases, a lamp-like feature hanging down from the central arch connected by rolled curtains to the flanking smaller arches.
- Part of a Round-Headed Grave Marker with a free-arm cross in relief with a band of Flat Moulding curving along the outer border.
- Part of a Grave Cover with an incomplete Inscription in Runes.
- Most of a Grave Marker with what might be described as a Ring-Head Crosshead with the ring placed on top of a free-arm cross, however in this instance it is more like a free-arm cross with the ring added.
- A coped Grave Cover with an Inscription which has been translated "Here lies Gunni, Eorl's companion"; an incomplete groove divides the top from the side walls.
- Part of a large Frieze with two Human Figures: a vertical walking mailed Warrior with sword (head and top right half of body is missing); a horizontally placed head and shoulders of a figure confronting the raised head of an animal.
- Part of a large Frieze with the head and part of the neck of an Animal in profile to the right - the end of its snout is up against a wide curved band of stonework decorated with

An Introduction to Anglo-Saxon Church Architecture &   **149**
Anglo-Saxon & Anglo Scandinavian Stone Sculpture

- indented rectangles which are adjacent to a Plant-Scroll Design.
- Part of Circular Cross-Shaft with abstract and figurative designs including: Bush-Scroll Design, Flat Moulding, Interlace Design. Inhabited Interlace Design with an Animal.
- Part of Angular Cross-Shaft with abstract designs including: Roll Moulding, Scroll Design.
- Fragment of Wall Painting showing most of head and shoulders and one hand of a Human.

121. WING, Buckinghamshire - All Saints Church.
- Nave: Coursed Rubble Walling. Vestiges of Side Alternate Quoining. Round-Headed Arches. First Floor Round-Headed Doorways for external access to Western Gallery – one partially blocked.
- North Aisle: Coursed Rubble Walling. Square Rubble Single Plinth. Blocked Round-Headed Doorway.
- Seven Sided Apsidal Chancel: Coursed Rubble Walling. Restored Chancel Arch with Hood Moulding which unusually is not separate from the arch but provides the edge of the arch itself. Restored Round-Headed Double Windows reusing Roman Bricks with mid-wall baluster shaft. Pilaster-Strips and Strip-Work forming a Blind Arcade of tall Round-Headed Arches. Incomplete Blind Arcade of Triangular-Headed Openings. Blocked Round-Headed Single-Splayed Windows. Vestiges of Round-Headed Windows. Round-Headed Windows – one adapted to provide access to Crypt.
- Octagonal Crypt with a central chamber surrounded by an Ambulatory: Coursed Rubble Walling. Arched Openings. Passages. Barrel Vaulted Roofs.

122. WINTERBOURNE STEEPLETON, Dorset – St Michael's Church.
- Nave: Coursed Rubble Walling. Side Alternate including Megalithic Quoining. Round-Headed Doorways with Hood Moulding which could be Anglo-Saxon.
- Panel with most of an Angel placed horizontally and in high relief with head turned back and legs and feet upturned; the halo and the wings are incomplete.
- Stone with incomplete Inscription – the surviving letters are very faint and difficult to identify, they provide no obvious wording.

123. WIRKSWORTH, Derbyshire – St Mary's Church.
- Almost complete coped Grave Cover (known as the "Wirksworth Stone", a "Tomb Lid" for the seventh century Northumbrian missionary "Betti") with figurative designs including: Christ washing the disciples' feet, Crucifixion Scene, The Blessed Virgin being borne out for burial, Presentation of Christ in the Temple, The Descent into Hell, The Ascension of Christ, The Annunciation, The Mission. Damaged Flat Moulding along the top ridge "gable" dividing the Grave Cover.
- Fragment from probably an Angular Cross-Shaft with "Adam (almost complete), the Serpent (neck and head – eye, open jaw around fruit) and the Tree of Life (incomplete)".

124. WITTERING, Cambridgeshire – All Saints Church.
- Nave: Coursed Rubble Walling. Square Single Plinth. "Cut-Back" Long and Short Quoining.
- Chancel: Coursed Rubble Walling. Square Single Plinth. "Cut-Back" Long and Short Quoining. Chancel Arch with Hood Moulding and Strip-Work.

125. WOOTTON WAWEN, Warwickshire – St Peter's Church Former Cruciform Church.
- Central Crossing and Square Tower: Coursed Rubble Walling. Long and Short Quoining. Round-Headed Archways with "Escomb" Jambs – some with Hood Moulding; the northern Archway is blocked and a window has been inserted - not Anglo-Saxon. Externally indications of blocked Round-Headed Openings probably the former single belfry openings.

- Shallow Free-Armed Cross – the south arm is missing; it is located in the centre of the Arch on the east face of the eastern Archway.

126. WORTH, Sussex – St Nicholas Church. Restored Cruciform Church.
- Nave: Coursed Rubble Walling. Square Single Plinth and Square Double Plinth. Pilaster-Strips. "Cut-Back" Long and Short Quoining some "Sussex Variation". Chamfered String Course which also provides the sills for the Round-Headed Double Windows with bulbous mid-wall shafts. Blocked Round-Headed Doorway with "Escomb" Jambs. Incomplete Round-Headed Doorway altered in the fourteenth century.
- Transepts: Coursed Rubble Walling. Square Single Plinth. Pilaster-Strips. "Cut-Back" Long and Short Quoins. Original and Restored Round-Headed Archways with Hood Moulding and Strip-Work.
- Apsidal Chancel: Coursed Rubble Walling. Square Double Plinth. Pilaster-Strips. Square String Course. Chancel Arch with Hood Moulding and Strip-Work.

PHOTO 147 – Site 126. St Nicholas Church, Worth, Sussex. Nave Interior: Round-Headed Double Windows with bulbous mid-wall shafts. Blocked Round-Headed Doorway with "Escomb" Jambs.

127. WROXETER, Shropshire – St Andrew's Church.
- Nave: Coursed Stone Walling including Megalithic work from reused Roman Stonework. Side Alternate including Megalithic Quoining. Square String Course. Blocked Flat-Headed Window.
- Incomplete Angular, Collared Cross-Shaft with abstract and figurative designs including: Cable-Pattern Moulding, Flat Moulding, Plant-Scroll Design. Mixture of Inhabited Interlace and Ring-Knot Design with an upright (now horizontal) Dragon-like Animal.
- Parts of two Panels from the Collar of the same Angular, Collared Cross-Shaft as identified above. Each is decorated with a Dog-like Animal in profile.
- Part of a Decorative Panel with geese-like Birds and S-shaped worms.
- Anglo-Saxon Font cut from a reused Roman column base.

PHOTO 148 – Site 127. St Andrew's Church, Wroxeter, Shropshire. Collar from Angular Cross-Shaft with Dog-Like Animal.